P9-DHC-601

The Civil Rights Movement

REFERENCES AND RESOURCES

PAUL T. MURRAY

"Designating the beginning and ending points of any social movement is, to a large extent, an arbitrary decision. The years from 1955 to 1968, however, do constitute a coherent chapter of American history. It was during this period that the question of black civil rights was foremost on the national agenda. These years bracket an explosion of black protest activities that shared common objectives, leadership, and a philosophy on nonviolent resistance. This is the period most often identified by students of the movement as the Civil Rights Era." So states Paul T. Murray in the introduction to *The Civil Rights Movement*, his bibliographic guide to one of the most important periods in U.S. history. Following his review of the published literature through 1991, Murray presents insightful annotations on the key general and collected works as well as publications addressing such topics as the history of the civil rights movement in individual states, civil rights organizations, the federal government, participants in the movement, and phases of the movement. Extensively indexed and cross-referenced, this work will be an invaluable reference tool for researchers in the fields of history, sociology, political science, and psychology.

THE CIVIL RIGHTS MOVEMENT

References and Resources

Reference Publications on American Social Movements

Irwin T. Sanders
Editor

THE CIVIL RIGHTS MOVEMENT

References and Resources

Paul T. Murray

NO LONGER
the property of
Whitaker Library

Whitaker Library
Chowan College
Murfreesboro, North Carolina

G.K. HALL & COMPANY
An Imprint of Simon & Schuster Macmillan
New York

Prentice Hall International
London • Mexico City • New Delhi • Singapore • Sydney • Toronto

108236

Copyright © 1993 by Paul T. Murray

All rights reserved. No part of this book may be reproduced or
transmitted in any form or by any means, electronic or mechanical,
including photocopying, recording, or by any information storage
and retrieval system, without permission in writing from the
Publisher.

Twayne Publishers
An Imprint of Simon & Schuster Macmillan
866 Third Avenue
New York, N.Y. 10022

Macmillan Publishing Company is part of the Maxwell Communication Group of Companies.

Library of Congress Catalog Card Number: 92–34223

Printed in the United States of America

printing number
2 3 4 5 6 7 8 9 10

Library of Congress Cataloging-in-Publication Data
Murray, Paul T.
    The civil rights movement : references and resources / Paul T.
Murray.
       p. cm.—(Reference publications on American social
movements)
    Includes index.
    ISBN 0–8161–1837–X (alk. paper)
    1. Afro-Americans—Civil rights—Bibliography. 2. Civil rights
movements—United States—History—20th century—Bibliography.
3. United States—Race relations—Bibliography. I. Title.
II. Series.
Z1361.N39M93 1993
[E185.61]
016.3231′196073—dc20
                                   92–34223
                                   CIP

The paper used in this publication meets the minimum requirements of American National
Standard for Information Sciences—Permanence of Paper for Printed Library Materials. ANSI
Z39.48-1984.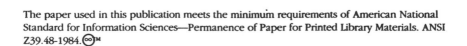

Contents

Preface

It hardly seems possible that more than a quarter century has passed since I was introduced to the civil rights movement. I vividly remember that day in June 1966 when I left my comfortable life as a college student and traveled south to Madison County, Mississippi, where I had volunteered to work for two months in a summer work camp that functioned under the auspices of the American Friends Service Committee. It was the most radical step I had ever taken and it changed my life.

I learned a great deal that summer. Living among people who viewed as luxuries many of the conveniences that I took for granted, such as indoor plumbing and milk for breakfast, I acquired a more immediate understanding of poverty. Listening to their tales of midnight raids by the Klan and being thrown in jail for attempting to register to vote, I began to appreciate the remarkable courage of ordinary men and women. When some of these same people appeared among the students in the adult classes I taught after the children went home, I realized how little I really knew.

During that summer I also discovered that the civil rights movement was changing. By 1966 many of the decisive battles had been won and the most blatant forms of legalized racism were rapidly fading, only to be replaced by other, more subtle, forms of discrimination. This was also the summer of the Black Power ideology and the message was clear—white volunteers were no longer welcome in the movement.

I spent much of that summer working in the local Head Start center—playing with the children and getting to know their teachers. It was a hopeful job because, for the first time, these inquisitive and cheerful youngsters were receiving some of the educational and medical services they needed so badly. Sometimes I wonder what happened to these children of Madison County, Mississippi. Do they enjoy a better life than their parents? Have they benefited from the civil rights movement? Do they remember the heady days when freedom was in the air? And what do they recall about the white students who spent the summer with them?

Today I spend much of my time teaching about the civil rights movement. Much to my dismay, I find that today's college students know very little about the movement. Of course, nearly everyone can identify Martin Luther King, Jr., and recognize his "I Have A Dream" speech. Most know about Rosa Parks and her role in the Montgomery bus boycott. Some are able to explain the significance of the *Brown v. Board of Education* decision. But all too often this is the limit of their knowledge. There is so much more they need to know.

Do they know the story of Fannie Lou Hamer, the Mississippi plantation worker who was savagely beaten for encouraging other poor people to register to vote? Have they learned about Robert Moses, the soft-spoken Harvard graduate who left a comfortable teaching position in New York to risk his life as an organizer for the Student Nonviolent Coordinating Committee? What do they know about the hundreds of dedicated local leaders like C.K. Steele in Tallahassee, Annie Devine in Canton, Mississippi, and Daisy Bates in Little Rock?

And what do they understand about the movement? Do they realize that it was a force for social change more powerful than any other America has seen in this century? Do they appreciate that it was not the creation of any single individual, but the collective effort of thousands of ordinary men and women who risked their lives so that they could live with freedom and dignity? Do they comprehend that the movement sought to attain something more than the right to enjoy a cup of coffee at a lunch counter or to ride on the front seat of a bus or to register to vote?

Those of us who were privileged to be part of the movement must preserve the story of this struggle and keep alive its vision of "the beloved community" so often referred to by Martin Luther King, Jr. We must pass on this legacy to future generations of students and scholars. We must help them discover the meaning of the movement, and show them how to reinterpret it and apply its lessons to their own unique situations.

Teaching about the civil rights movement must include equal parts of preservation and inspiration. The story of the movement must be preserved by continually retelling our children and grandchildren about the southern freedom struggle. Only then will they be able to appreciate the magnitude of the changes that the movement accomplished and the heroism of the people who made it happen. Teaching about the movement will also provide them with a model of successful social change based on grass-roots organization and nonviolent direct action. From the Berlin Wall to Tianamen Square, oppressed people around the world have borrowed the tactics which originated and were refined in the southern freedom struggle. Future generations of American youth must also learn these lessons and be encouraged to apply them to their own situations.

Studying the civil rights movement will help historians and social scientists to better understand our social institutions—how they changed and how they failed to change. Law, politics, public opinion, the media, education, religion, corporations, and the government all were affected by the movement and, in turn, helped define the direction and extent of change that was possible. Studying the movement can be a powerful tool for exploring the potential and the limitations of American society.

During the past thirty years the civil rights movement has been viewed from a variety of perspectives, and no doubt it will continue to be examined and debated for many years to come. It is my hope that this bibliography will help keep the memory of the movement alive and make easier the efforts of future generations of students and scholars. Its goal is to guide them through the abundance of published studies on the movement and help them locate those which are most valuable and relevant for their own purposes.

Acknowledgments

A work of this magnitude is not possible without the assistance and cooperation of many people. My friend and fellow student of the civil rights movement, Rhoda Lois Blumberg, first suggested that I undertake this task. She also provided helpful comments on the section "Women in the Movement." My colleague and former student, Donald Cunnigen, provided valuable suggestions for the section "Whites in the Movement."

Denise Faughnan and Amy Studdard, my student assistants for the past three years, were conscientious and persistent in tracking down hundreds of bibliographic references and making innumerable inter-library loan requests. The staff of the Siena College Library was consistently courteous and unfailingly resourceful in locating even the most obscure works I had requested. I am convinced that there is nothing in print which they cannot find. I am especially indebted to Sean Maloney, Mary Tully, and Cathy Williams for their special assistance.

For financial support in the form of a Summer Research Fellowship, I am grateful to the Siena College Committee on Teaching. Finally, I would like to thank my wife, Suzanne, for her constant encouragement and proofreading services. I couldn't have done it without her.

THE CIVIL RIGHTS MOVEMENT

References and Resources

Introduction

The library of works about the civil rights movement is large and steadily growing. The events of the black freedom struggle, their causes and consequences, have been the subject of hundreds of books and articles by journalists, historians, social scientists, jurists, government officials, and the participants themselves. These studies are so numerous that it is nearly impossible for any one person to keep track of them all.

This bibliography attempts to gather all of the published studies about the civil rights movement into one source and to offer some guidance regarding their contents. To complete this task in a reasonable time, however, it became necessary to adopt a somewhat restricted definition of the movement, thus limiting the scope of this work.

I define the civil rights movement as the social movement that operated primarily in the southern United States between 1955 and 1968 using the tactics of nonviolent direct action and community organizing to seek the elimination of legalized segregation and racial discrimination and the full political participation of African Americans.

This definition takes the arrest of Rosa Parks in Montgomery, Alabama, on 1 December 1955 as the movement's starting date, and the assassination of Martin Luther King, Jr., in Memphis, Tennessee, on 4 April 1968 as its end. I realize that many scholars may disagree with my choice of dates. Vincent Harding, among others, has argued that the history of the African diaspora in America consists of an unbroken tradition of struggle for civil rights which began three centuries before the Montgomery bus boycott. Lerone Bennett, Jr., places the movement's origin in 1905 when the Niagara movement was organized. Others point to the March on Washington Movement of 1940 as the opening salvo of the modern civil rights movement. Aldon Morris emphasizes the significance of the Baton Rouge bus boycott in 1953. But most observers will agree that the events in Montgomery marked the opening of a critical new chapter in the black freedom struggle.

Similarly, most students of the movement cannot agree on a date to mark its end. Some contend that the integrated civil rights movement came to a close with the Selma to Montgomery march in 1965. Others maintain that the movement did not die in the late 1960s, but continues even today, albeit with different leadership and strategies. Most would concur, however, that the death of Martin Luther King, Jr., marks the symbolic end of one era and the beginning of another in the ongoing struggle for human rights and racial equality.

Designating the beginning and ending points of any social movement is, to a large extent, an arbitrary decision. The years from 1955 to 1968, however, do constitute a coherent chapter of American history. It was during this period that the question of black civil rights was foremost on the national agenda. These years bracket an explosion of black protest activities that shared common objectives, leadership, and a philosophy of nonviolent resistance. This is the period most often identified by students of the movement as the Civil Rights Era.

The definition employed in compiling this bibliography focuses on the nonviolent movement for racial integration and equality. As such, it excludes studies of black nationalist leaders and organizations. Although Malcolm X and the Black Muslims, among others, exercised a profound influence on the direction of the civil rights movement, the study of black nationalism is properly the subject for another work. I do, however, include a substantial number of references devoted to the debate over the meaning of Black Power that raged within the movement between 1966 and 1968.

This bibliography also includes a separate section dealing with organized white resistance to the civil rights movement. Studies of groups such as the White Citizens' Council and the Ku Klux Klan belong in this volume because these organizations flourished in direct response to the push for black equality and created formidable obstacles which the movement had to overcome if it was to succeed. To fully understand the dynamics of the movement, these works dealing with the counter-movement by white segregationists must be consulted.

Although the civil rights movement was national in scope, most of the works included in this bibliography concentrate either on events in the southern states or in the national political arena of Washington, D.C. This omission is not the result of a conscious decison on my part, but rather it is because only a relative handful of studies have examined the movement outside the South.

Readers will immediately note that this bibliography omits any works by or about Martin Luther King, Jr. Although King undoubtedly was the central figure in the modern civil rights movement, three comprehensive bibliographies on his life and work have been compiled by Fisher (1976, see entry 1384); Pyatt (1986, see entry 1387); and Carson (1989, see entry 1383). Since readers can easily consult these works, I see no need to duplicate their efforts here.

Similarly, this bibliography contains relatively few studies dealing with school desegregation. Those included here were selected because they involved substantial community protest such as in Little Rock or New Orleans.

Both Quay (1977, see entry 1388) and Jones (1979, see entry 1385) have compiled exhaustive bibliographies covering the battle for integrated education. The student who needs more extensive references on school desegregation should consult these works.

Weatherspoon (1985, see entry 1389) has assembled a comprehensive bibliography on employment discrimination and affirmative action. Thus, this subject is not treated here.

The works selected for this bibliography consist of articles and books published in English about the civil rights movement. Included are articles appearing in general interest and specialized periodicals; articles in scholarly journals that focus mainly on history and the social sciences; academic monographs; books intended for a general audience; and biographies and memoirs of movement activists.Since they are not readily available to the general reader, unpublished manuscripts and dissertations have not been included. Also excluded due to their sheer volume are contemporaneous news stories appearing in newspapers and news magazines such as *Time* or *Newsweek*. Because of their technical nature, most of the numerous articles on civil rights in law journals have also been excluded.

Within the restrictions outlined above, I have attempted to make this bibliography as comprehensive as possible. Despite the impossibility of including every work on the subject, I am confident that it includes nearly all of the significant articles and books dealing with the civil rights movement in America.

1

A Review of the Literature

In the thirty-eight years since Rosa Parks was arrested for refusing to give up her seat on a Montgomery bus, hundreds of articles and books have been written about the civil rights movement. Many of these works deal with events in a specific community or the work of a particular organization. A large number chronicle the contributions of distinguished indivuduals. Others are primarily concerned with testing academic hypotheses or debating the merits of competing theoretical perspectives. Only a handful of these works attempt to present a general overview of the movement. Of these efforts, the most impressive to date is Taylor Branch's *Parting the Waters* (1988, see entry 15). The first of a projected two-volume work, this comprehensive account covers the years from the Supreme Court's *Brown* decision to the assassination of John F. Kennedy. Most studies of the movement tend to concentrate on either the actions of the federal government in Washington or the confrontations between protestors and lawmen in the cities and towns of the Deep South. Branch, however, moves smoothly from the national to the local level and shows the many connections between these two fronts in the struggle.

Several scholars have attempted more concise summations of the movement's history. Thomas Brooks's *Walls Come Tumbling Down* (1974, see entry 18), is an early work that has been supplanted by more recent scholarship. Harvard Sitkoff's *The Struggle for Black Equality* (1981, see entry 87) is an able synthesis, but breaks no new ground. Rhoda L. Blumberg's *Civil Rights: The 1960's Freedom Struggle* (1991, see entry 12) presents a sociological analysis of the movement. In *Race, Reform and Rebellion* (1984, see entry 67), Manning Marable examines the movement from a critical, radical perspective. Perhaps the best brief history of the movement is Robert Weisbrot's *Freedom Bound* (1990, see entry 103), which concentrates on the period between 1960 and 1968. He attributes the movement's successes to the alliance between white liberals and black activists, which resulted in the civil rights laws of 1964 and 1965. He sees its failures as being

5

due to the inability of liberal reformers to make the fundamental social changes needed to bring about true equality.

Another important source of information about the civil rights movement is the work of journalists who covered the South during the 1960s. Anthony Lewis's *Portrait of a Decade* (1965, see entry 60) draws heavily on dispatches he filed with *The New York Times* from Montgomery, Little Rock, Oxford, Birmingham, and other scenes of racial conflict. Lewis Lomax's *The Negro Revolt* (1962, see entry 63) stresses the emergence of young, militant leaders during the sit-ins and freedom rides. Paul Good's *The Trouble I've Seen* (1975, see entry 39) contains his observations as an insider on media coverage of the movement. Fred Powledge's *Free At Last?* (1991, see entry 81) humanizes the movement by including the reflections of numerous civil rights activists. Pat Watters's *Down To Now* (1971, see entry 100) is a highly personal account of the transformation that he as a white southern reporter experienced while covering the movement.

Numerous anthologies of articles and documents about the civil rights movement have been published, but most are no longer in print. Fortunately, the most comprehensive collection is also the most recent. David Garrow's three-volume work *We Shall Overcome* (1989, see entry 135), is an ecclectic compilation of fifty-two seminal articles by historians, journalists, and social scientists. Clayborne Carson, Jr., and his associates have assembled a valuable collection of short selections from primary source material in their reader *Eyes On the Prize* (1987, see entry 121) for the PBS video series of the same name. The best of the earlier works is Joanne Grant's *Black Protest* (1968, see entry 137), which links the movement to earlier black freedom struggles. Two oral history collections are essential references because of their interviews with key civil rights activists: both Howell Raines's *My Soul Is Rested* (1977, see entry 154), and *Voices of Freedom* (1990, see entry 138) by Henry Hampton, Steve Fager, and Sarah Flynn include the recollections of rank and file movement participants as well as the views of nationally recognized civil rights leaders.

Clayborne Carson, Jr., (1986, see entry 1374) contends that the movement must be viewed as a series of local struggles, each with its own distinctive goals, tactics, and leadership. One of the greatest resources for the student of the movement is the wealth of detailed case studies of the fight for civil rights in specific southern communities. Two outstanding examples are Robert Norrell's *Reaping the Whirlwind* (1985, see entry 221), a well-documented account of the decades-long struggle for black political power in Tuskeegee, Alabama, and William Chafe's *Civilities and Civil Rights* (1980, see entry 430), which examines both the sources of black insurgency and the deeply rooted white resistance in Greensboro, North Carolina. Elizabeth Jacoway and David Colburn's *Southern Businessmen and Desegregation* (1982, see entry 140), includes original accounts of the desegregation process in fourteen diverse southern cities. Other important community studies include Frederick Wirt's political analysis of Panola County, Mississippi, *The Politics of Southern Equality* (1970, see entry 425), Charles Fager's vivid description of the Selma to Montgomery march, *Selma 1965* (1985, see entry 343), and David Colburn's examination of the forces behind the civil rights protests in St. Augustine, Florida, *Racial Change and Community Crisis* (1985, see entry 258). *Minds Stayed on Freedom* (1991, see entry 426) describes events in Holmes County, Mississippi, in the words of independent black farmers who were the nucleus of the movement there. Few studies of the movement in northern cities have been published, but one notable effort is Alan B. Anderson and George W. Pickering's *Confronting the Color Line* (1986, see entry 448), which describes the struggle for civil rights in Chicago during the mid-sixties.

The various civil rights organizations have been another fertile area for research on the movement. Clayborne Carson, Jr.'s *In Struggle* (1981, see entry 505) is the definitive study of the Student Nonviolent Coordinating Committee, but Howard Zinn's early account, *SNCC* (1964, see entry 548), captures the fervor and dedication of SNCC's young militants. Adam Fairclough's *To Redeem the Soul of America* (1987, see entry 558) is a careful analysis of origins and evolution of the Southern Christian Leadership Conference. David Garrow also documents SCLC's development in his biography of Martin Luther King, *Bearing the Cross* (1986, see entry 559). August Meier and Elliot Rudwick's *CORE* (1973, see entry 592) is a comprehensive history of the Congress of Racial Equality, but Inge Powell Bell's sociological study *CORE and the Strategy of Nonviolence* (1968, see entry 575) is also worth consulting. The best of several studies of the role of the Highlander Folk School is Frank Adams and Myles Horton's *Unearthing Seeds of Fire* (1975, see entry 642). Unfortunately, there is relatively little scholarship on the NAACP's contributions to the movement.

No aspect of the movement has received more attention than the role of the federal government. The civil rights record of each presidential administration has been examined in great detail. William Berman focuses on the Truman administration in *The Politics of Civil Rights in the Truman Administration* (1970, see entry 658). Robert Burk considers the government under Eisenhower in *The Eisenhower Administration and Black Civil Rights* (1984, see entry 663). Carl M. Brauer praises the civil rights initiatives of the Kennedy administration in *John F. Kennedy and the Second Reconstruction* (1977, see entry 661). In *Kennedy Justice* (1971, see entry 695) however, Victor Navasky presents a more critical view. James C. Harvey chronicles Lyndon Johnson's accomplishments in *Black Civil Rights During the Johnson Administration* (1973, see entry 672). Hugh Davis Graham examines the formulation, enactment, and implementation of civil rights legislation from Kennedy to Nixon in *The Civil Rights Era* (1990, see entry 668). Kenneth O'Reilly exposes the FBI's ineffective record on civil rights protection and enforcement in *"Racial Matters"* (1989, see entry 697). The political forces and legislative maneuvering behind the passage of the 1964 Civil Rights Act are described by Charles and Barbara Whalen in *The Longest Debate* (1985, see entry 731), and by Robert D. Loevy in *To End All Segregation* (1990, see entry 723).

From the *Brown* to the *Baake* decisions, the federal courts were in the forefront of civil rights enforcement. Richard Kluger's *Simple Justice* (1976, see entry 614) is the definitive history of the Supreme Court's monumental 1954 *Brown* decision. Several works focus on southern federal judges who had the uncomfortable task of enforcing unpopular edicts on their home ground. Jack Bass's *Unlikely Heroes* (1981, see entry 738) profiles the justices of the Fifth Circuit Court of Appeals, which covered the six Deep South states. Frank T. Read and Lucy S. McGough explore the bitter division between liberal and conservative justices on the Fifth Circuit in *Let Them Be Judged* (1978, see entry 790). Charles V. Hamilton's *The Bench and the Ballot* (1973, see entry 762) examines the enforcement of voting rights by federal judges in Alabama and Mississippi. Jack W. Peltason's *Fifty-Eight Lonely Men* (1961, see entry 788) scrutinizes the school desegregation rulings of southern federal district judges. Tinsely E. Yarbough has produced biographies of two of the most courageous and controversial federal judges: *Judge Frank Johnson and Human Rights in Alabama* (1981, see entry 801), and *A Passion for Justice: J. Waties Waring and Civil Rights* (1987, see entry 802).

Sociologists and psychologists were quick to seize the opportunity to study the characteristics and motivations of participants in the civil rights movement. Anthony M. Orum studied black college students who joined the sit-in movement in *Black Students in Protest* (1972, see entry 819), as did Frederic Solomon and Jacob R. Fishman (1964, see entry 824), and Ruth R. Searles and J. Allen Williams, Jr. (1962, see entry 822). More often, however, it was white civil rights protestors who were used in these studies. Alphonso Pinkney studies white activists in *The Committed* (1968, see entry 838). *The Dynamics of Idealism* (1971, see entry 831) by N. J. Demerath, Gerald Marwell, and Michael T. Aiken examines 300 whites who volunteered to work for SCLC in the summer of 1965. Doug McAdam focuses on the recruitment and subsequent careers of volunteers for the 1964 Mississippi Summer Project in *Freedom Summer* (1988, see entry 383). Many of the same white northern volunteers are studied by Mary Aickin Rothschild in *A Case of Black and White* (1982, see entry 402). James M. Fendrich (see entries 807–813) has conducted one of the few comparative studies of black and white civil rights activists. He and his associates follow a sample of former protestors and chart their subsequent political values and career paths.

The contributions of women to the civil rights movement have only recently begun to be appreciated and acknowledged. Rhoda L. Blumberg (1991, see entry 846) argues that sexism within the movement limited women's chances to occupy leadership roles and denied them the recognition they deserve. Jo Ann Gibson Robinson describes the key role of women in launching the movement in *The Montgomery Bus Boycott and the Women Who Started It* (1987, see entry 227). *Women in the Civil Rights Movement*, edited by Vicki L. Crawford, Jacqueline Anne Rouse, and Barbara Woods (1990, see entry 856) brings together fourteen original articles describing the varied roles of women in the movement. Charles Payne (1990, see entry 879) documents the surprisingly large portion of movement participants in

Mississippi who were women. In *Personal Politics* (1979, see entry 859) Sara Evans argues that young female participants in the civil rights movement were a significant force in launching the modern women's movement. The role of black women in the movement is also covered in Paul Gidding's comprehensive analysis, *When and Where I Enter* (1984, see entry 514).

Several notable autobiographies by key civil rights activists contribute important insights into the inner workings of the movement. Three of the most compelling self-portraits come from veteran SNCC activists. Although Cleveland Sellers' *River of No Return* (1973, see entry 537), James Forman's *The Making of Black Revolutionaries* (1985, see entry 926), and Mary King's *Freedom Song* (1987, see entry 518) all cover SNCC's evolution from the sit-ins to Black Power, their differing perspectives reveal the variety of personal experiences within that volatile organization. Anne Moody's *Coming of Age in Mississippi* (1968, see entry 390) offers an unmatched description of the day-to-day work in a voter registration project. Ralph Abernathy's *And the Walls Came Tumbling Down* (1989, see entry 549) provides his personal observations on the origins and evolution of SCLC. James Farmer's *Lay Bare the Heart* (1985, see entry 582) traces his career with CORE, and Roy Wilkins's *Standing Fast* (1982, see entry 632) focuses on the NAACP. Autobiographies are also a key source of information for the role of women in the movement. In addition to the previously mentioned works of King, Moody, and Robinson, the reader should consult Septima P. Clark's *Ready from Within* (1988, see entry 553), Virginia Durr's *Outside the Magic Circle* (1985, see entry 185), and Florence Mars's *Witness in Philadelphia* (1977, see entry 387). Also of interest is William R. Beardslee's psychiatric evaluation of veteran civil rights workers in *The Way Out Must Lead In* (1983, see entry 896).

Social scientists have devoted considerable effort to unraveling the origins of the civil rights movement. Three distinctive theoretical perspectives have acted as a basis for their efforts to explain why the movement happened: rising expectations, resource mobilization, and political process. Although they differ in many details, James A. Geschwender (1964, see entry 1004) and James C. Davies (1969, see entry 1003) both contend that improving economic conditions and the resultant rising expectations among African Americans during the 1940s and 1950s were critical in launching the modern protest movement. Anthony Oberschall and Aldon Morris both employ the resource mobilization theory to explain the rise of the movement. In *Social Conflict and Social Movements* (1973, see entry 1368) Oberschall emphasizes the importance of "outside resources," such as the support of northern liberals and the federal government. In *The Origins of the Civil Rights Movement* (1984, see entry 1016), Morris argues that the increased strength of "internal resources," especially the black church, made the movement possible. Doug McAdam advances a political theory in *Political Process and the Development of Black Insurgency* (1982, see entry 1009); he argues that the growing power of northern blacks in Democratic politics was a critical factor in persuading the federal government to actively protect blacks' constitutional rights. Jack M. Bloom follows a similar path in *Class, Race and the Civil Rights Movement* (1987, see entry 11), but stresses the declining political power of the old southern plantation aristocracy.

The student sit-ins which began in 1960 breathed new life into the movement. There are several case studies of sit-in communities and analyses of sit-in participants, but the best general studies of the sit-ins are Martin Oppenheimer's dissertation *The Sit-In Movement of 1960* (1989, see entry 1037), and Aldon Morris's essay "Black Student Sit-In Movement" (1981, see entry 1033), which analyzes the institutional framework that made them possible.

The emergence of the Black Power ideology in 1966 marked the demise of the integrated civil rights movement. Many advocates advanced their definitions of the concept, but the most widely circulated statement is *Black Power* (1967, see entry 1071), by Stokely Carmichael and Charles V. Hamilton. Bayard Rustin offers a liberal critique in his "Black Power and Coalition Politics," (1966, see entry 1115) while Lewis M. Killian traces the social and historical forces that contributed to its emergence in *The Impossible Revolution?* (1968, see entry 1105). Doug McAdam (1983, see entry 1105) develops an explanation for the decline of the movement that stresses both the internal weaknesses of civil rights organizations and their repression by external forces, especially the federal government.

The civil rights movement had a major impact on American attitudes toward race relations. In her review of public opinion research, *Trends in White Attitudes toward Negroes* (1967, see entry 1142), Mildred Schwartz concludes that whites' views of racial integration became much more favorable during the 1960s and their support for the goals of the movement increased substantially. Surveys of opinion within the black community such as Peter Goldman's *Report from Black America* (1970, see entry 1136) report that even as the movement grew more militant, a large majority of blacks remained committed to the goal of racial integration and the methods of nonviolent protest.

Studies of black leadership during the civil rights era repeatedly emphasize the rejection of traditional, accommodating spokesmen by younger, more militant protest leaders. This theme was first sounded by Louis Lomax (1960, see entry 1155), and subsequently was documented in Tallahassee by Lewis M. Killian (1962, see entry 1151), in Atlanta by Jack L. Walker (1989, see entry 1161), and in Winston-Salem by Everett C. Ladd (1966, see entry 1154). These changes were not always long-lasting, however, as Hines and Pierce (1965, see entry 204) and Nelson (1971, see entry 1158) report the return of non-charismatic leaders after the most intense phase of the civil rights struggle had subsided.

No analysis of the civil rights movement would be complete without considering the forces of white resistance to racial integration which were constantly working against the goals of the movement. Numan V. Bartley's *The Rise of Massive Resistance* (1969, see entry 1165) profiles the southern politicians who used the promise of preserving racial segregation to rise to power during the late 1950s. Neil R. McMillen's *The Citizens' Council* (1971, see entry 1182) describes the tactics and programs of the largest anti-civil rights organization, which was long a dominant force in Mississippi politics. No comparable study of the Ku Klux Klan during this period exists, although Edward W. Kallal (1989, see entry 266); Gary Thomas Rowe (1976, see entry 1189); Bill Shipp (1981, see entry 1192); and James W. Vander Zanden (1960, see entry 1197) offer some glimpses into this secretive organization.

Nearly every account of the civil rights movement includes some mention of the rousing and inspirational singing which accompanied mass meetings and demonstrations. Guy and Candie Carawan have collected the lyrics to more than 100 Freedom Songs in *Sing for Freedom* (1990, see entry 1206). Bernice Johnson Reagon (1987, see entry 1210) and Jon Michael Spencer (1987, see entry 1212) have published some helpful material, but the definitive study of the music which sustained the movement has yet to be published.

A spirited debate surrounds any discussion of the consequences of the civil rights movement. The most visible changes occurred in the political arena where the number of black registered voters and the number of black elected officials increased dramatically. Steven F. Lawson's *Black Ballots* (1976, see entry 722) chronicles the struggle for black voting rights which culminated in the passage of the Voting Rights Act of 1965, and his *In Pursuit of Power* (1985, see entry 1240) traces its subsequent implementation by the Justice Department. In *Whose Votes Count?* (1987, see entry 728), Abigail Thernstrom argues that the original congressional intent was subverted by a series of judicial decisions that interpreted the Voting Rights Act as a guarantee of maximum black political effectiveness. *Black Votes Count* (1990, see entry 398) is a rejoinder by Frank R. Parker who contends that these decisions were needed to overcome a variety of disenfranchising devices created by southern legislatures. Lawrence J. Hanks' study *The Struggle for Black Political Empowerment in Three Georgia Counties* (1987, see entry 287) is a useful reminder that the political consequences of the movement vary greatly from one community to another.

Several studies have revealed the difficulties that black voters face in translating their newly acquired political power into tangible gains. Mack Jones's study of rural, mainly black counties (1976, see entry 1239) reports only limited success in delivering more benefits or services. James W. Button's survey of six Florida communities, *Blacks and Social Change* (1989, see entry 257), notes only a few small economic gains. Margaret Edds's survey of eight southern communities, *Free at Last* (1987, see entry 1226), concludes that achieving concrete gains from voting is proving to be a slower process than many had hoped. Not all assessments, however, are as pessimistic as those mentioned above. In *Ain't Gonna Let Nobody Turn Me Round* (1991, see entry 1224), Richard A. Couto shows how four rural southern communities have benefitted as a result of community health centers which were established in response to the civil rights movement.

Statistical studies of the social and economic status of African Americans provide evidence of only limited progress. James E. Blackwell (1982, see entry 1217) reports that the movement did not improve the lives of millions of blacks who remain mired in poverty. Though somewhat more optimistic, Reynolds Farley (1977, see entry 1228) agrees that reductions in inequality are small, in light of the large differences remaining between blacks and whites.

Despite the plethora of studies dealing with the civil rights movement, there remain plentiful opportunities for the next generation of scholars. One critical area which has barely been touched is the impact of the mass media on the movement. Richard Lentz's study of reporting of the 1968 Memphis sanitation workers' strike (1989, see entry 444) is one notable exception, but no author has yet attempted to analyze television's coverage of the movement and its role in shaping public opinion on civil rights. Another neglected topic is the decline of the movement during the late 1960s. With the exception of Doug McAdam's essay (1983, see entry 1105), no work has seriously addressed the organizational weaknesses, strategic blunders, and rhetorical excesses which led to the movement's collapse.

Surely much more work is needed to document the hundreds of local struggles against segregation. Where, for example, is the historical study of the movement in Nashville, a city that was so instrumental in launching the sit-ins, and that contributed nearly all of SNCC's early leadership? Future scholars could also focus on the movement in states like Louisiana, Arkansas, South Carolina, and Virginia, which thus far have been virtually excluded from serious scholarship. With the exception of Chicago, the same can be said about the study of the movement in the North.

The biographical coverage of key movement activists is also far from complete. Although she is featured in a fine documentary film, "Fundi" by Joanne Grant, Ella Baker's long and influential career as a civil rights organizer certainly deserves a full-length study. Other potential subjects include Robert Moses, SNCC's charismatic organizer; Fred Shuttlesworth, Birmingham's fiery leader; James Lawson, the inspiration for nonviolence of the Nashville movement; and Stokely Carmichael, the apostle of Black Power.

More difficult, but no less important, is the study of organized white resistance to integration. Its splintered and secretive means of organization make any comprehensive study of the Ku Klux Klan an imposing task, but one that needs to be attempted. Also missing are the biographies of ardent segregationists such as Eugene "Bull" Connor of Birmingham; Leander Perez of Plaquemine Parish, Louisiana; and Mississippi's Ross Barnett.

Certainly, one of the largest opportunities for further research is the study of the NAACP's role in the movement. During the 1960s it was frequently criticized for its bureaucratic organization and "conservative" leadership—the same forces which limit access to its records today. Nevertheless, the NAACP was directly involved in virtually every major phase of the struggle for civil rights. Local NAACP chapters produced courageous leaders like Daisy Bates in Little Rock; E. D. Nixon in Montgomery; Robert F. Williams in Monroe, North Carolina; and Medgar Evers and Aaron Henry in Mississippi. Unfortunately, our knowledge of the NAACP's contributions to the movement is limited to the biographies of three national figures: Rendall Bland's biography of Thurgood Marshall (1973, see entry 609), Genna Rae McNeil's study of Charles Hamilton Houston (1983, see entry 617), and Denton L. Watson's life of Clarence Mitchell (1990, see entry 630).

Most observers would agree that the civil rights movement has been the most important domestic upheaval in the United States during the twentieth century. Its meaning and ultimate significance will remain the subject of debate for generations to come. The books and articles listed in this bibliography represent a large and impressive body of literature, but they are only a beginning. New sources of information and fresh theoretical perspectives will result in improved understanding of the movement's causes and consequences, the evolution of its tactics and ideology, the dynamic interaction between a mass movement and national institutions, and its lasting impact on American democracy. The passage of time inevitably will result in the reinterpretation and reassessment of the civil rights movement. It can be stated with confidence, however, that the movement will remain a testament to the faith and courage of those men and women who joined the crusade to bring freedom to all Americans, and its study will continue to reward and inspire future generations of students and scholars.

2

General Works

1   ADAMS, A. JOHN, and JOAN MARTIN BURKE. *Civil Rights: A Current Guide to the People, Organizations, and Events.* New York: R. R. Bowker, 1970. 194 pages.

This reference work contains an alphabetical guide to more than 300 individuals and organizations involved in the civil rights movement. Four appendices provide congressional voting records on civil rights bills, information about state civil rights laws and agencies, a chronology of the movement from 1954 to 1970, and a list of leading black elected officials.

2   ASANTE, KETE MOLEFI. "Rhetorical Alliances in the Civil Rights Era. *Negro Educational Review* 36, no. 1 (1985): 6–12.

Asante calls attention to the "whole school of literature which was allied to the rhetorical discourse" of the civil rights movement. He singles out Ellison's *Invisible Man* (1952) as "an abiding symbol" for early civil rights protests, and the work of James Baldwin as a complement to the Black Power phase of the movement.

3   ASHMORE, HARRY S. *Hearts and Minds: A Personal Chronicle of Race in America.* Cabin John, MD: Seven Locks Press, 1988. 513 pages.

Ashmore reflects on the changes in American race relations from his boyhood in the segregated South of the 1920s to the Reagan presidency of the 1980s. Much of this account focuses on the struggle for school desegregation, especially the NAACP's strategy in bringing the *Brown* case to the Supreme Court and the Little Rock crisis, which Ashmore observed as editor of the *Arkansas Gazette.* His emphasis is on leaders and events that attracted national attention during the civil rights era.

4   BAILEY, HARRY A., JR. "Negro Interest Group Strategies." In *The Black Revolt,* edited by James A. Geschwender, 126–35. Englewood Cliffs, NJ: Prentice Hall Press, 1971. Orig. pub. in *Urban Affairs Quarterly* 4 (September 1969): 26–38.

Bailey contrasts the middle-class political strategy of the NAACP with the direct action strategy of more militant civil rights organizations. He concludes that "only the nonviolent direct action strategy can have the power to override those pressures which stand in the way of the achievement of future race goals."

5 BARKAN, STEVEN. "Interorganizational Conflict in the Southern Civil Rights Movement." *Sociological Inquiry* 56, no. 2 (1986): 190–209.

Barkan analyzes the development of hostility between moderate and radical organizations in the southern civil rights movement over the issues of communist participation, the Vietnam War, and Black Power. He concludes that the moderates' perceived need for external support from federal officials and white liberals resulted in their "criticism of militant views and actions that aggravated interorganizational conflict within the movement."

6 BARNES, CATHERINE A. *Journey from Jim Crow: The Desegregation of Southern Transit.* New York: Columbia University Press, 1983. 313 pages.

Barnes traces the origins of Jim Crow transit, early challenges to the segregation policy, and its eventual demise under federal pressure in the early 1960s. She includes chapters on the Montgomery bus boycott; the protests over segregation in southern bus, rail, and air terminals; and the Freedom Rides of 1961. She concludes that action by the federal government was essential to ending Jim Crow transit, but that this change would not have occurred without the initiative and pressure from black organizations such as the NAACP.

7 BATCHELDER, ALAN B. "Economic Forces Serving the Ends of the Negro Protest." *Annals of the American Academy of Political and Social Science* 357 (1965): 80–88.

Batchelder argues that economic forces during the 1950s were not favorable to realizing the objectives of Negro protest, but that conditions during the 1960s will lead to increased employment opportunities and economic advancement for blacks.

8 BENNETT, LERONE, JR. *Confrontation Black and White.* Chicago: Johnson Publishing Co., 1965. 321 pages.

Bennett explores the antecedents and origins of the modern civil rights movement. He insists that the "Negro rebellion began not in Montgomery in 1955, not in Greensboro in 1960, not in Birmingham in 1963, but in Boston in 1905." He demonstrates that the black freedom movement of the 1960s was just the most recent wave of an ongoing struggle for racial equality in America.

9 ———. *The Negro Mood and Other Essays.* Chicago: Johnson Publishing Co., 1964. 104 pages.

A collection of five interpretive essays all dealing with questions raised by the "Negro revolution." Included are Bennett's reflections on "the Black Establishment" and "White Liberals."

10 BLOOM, JACK M. "The Civil Rights Movement: Upheaval and Organization." In *Dream and Reality: The Modern Black Struggle for Freedom and Equality*, edited by Jeannine Swift, 29–41. Westport, CT: Greenwood Press, 1991.

Bloom attempts to find a middle ground between those who view the civil rights movement as a spontaneous upheaval and those who stress the importance of organizations in the movement. He argues that "organizations were crucial to advancing the civil rights movement," but they arose in "response to upheavals . . . that emerged from a changing black consciousness and a new sense of efficacy."

11 _____. *Class, Race and the Civil Rights Movement*. Bloomington: Indiana University Press, 1987. 267 pages.

Bloom's sociohistorical analysis of the emergence of the civil rights movement focuses on economic changes in the South. He contends that the erosion of the political power of the old agricultural upper class made it possible for blacks to forge a coalition with southern business and middle classes, the northern middle class, the national Democratic party, and the federal government, which ultimately changed the racial practices of the South.

12 BLUMBERG, RHODA L. *Civil Rights: The 1960's Freedom Struggle*. Rev. ed. New York: Twayne Publishers, 1991. 244 pages.

Blumberg gives a brief, comprehensive account of the origin and evolution of the civil rights movement from a sociological perspective. She includes an appendix on "The Civil Rights Movement as a Social Movement."

13 BOOKER, SIMEON. *Black Man's America*. Englewood Cliffs, NJ: Prentice Hall Press, 1964. 230 pages.

Booker offers his observations on race relations and the civil rights movement from his perspective as Washington bureau chief for Johnson Publications, publisher of *Ebony* and *Jet*.

14 BRADEN, ANNE. "The Southern Freedom Movement in Perspective." In *We Shall Overcome*, edited by David J. Garrow, vol. 1, 55–150. Brooklyn, NY: Carlson Publishers, 1989. Orig. pub. in *Monthly Review* 17 (July 1965): 1–93.

Braden reviews the history of the southern civil rights movement. While she praises the movement for encouraging "grass roots leadership and independent thinking," she faults it for not seriously considering socialist solutions to the problems of the South and not pursuing broad social and economic goals.

15 BRANCH, TAYLOR. *Parting the Waters: America in the King Years, 1954–63*. New York: Simon & Schuster, 1988. 1062 pages.

This is the first of a projected two-volume comprehensive history of the civil rights movement covering the period from the Montgomery bus boycott to the assassination of John F. Kennedy. Branch makes use of a wide variety of source material, including many interviews with key figures in the movement. Although Martin Luther King is the central character of this account, Branch does not neglect the contributions of other, less well known activists. He strikes a judicious balance between national developments, such as the civil rights strategy of the Justice Department under Robert Kennedy, and the bitter struggles in southern communities like Montgomery, Albany, Birmingham, and Greenwood.

16   BREED, WARREN. "Group Structure and Resistance to Desegregation in the South." *Social Problems* 10, no. 1 (1962): 84–94.

Breed tests the hypothesis that white resistance to desegregation was more intense in the Deep South because of the relative scarcity of organizational memberships. He argues that this lack of political pluralism allows traditional elites to exercise more control than they would in other sections of the nation, where organizations are more prominent.

17   BRISBANE, ROBERT H. *Black Activism: Racial Revolution in the United States, 1954–1970.* Valley Forge, PA: Judson Press, 1974. 332 pages.

The first third of this book deals with the southern civil rights movement, and includes a valuable discussion of the Mississippi Freedom Democratic party. Brisbane's major emphasis, however, is on the development of black nationalism in the mid- to late 1960s.

18   BROOKS, THOMAS R. *Walls Come Tumbling Down: A History of the Civil Rights Movement, 1940–1970.* Englewood Cliffs, NJ: Prentice Hall Press, 1974. 309 pages.

A brief, comprehensive overview of the civil rights movement beginning with the March on Washington Movement and the NAACP's legal challenge to segregation of the 1940s, and concluding with the southern campaigns of the 1960s.

19   BROOM, LEONARD, and NORVAL D. GLENN. *Transformation of the Negro American.* New York: Harper & Row, 1965. 207 pages.

Broom and Glenn assess the progress of black Americans toward equality with whites. They review the history of the civil rights movement in chapter 4 ("Action and Integration") and discuss the effectiveness of protest demonstrations in light of the growing "white backlash." They conclude that "a point of diminishing returns for civil rights activities may already have been reached" because "the more overt and flagrant forms of discrimination . . . will soon be largely removed."

20   BULLARD, SARA, ed. *Free At Last: A History of the Civil Rights Movement and Those Who Died in the Struggle.* Montgomery: Southern Poverty Law Center, 1989. 104 pages.

This magazine presents a brief general history of the civil rights movement together with profiles of forty people who died in the movement. Some of these martyrs are well-known figures such as Emmett Till, Medgar Evers, and Martin Luther King. Others are relatively obscure, such as William

Moore, the white Baltimore postal worker who was slain in 1963 while conducting a one-man march against segregation in Alabama.

21   BURNS, W. HEYWOOD. *The Voices of Negro Protest in America.* New
      York: Oxford University Press, 1963. 88 pages.

This short booklet consists of four chapters that cover black protest up to World War II, the program of the NAACP, nonviolent direct action against segregation, and the Black Muslims. Burns concludes that unless America moves rapidly to eradicate the effects of racial discrimination, the Muslims and other similar groups will continue to grow.

22   CARSON, CLAYBORNE. "Civil Rights Movement." In *Encyclopedia of
      American Political History: Studies of Principal Movements and
      Ideas*, edited by Jack P. Greene, 218–32. New York: Charles
      Scribner's Sons, 1984.

Carson offers a brief general overview of the civil rights movement that focuses on the principal campaigns beginning with the Montgomery bus boycott and ending with the Selma to Montgomery march. He sees the origins of the movement in the "federal government's reluctance to act swiftly and forcefully to enforce" the 1954 *Brown* decision. In addition to dramatically expanding "the political influence and institutional resources" of African Americans, he credits the movement with transforming "prevailing attitudes about the nature of citizenship rights and about the role of government in protecting those rights."

23   CASHMAN, SEAN DENNIS. *African-Americans and the Quest for Civil
      Rights, 1900–1990.* New York: New York University Press, 1991. 321
      pages.

This social and political history of America during the twentieth century includes four chapters on the civil rights movement.

24   CHAFE, WILLIAM H. "The Civil Rights Movement." In *The Unfinished
      Journey: America Since World War II*, 146–76. New York: Oxford
      University Press, 1986.

This brief but excellent summary of the civil rights movement covers the period from 1954 to 1962.

25   ———. "The End of One Struggle, the Beginning of Another." In *The
      Civil Rights Movement in America*, edited by Charles W. Eagles,
      121–56. Jackson: University Press of Mississippi, 1986.

In assessing the accomplishments of the civil rights movement, Chafe stresses the distinction between the individual goal of attaining greater personal freedom and the collective goal of achieving racial equality. With regard to the first, he believes that the movement was undoubtedly successful. The second, however, he feels remains far from realization. Ironically, increased opportunities for middle class blacks have helped widen the gap between the rich and the poor, according to Chafe. He credits the movement with clarifying the linkage between class, race, and gender in American society. Where it failed, he contends, is that it did not provide an effective political strategy for addressing these persistent problems.

26 CLEGHORN, REECE. "The Angels Are White: Who Pays the Bills for Civil Rights?" *New Republic,* 17 August 1963, 12–14.

Cleghorn describes the efforts of Stephen Currier, a wealthy young philanthropist, to raise money for the civil rights movement through the Council for United Civil Rights Leadership. By June 1963 he had raised $800,000, and another $700,000 was expected by the end of the summer. Cleghorn discusses how these funds are to be distributed and used by civil rights organizations.

27 CONGRESSIONAL QUARTERLY. *Revolution in Civil Rights, 1945–1968.* 4th ed. Washington, DC: Congressional Quarterly, Inc., 1968. 119 pages.

Although its title suggests a comprehensive survey of the civil rights movement, this volume focuses primarily on congressional action regarding civil rights legislation. Nearly half of the book is devoted to describing the provisions of civil rights legislation from 1957 to 1968. Also included are descriptions of other federal government actions that were intended to promote the civil rights of blacks, including Supreme Court decisions and efforts of the president and executive agencies.

28 COTHRAN, TILMAN C. "The Negro Protest against Segregation in the South." *Annals of the American Academy of Political and Social Science* 357 (1965): 65–72.

Cothran reviews the protest movement against segregation in the South and concludes that it has "made real" Myrdal's "American Dilemma" for white people, and has created a "social climate in which meaningful communication between the races can take place."

29 COUSINS, NORMAN. "Black Wind Rising." *Saturday Review,* 30 May 1964, 22.

Cousins editorializes against the growing "extremism" within the civil rights movement and urges "moderates among blacks and whites to close ranks against the pressure from their extremes."

30 DANZIG, DAVID. "The Meaning of Negro Strategy." *Commentary* 37 (February 1964): 41–46.

Danzig hails the "development of a new stage in Negro-white relations" following the massive civil rights demonstrations in the summer of 1963. He feels that this signals "the emergence of an organized Negro community . . . representing the interests of its members and able to negotiate for them." In Danzig's view, this emergence of communal solidarity and the resulting political power parallels the achievements of other American ethnic minorities.

31 DORMAN, MICHAEL. *We Shall Overcome.* New York: Delacorte Press, 1964. 340 pages.

Dorman was a reporter who covered the South from August 1962 to

August 1963 for *Newsday*. He witnessed James Meredith's entry to The University of Mississippi, SCLC's Birmingham campaign, and the reaction to the killing of Medgar Evers in Mississippi.

32   DUNBAR, LESLIE W. "Civil Rights Movement." In *Encyclopedia of Religion in the South*, edited by Samuel S. Hill, 172–75. Macon, GA: Mercer University Press, 1984.

In this brief assessment of the southern civil rights movement, Dunbar concludes that the movement "essentially achieved its modest, though bitterly resisted, goals" of personal security, the right to vote, and the end of segregation.

33   _____. "The Enduring American Dilemma." *Virginia Quarterly Review* 59, no. 3 (1983): 369–83.

The former head of the Southern Regional Council reflects on the lasting impact of the civil rights movement on American society. He views the movement as a moral decision on the part of political leaders to respect and obey the constitution.

34   EISINGER, PETER K. "The Conditions of Protest Behavior in American Cities." *American Political Science Review* 67 (March 1973): 11–28.

Eisinger examines the frequency and intensity of protest behavior in forty-three U.S. cities between May and October of 1968. He concludes that "the incidence of protest is mildly related to the nature of a city's political opportunity structure."

35   ELINSON, HOWARD. "Radicalism and the Negro Movement." In *Problems and Prospects of the Negro Movement*, edited by Raymond J. Murphy and Howard Elinson, 355–75. Belmont, CA: Wadsworth, 1966.

Elinson discusses the role of three radical groups within the civil rights movement—black nationalists, "the authoritarian left," and "the new anarchists." He credits the radicals with raising two fundamental issues: (1) "where Negroes fit into the pattern of American ethnic life," and (2) "how radically must American society change to satisfy the just demands of the American Negro?"

36   FULLINWIDER, S. P. *The Mind and Mood of Black America: Twentieth Century Thought*. Homewood, IL: Dorsey Press, 1969. 255 pages.

This intellectual history of twentieth-century African Americans contains only twenty pages dealing with the civil rights movement, but traces the origins of the movement to the black protest thought of previous generations.

37   GESCHWENDER, JAMES A. "The Changing Role of Violence in the Black Revolt." *Sociological Symposium* 9 (1973): 1–15.

Geschwender examines the use of violence and black protest in the twentieth century, and concludes that "violence is neither intrinsically effective nor intrinsically ineffective in achieving movement objectives. The relationship between violence and the attainment of movement objectives is a function of many situational variables."

38   GOOD, PAUL. "Beyond the Voting Rights Act." *The Reporter*, 7 October 1965, 25–29.

Good uses the example of the election of four black legislators in Georgia to reflect on the limited ability of the political system to solve the underlying economic problems of southern blacks. He also describes the resurgence of moderate civil rights leaders allied with the NAACP and the waning influence of more radical voices as exemplified by the decline of the Mississippi Freedom Democratic party.

39   _____. *The Trouble I've Seen: White Journalist/Black Movement.* Washington, DC: Howard University Press, 1975. 272 pages.

In November 1963 Paul Good was assigned to open an ABC News Bureau in Atlanta. This position gave him an ideal view of the southern civil rights movement during its most eventful year. His book contains eyewitness accounts of sit-ins in Atlanta, school desegregation in Tuskegee, the murders in Neshoba County, the Mississippi Summer Project, and the trial of Lemuel Penn's killers in Georgia. In July 1964 Good quit/was fired by ABC, but he continued to cover the movement as a free-lance journalist. What makes this book especially valuable are his critical observations on the way in which the media covered the movement. He gives an insider's view of how stories are selected for coverage and which images the networks choose to broadcast.

40   GORDON, DAVID M. "Communities of Despair and the Civil Rights Movement." *Harvard Review* 4 (June 1966): 49–68.

Gordon examines the "revolutionary" nature of the civil rights movement. He concludes that "the movement may be heading toward a 'revolution'" if black communities shift from socioeconomic tactics to issues of political control. Gordon feels that this change could be inherently revolutionary if it leads to attacks on the "legitimacy of jurisdiction which our established governmental bodies now enjoy."

41   HAINES, HERBERT H. "Black Radicalization and the Funding of Civil Rights, 1957–1970." In *We Shall Overcome*, edited by David J. Garrow, vol. 1, 299–312. Brooklyn, NY: Carlson Publishing, 1989. Orig. pub. in *Social Problems* 32 (October 1984): 31–43.

Haines investigates "the effect of black radicalization during the 1960s on the ability of moderate civil rights groups to attract financial contributions from outside supporters." He concludes that the radicalization "stimulated increased financial support by white groups of more moderate black organizations."

42   _____. *Black Radicals and the Civil Rights Mainstream, 1954–1970.* Knoxville: University of Tennessee Press, 1988. 231 pages.

Haines studies "radical flank effects" on the civil rights movement. He finds that white support for black civil rights increased during this sixteen-year period despite black radicalization. When he examines the funding for civil rights organizations, he concludes that increasing black radicalism "led to a greater willingness among certain funding sources . . . to underwrite forms of black collective action which were more consistent with their interests." He also finds that the threat of violence, particularly as a result of black direct action, produced positive responses from the federal government.

43   HANSBERRY, LORRAINE. *The Movement: Documentary of a Struggle for Equality.* New York: Simon & Schuster, 1964. 127 pages.
A collection of excellent photos showing civil rights actions in the South and North, with a narrative by Hansberry.

44   HARDING, VINCENT. *Hope and History: Why We Must Share the Story of the Movement.* Maryknoll, NY: Orbis Books, 1990. 249 pages.
Harding urges teachers to share "the powerful and humanizing lessons" of the civil rights movement. His essays illustrate the ways in which the story of the movement can be used to explore the promise of American democracy, and to demonstrate the power of ordinary people to shape their destinies.

45   HEACOCK, ROLAND T. *Understanding the Negro Protest.* New York: Pageant Press, 1965. 138 pages.
This essay is an attempt to explain the objectives and methods of the civil rights movement. Heacock views black violence as the greatest threat to the movement's success, and the support of religious, middle-class whites as the critical determinant of the movement's future. Also included is a twenty-eight-page chronology of civil rights demonstrations from 1954 to 1964.

46   HIMES, JOSEPH S. *Racial Conflict in American Society.* Columbus, OH: Merrill Publishing Co., 1973. 205 pages.
Himes presents a sociological analysis of the factors contributing to the emergence of the civil rights movement. He identifies six key developments: (1) the forging of unifying common interests, (2) the spread of the belief that change through self-help was possible, (3) the rising level of aspirations among black people, (4) the availability of resources that could be expended in conflict, (5) the growing willingness to accept the risks of conflict, and (6) the stabilization of a conflict ideology.

47   JACKSON, MAURICE. "The Civil Rights Movement and Social Change." In *Social Movements and Social Change,* edited by R. L. Lauer, 174–89. Carbondale: Southern Illinois University Press, 1976. Orig. pub. in *American Behavioral Scientist* 12 (March/April 1969): 8–17.
In this preliminary examination of the effects of the civil rights movement on American society, Jackson finds sufficient evidence to conclude, that "the civil rights movement has resulted in a large measure of change" both in basic social institutions and in the self-respect of blacks and other ethnic groups.

48   JENKINS, J. CRAIG, and CRAIG M. ECKERT. "Channeling Black Insur-
      gency: Elite Patronage and Professional Social Movement Organiza-
      tions in the Development of the Black Movement." *American Socio-
      logical Review* 51 (December 1986): 812–29.

Jenkins and Eckert evaluate the effect of elite patronage on the civil
rights movement by tracing private foundation grants between 1953 and
1980. They do not find support for the thesis that elite patronage diverted
the movement from radical goals. Instead, they argue that the causes of the
movement's decline were "largely internal, rooted in the strategic
weaknesses and political obstacles to attacking the problems of the black
underclass."

49   KAHN, TOM. "Problems of the Negro Movement." In *Problems and
      Prospects of the Negro Movement*, edited by Raymond J. Murphy and
      Howard Elinson, 318–24. Belmont, CA: Wadsworth, 1966. Orig. pub.
      in *Dissent* 11, no. 1 (1964): 108–38.

During a lull in civil rights activity following the March on Washington,
Kahn argues that the civil rights movement needs "new tactics and fresh
approaches." He believes that the movement has not addressed the basic
social and economic problems of Negroes and cannot act on these problems
effectively unless it is part of broader social reform movement.

50   KAHN, TOM, and AUGUST MEIER. "Recent Trends in the Civil Rights
      Movement." In *We Shall Overcome*, edited by David J. Garrow, vol.
      2, 483–502. Brooklyn, NY: Carlson Publishing, 1989. Orig. pub. in
      New Politics 3 (Spring 1964): 34–53.

Kahn and Meier examine developments in the civil rights movement
during the nine months following the March on Washington. They report a
decline in the amount of direct action, but a proliferation of civil rights
activities. They predict that civil rights organizations will adopt "a varied and
flexible program in which no one type of activity will dominate."

51   KILLIAN, LEWIS M. "Organization, Rationality and Spontaneity in the
      Civil Rights Movement." In *We Shall Overcome*, edited by David J.
      Garrow, vol. 2, 503–16. Brooklyn, NY: Carlson Publishing, 1989.
      Orig. pub. in *American Sociological Review* 49 (December 1984):
      770–83.

Killian examines the 1956 Tallahassee bus boycott and 1960 sit-ins to
determine the relative importance of spontaniety and prior organization in
launching these protests. He concludes that "while organization and rational
planning are key variables, social movement theory must take into account
spontaneity and emergence and the forces which generate them."

52   KING, RICHARD H. "Citizenship and Self-Respect: The Experience of
      Politics in the Civil Rights Movement." *Journal of American Studies*
      22, no. 1 (1988): 7–24.

King discusses the psychological transformation that happened to participants in the civil rights movement. He claims that the movement estab-

lished "a new sense of individual and collective self . . . through political mobilization and participation." He argues that by participating in the movement "one also realized new powers and capacities, one acquired self-respect as well as interests, through engaging in politics."

53 KUNSTLER, WILLIAM M. *Trials and Tribulations.* New York: Grove Press, 1985. 201 pages.
This collection of 102 sonnets by the veteran civil rights lawyer includes several dealing with leaders, organizations, events, and locations related to the movement, such as Medgar Evers, the Mississippi Summer Project, Birmingham, the Freedom Riders, Rosa Parks, SNCC, and Fannie Lou Hamer.

54 LAUE, JAMES H. "The Civil Rights Movement." In *Modern Social Movements,* edited by William Bruce Cameron, 111–20. New York: Random House, 1966.
Laue presents a brief account of the civil rights movement as a case study of an ongoing social movement. He says the movement began in 1960 with the first student sit-in. His account focuses on the "constant tension and interplay between spontaneity and institutionalization." He writes: "What began as an uncontrolled, spontaneous, rapidly spreading movement in the 1960s was soon virtually taken over by various organizations as a program."

55 ———. *Direct Action and Desegregation, 1960–1962: Toward a Theory of the Rationalization of Protest.* Brooklyn, NY: Carlson Publishing, 1989. 112 pages. Ph.D. dissertation, Harvard University, 1965.
Laue was a participant-observer of the civil rights movement in the critical period between 1960 and 1962. This account of the movement's early days focuses on the student sit-ins of 1960, the Freedom Rides of 1961, and the Albany movement of 1962.

56 ———. "The Movement, Negro Challenge to the Myth." In *We Shall Overcome,* edited by David J. Garrow, vol. 2, 537–46. Brooklyn, NY: Carlson Publishing, 1989. Orig. pub. in *New South* 18 (July 1963): 9–17.
Laue views the civil rights movement as attacking the "Myth of the South." This process is done according to him in seven stages: challenge, conflict, crisis, confrontation, communication, compromise, and change.

57 ———. "Power, Conflict and Social Change." In *Riots and Rebellion: Civil Violence in the Urban Community,* edited by Louis Masotti and Don Bowen, 85–96. Beverly Hills, CA: Sage Publications, 1968. Reprinted in *Racial Conflict,* edited by Gary T. Marx, 256–62. Boston: Little, Brown & Co., 1971.
Laue uses his seven-stage model to describe the process of community change he observed in response to the civil rights movement. Laue gives examples of this process at work, but raises questions regarding its long-range applicability.

58   LEE, BERNARD S. "We Must Continue to March." *Freedomways* 6, no. 3
     (1966): 255–61.
Lee argues for the continuation of nonviolent direct action as the best
tactical means for bringing about social change in the United States.

59   LESTER, JULIUS. *Search for the New Land: History as Subjective Experi-
     ence.* New York: Dial Press, 1969. 195 pages.
This "history" of America during the 1960s consists of Lester's reflections on the relationship between the civil rights movements and other
forces of change in American society.

60   LEWIS, ANTHONY. *Portrait of a Decade: The Second American Revolu-
     tion.* New York: Random House, 1965. 322 pages.
New York Times reporter Lewis relates here his observations of social
change in the South during the decade of 1954 to 1964. Among the topics
he covers are the Supreme Court's *Brown* decision, the Little Rock crisis, the
Montgomery bus boycott, the sit-ins, and the movement in Alabama and
Mississippi. He draws heavily on reports and dispatches which appeared in
the *Times* during this period.

61   LEWIS, MICHAEL. "The Negro Protest in Urban America." In *Protest,
     Reform, and Revolt,* edited by Joseph R. Gusfield, 149–90. New York:
     John Wiley & Sons, 1970.
Lewis assesses the prospects for successful black protest activities in the
urban North in light of the historical experience of organizations such as
Marcus Garvey's Universal Negro Improvement Association, the March on
Washington Movement, and the Black Muslims. He concludes that the only
viable strategy is mass dissidence. He feels that such a strategy would be
successful because it would unite two key characteristics of previous black
protests: large-scale organization and militant civil disobedience.

62   LINCOLN, C. ERIC. "Patterns of Protest." *Christian Century* 81 (3 June
     1964): 733–36.
Lincoln considers the extent of civil rights protests during 1963 as a
healthy development in American society. He sees the demonstrations as
leading to an opening of honest communication between blacks and whites
and concludes that "it is inevitable that a reconstruction in race relations is
at hand."

63   LOMAX, LOUIS E. *The Negro Revolt.* New York: Harper & Row, 1962.
     288 pages.
Lomax's journalistic account of American race relations in the early
1960s contains important observations on the early civil rights movement
including the sit-ins, the Freedom Rides, SCLC, the NAACP, and the revolt
against the Negro leadership.

64   MABEE, CARLETON. "Will Commitment to Nonviolence Last?" *Libera-
     tion* 8 (April 1963): 14–17.
Mabee examines the commitment to nonviolence among civil rights

workers in the South. He reports many violations of the nonviolent spirit among civil rights demonstrators. He observes that most of the youthful civil rights workers accept nonviolence only as a tactic, and that their commitment "will not necessarily continue . . . [unless] they receive a rigorous training in nonviolence and achieve a fair number of victories over segregation."

65 MCADAM, DOUG. "Tactical Innovation and the Pace of Insurgency." In *We Shall Overcome*, edited by David J. Garrow, vol. 2, 617–36. Brooklyn, NY: Carlson Publishing, 1989. Orig. pub. in *American Sociological Review* 48 (December 1983): 735–54.

McAdam examines the cyclical pattern of civil rights activity and argues that it is a function of "tactical interaction between insurgents and their opponents." He states that a problem for any movement of powerless people is devising effective protest techniques, and argues that new tactics provide only a temporary advantage as opponents soon learn how to neutralize them. Thus, he believes that the challengers must continually "search for new and effective tactical forms" in order to be successful.

66 MCMILLAN, GEORGE. "Racial Violence and Law Enforcement." *New South* 15 (November 1960): 4–32.

McMillan describes three incidents: (1) several days of rioting in Chattanooga, Tennessee, following the sit-ins in February 1960, (2) a near-riot in Montgomery, Alabama, in March 1960, and (3) police dispersal of a disorderly crowd in Little Rock, Arkansas, in August 1959. These incidents were chosen by McMillan to illustrate a variety of law enforcement responses to threatened racial conflicts.

67 MARABLE, MANNING. *Race, Reform and Rebellion: The Second Reconstruction in Black America from 1945 to 1982*. Jackson: University Press of Mississippi, 1984. 249 pages.

Marable offers a radical interpretation of black political struggles in the United States since 1945. Among his original insights is the hypothesis that the anti-communist hysteria of the postwar era retarded the fight for desegregation by at least a decade. He also pays close attention to black nationalist organizations, which he credits with "most of the original and innovative political theory and programmes advanced by blacks." He faults the movement for seeking the narrow goals of integration and political rights rather than the "transformation of the entire American political economy and society."

68 MEIER, AUGUST. "Dynamics of Crisis and Unity in the Southern Movement." In *We Shall Overcome*, edited by David J. Garrow, vol. 2, 777–82. Brooklyn, NY: Carlson Publishing, 1989. Orig. pub. in *New America* (10 January 1964): 4–5.

Meier presents five case studies of civil rights protests to illustrate "how, in a crisis situation, the more militant elements compel the more conservative elements in the community to support their strategy."

69 _____. "New Currents in the Civil Rights Movement." In *We Shall Overcome*, edited by David J. Garrow, vol. 2, 737–62. Brooklyn, NY: Carlson Publishing, 1989. Orig. pub. in *New Politics* 2 (Summer 1963): 7–32.

Meier discusses here changes within the civil rights movement during 1963. He stresses its new militancy, the rivalries among civil rights organizations, the growing mass involvement in protests, and the declining role of whites.

70 MENDELSHON, JACK. *The Martyrs.* New York: Harper & Row, 1966. 227 pages.

Mendelshon profiles sixteen people who died in the struggle for civil rights between 1955 and 1965. Among those included are Medgar Evers, Viola Liuzzo, Jonathan Daniels, the four girls killed in the 1963 bombing of Birmingham's 16th Street Baptist Church, and the three civil rights workers murdered in Neshoba County, Mississippi, in the summer of 1964.

71 MILLER, LOREN. "Farewell to Liberals." In *Black Protest Thought in the Twentieth Century*, edited by August Meier, Elliot Rudwick, and Francis L. Broderick, 373–80. Indianapolis: Bobbs-Merrill, 1971. Orig. pub. in *The Nation*, 20 October 1962, 235–238.

Miller expresses the impatience felt by many black activists toward white liberals because of their commitment to "gradualism" and willingness "to see both sides" when dealing with issues of racial discrimination.

72 MUSE, BENJAMIN. *The American Negro Revolution: From Nonviolence to Black Power, 1963–1967.* Bloomington: University of Indiana Press, 1968. 406 pages.

This sequel to Muse's *Ten Years of Prelude* (1964, see entry 73) traces the evolution of the civil rights movement from the 1963 March on Washington to the 1968 Report of the National Advisory Commission on Civil Disorders. The scope of this work extends beyond the South and includes chapters on school boycotts in the North and the ghetto uprisings in the Watts section of Los Angeles and other cities. Muse also chronicles the congressional response to the movement and the role of civil rights in the 1964 presidential election.

73 _____. *Ten Years of Prelude: The Story of Integration Since the Supreme Court's 1954 Decision.* New York: Viking, 1964. 308 pages.

Muse traces southern reaction to the *Brown* decision and the gradual implementation of school desegregation in the South. He characterizes the nine years of turmoil following the decision as "the prelude to an even greater upheaval . . . whose end is not yet in sight."

74 NEWMAN, DOROTHY K., NANCY J. AMIDEI, BARBARA L. CARTER, DAWN DAY, WILLIAM J. KRUVANT, and JACK S. RUSSELL. *Protest, Politics, and Prosperity: Black Americans and White Institutions, 1940–1975.* New York: Pantheon Books, 1978. 348 pages.

The authors examine progress toward economic equality between blacks and whites in the United States from 1940 to 1975. They conclude that "black Americans achieved most when they themselves took up the fight, and also when economic advances were being made in the society at large, so that everyone was gaining and no one group was losing."

75 O'DELL, JACK H. "Climbin' Jacob's Ladder: The Life and Times of the Freedom Movement." *Freedomways* 9, no. 1 (1969): 7–23.
O'Dell reviews the history of the civil rights movement and assesses its future. He emphasizes the role of SCLC and stresses the need to shift priorities from civil rights to the problem of poverty.

76 OPPENHEIMER, MARTIN, and GEORGE LAKEY. "The Civil Rights Movement in American History." In *Problems and Prospects of the Negro Movement*, edited by Raymond J. Murphy and Howard Elinson, 309–17. Belmont, CA: Wadsworth, 1966. Excerpt from *Manual for Direct Action* by Martin Oppenheimer and George Lakey. Chicago: Quadrangle Books, 1965.
Oppenheimer and Lakey identify factors contributing to the emergence of the civil rights movement, and trace its development through 1964.

77 PATTERSON, JAMES. "Business Response to the Negro Movement." *New South* 21, no. 1 (1966): 68–74.
Patterson uses Mississippi as a location to study the role of businessmen in the civil rights movement. He finds that "business managers, acting under pressure to defend their economic welfare, have joined other community groups to make concessions to Negro demands, especially as these demands were backed by new federal legislation." He also discovers, however, that their response was limited since many of the movement's demands "were not things businessmen alone could grant," and it usually required a community crisis to force business leaders to take action as well.

78 PEEKS, EDWARD. *The Long Struggle for Black Power*. New York: Charles Scribner's Sons, 1971. 448 pages.
Peeks links the civil rights movement to the long tradition of black self-help organizations such as Garvey's Universal Negro Improvement Association, the NAACP, and the Black Muslims.

79 PETERS, WILLIAM. *The Southern Temper*. Garden City, NY: Doubleday, 1959. 283 pages.
Peters presents a journalistic account of black and white reaction to the first attempts at desegregation in the South during the 1950s.

80 PIVEN, FRANCES F., and RICHARD CLOWARD. *Poor People's Movements: Why They Succeed, How They Fail*. 1977. Reprint. New York: Vintage Books, 1979. 381 pages.
The civil rights movement is one of four movements included in this sociological analysis. Piven and Cloward stress here the economic origins of social movements. With regard to the civil rights movement, they argue that economic modernization of the South coupled with the urbanization of its

black population "freed blacks from feudal constraints and enabled them to construct the occupational and institutional foundation from which to mount resistance to white oppression."

81 POWLEDGE, FRED. *Free At Last? The Civil Rights Movement and the People Who Made It.* Boston: Little, Brown & Co., 1991. 771 pages.

Powledge covered the civil rights movement for the *Atlanta Journal* and *The New York Times.* His book is a general portrait of the movement written by a journalist who is sympathetic to its goals and objectives. The emphasis is on the people who made up the movement. He shows this by liberally sprinkling each chapter with exerpts from interviews with more than fifty movement activists who relive their experiences and reflect on their significance.

82 ROLAND, CHARLES. *The Improbable Era: The South Since World War II.* Lexington: University Press of Kentucky, 1975. 228 pages.

This account of social and political change in the South includes two relatively brief chapters recounting "the challenge to racial inequality" in the late 1950s and the "achievement of legal equality" in the 1960s.

83 RUSTIN, BAYARD. "New Directions for the Unfinished Revolution." *New America* (24 September 1963): 6–7.

Rustin stresses that the civil rights movement needs to "go deeper into the economic and social questions" and urges a coalition of the labor and civil rights movements to address the problem of unemployment.

84 _____. *Strategies for Freedom: The Changing Patterns of Black Protest.* New York: Columbia University Press, 1976. 82 pages.

This book consists of three lectures delivered at Columbia University. Rustin traces the origins of the civil rights movement back to the 1940s and 50s, through its peak of influence in the 1960s, and describes its future in the 1970s. He repeats the theme he sounded in "From Protest to Politics" (1965, see entry 1116)—that the movement must adopt strategies more suited to compromise and coalition. He faults SCLC and other civil rights organizations for their "continued reliance on the tactics of protest after the potential usefulness of those tactics had been exhausted."

85 RUSTIN, BAYARD, and A. J. MUSTE. "Fundamentals of Strategy for the Struggle for Integration." *Liberation* 5 (May 1960): 5–9.

Rustin and Muste assess the possible strategies for the civil rights movement in the South. They see the greatest chance for success in mass demonstrations which lead to mass arrests. They stress that the movement must be "church-centered and preacher-led." They claim that the nonviolent civil rights movement will result in the liberation of white southerners as well as bringing freedom to southern blacks.

86 SEEGER, PETE, and BOB REISER. *Everybody Says Freedom.* New York: W. W. Norton & Co., 1989. 266 pages.

This popular history of the civil rights movement from 1955 to 1968 emphasizes the music of the movement and includes words and music to most of the best known freedom songs. Another feature is a series of profiles of civil rights activists such as Bernard Lafayette, Dorothy Cotton, Bob Zellner, Annie Devine, and Bob Moses.

87   SITKOFF, HARVARD. *The Struggle for Black Equality, 1954–1980.* New York: Hill & Wang, 1981. 259 pages.

This brief, general history of the civil rights movement covers the period from the *Brown* decision to the assassination of Martin Luther King. Sitkoff focuses on the grass-roots struggle in southern communities more than the political maneuvering in Washington, D.C.; he provides an able synthesis of existing research.

88   SMITH, DONALD H. "Civil Rights: A Problem in Communication." *Phylon* 27 (1966): 379–89.

Smith views the civil rights movement "as an effort to establish communication between two dissonant groups: the have-nots and the haves."

89   SMITH, CHARLES U., and LEWIS M. KILLIAN. "Sociological Foundations of the Civil Rights Movement." In *Sociology in America*, edited by Herbert J. Gans, 105–16. Newbury Park, CA: Sage Publications, 1990.

Smith and Killian examine the limited role of sociologists in the civil rights movement. They cite W. E. B. Du Bois as both a protest leader and a sociologist, but his work was largely ignored by the sociological mainstream. Sociologists did make many important contributions to Myrdal's *An American Dilemma* (1944), but most failed to anticipate the emergence of the movement. Smith and Killian maintain this was due to the discipline's commitment to evolutionary theories of social change, its conception of racial problems as the result of white prejudice, and its tendency to view blacks as passive victims rather than a dynamic force for social change.

90   SOLOMON, FREDERIC, WALTER L. WALKER, GARRETT J. O'CONNOR, and JACOB R. FISHMAN. "Civil Rights Activity and Reduction of Crime among Negroes." *Archives of General Psychiatry* 12 (1965): 227–36.

Fishman and his associates present evidence from three southern cities that a well-organized campaign for civil rights contributes to "a substantial reduction of crimes of violence committed by Negroes."

91   SYNNESTVEDT, SIG. *White Response to Black Emancipation.* New York: Macmillan Publishing Co., 1972. 248 pages.

Synnestvedt traces the history of "the white problem" in America from the Civil War through the civil rights movement, and includes one chapter that summarizes the highlights of the movement. His work here is based largely on secondary sources.

92   TURNER, JOHN B., and WHITNEY M. YOUNG, JR. "Who Has the Revolution or Thoughts on the Second Reconstruction." In *The Negro American*, edited by Talcott Parsons and Kenneth B. Clark, 678–92. Boston: Beacon Press, 1966.

Turner and Young reject the "melting pot" as a model for the Negro revolution. They suggest instead a "group-exploitation deterrance" approach that would include the following elements: "sources of power, the will to use power for group ends, and skill, knowledge, and organization designed to change the rules of the system and to teach the Negro to play a more skilled game within the existing rules."

93   VANDER ZANDEN, JAMES W. "The Nonviolent Resistance Movement against Segregation." *American Journal of Sociology* 68 (March 1963): 540–50.

Vander Zanden argues that the popular support for the nonviolent resistance movement among southern blacks "can be understood as an effort to mediate between the conflicting roles and traditions of the accommodating Negro and the new militant Negro." The psychological appeal of nonviolence, he claims, lies in its ability to offer southern blacks an opportunity to express their hostility towards whites in a socially acceptable manner. Any guilt that protest leaders and participants may feel because of their aggressive actions is mitigated by the movement's emphasis on suffering.

94   VIORST, MILTON. *Fire in the Streets: America in the 1960's.* New York: Simon & Schuster, 1979. 591 pages.

Viorst tells the story of social unrest in the 1960s through his profiles of people who were deeply involved in the movements of this decade. The civil rights leaders Viorst interviewed include E. D. Nixon on the Montgomery bus boycott, John Lewis on the sit-ins, James Farmer on the Freedom Rides, Bayard Rustin on the march on Washington, Joseph Rauh on the 1964 Democratic convention, and Stokely Carmichael on Black Power.

95   WAKEFIELD, DAN. *Revolt in the South.* New York: Grove Press, 1960. 128 pages.

Wakefield describes the first phase of the civil rights movement between 1954 and 1960, which he covered for *The Nation* magazine. Among the topics he reports on are the growth of the White Citizens' Council in Mississippi, the plight of white moderates, and the growing militance of young blacks.

96   WALKER, ALICE. "The Civil Rights Movement: What Good Was It?" *American Scholar* 36 (Autumn 1967): 550–54.

Walker responds to skeptics who question the value of the civil rights movement. She argues that it was responsible for transforming the attitudes and personal lives of many black Americans: "It gave us history and men far greater than Presidents. It gave us heroes, selfless men of courage and strength, for our little boys to follow. It gave us hope for tomorrow. It gave us life."

97   WALKER, WYATT T. "The Techniques of Winning Freedom Now." *Negro Digest*, March 1964, 6–10.

Walker proposes national campaigns of "economic withdrawal," civil disobedience, and work stoppage to draw national attention to civil rights.

98 WASKOW, ARTHUR I. "'Creative Disorder' in the Racial Struggle." In *Problems and Prospects of the Negro Movement*, edited by Raymond F. Murphy and Howard Elinson, 324–37. Belmont, CA: Wadsworth, 1966. Orig. pub. in *The Correspondent* 32 (Autumn 1964).

Waskow describes the "politics of disorder" employed by the civil rights movement, and assesses its future. He identifies three factors which will determine its continued use in the movement: (1) the response of the government, (2) its success in resolving conflicts, and (3) "the degree of inventiveness and self-discipline in the Negro community."

99 _____. *From Race Riot to Sit-in: 1919 and the 1960s*. Garden City, NY: Doubleday, 1966. 380 pages.

Waskow contrasts the race riots of 1919 with the nonviolent movement for racial equality of the 1960s.

100 WATTERS, PAT. *Down to Now: Reflections on the Southern Civil Rights Movement*. New York: Pantheon Books, 1971. 426 pages.

Watters covered the civil rights movement first as a reporter and later as a writer for the Southern Regional Council. His book about the rise and fall of the southern nonviolent direct action movement for racial integration is based on his personal recollections and reflections. He views the movement as offering "salvation" to American society—the chance to break down "the artificial barriers to fellowship" between blacks and whites. Although he describes civil rights efforts in many communities, he views the campaign in Albany, Georgia, as the epitome of the movement. He also offers important observations on the role of music and the shortcomings of media coverage.

101 _____. "The Mob Behind the Marchers." *The Reporter*, 18 June 1964, 34–35.

Watters examines here the possibility "that direct action in the South this summer may bring an end to the near-miracle of Negro nonviolence." He reviews several incidents in which black-initiated violence flared in conjunction with civil rights protests, and discusses the difficulty faced by leaders in keeping the movement nonviolent.

102 _____. "The Spring Offensive: Negroes Plan the Future." *The Nation*, 3 February 1964, 117–20.

Watters discusses plans for civil rights actions in 1964 based on interviews with Martin Luther King, John Lewis, and James Forman. None of the leaders expresses any willingness to curtail demonstrations because of the coming presidential election. Rather, they stress the need to create a situation that would give Lyndon Johnson the opportunity "to prove himself" on civil rights.

103 WEISBROT, ROBERT. *Freedom Bound: A History of the Civil Rights Movement*. New York: W. W. Norton & Co., 1990. 350 pages.

Weisbrot traces the history of the civil rights movement from 1960 to 1970. He argues that the liberal coalition of the 1960s wrought "a self-limiting revolution that abolished formal barriers to equality while leaving intact the basic features of a system in which blacks had played a subordinate, marginal role."

104   WEST, CORNEL. "The Paradox of the Afro-American Rebellion." In *The Sixties without Apology*, edited by Stanley Aronowitz, 44–58. Minneapolis: University of Minnesota Press, 1984.

West presents a Marxist analysis of the civil rights movement. The paradox he refers to is that the aims of the "small yet determined petite bourgeoisie" who initiated the movement were essentially liberal, but the black masses whose support made the movement possible had more radical aspirations. He divides the movement into two stages: before and after the March on Washington. Following the march, the newly radicalized students increasingly questioned the legitimacy of the established black leadership. The subsequent revolt of the black masses led to the development of black nationalism, which West dismisses as "the activity of black petite bourgeois self-congratulation and self-justification upon reaching an anxiety-ridden middle class status."

105   WILLIAMS, JUAN. *Eyes on the Prize: America's Civil Rights Years, 1954–1965.* New York: Viking, 1987. 320 pages.

Williams gives a brief general history of the civil rights movement based on the PBS "Eyes on the Prize" television documentary series.

106   WILSON, JAMES Q. "The Strategy of Protest: Problems of Negro Civic Action." *Journal of Conflict Resolution* 5 (September 1961): 291–303.

Wilson discusses the conditions necessary for successful protest activity, both in northern cities and in the South. He concludes that protest is best suited to "situations in which the goal sought is defensive, specific, of a welfare character, relevant to the wants of the Negro rank-and-file and has an explicit target."

107   WIRMARK, BO. "Nonviolent Methods and the American Civil Rights Movement, 1955–1965." *Journal of Peace Research* 11 (1974): 115–32.

Wirmark examines the role of nonviolent tactics in the civil rights movement. Drawing heavily on the work of Oppenheimer (1989, see entry 1037) and Laue (1989, see entry 55), he develops a model of an ideal typical civil rights campaign. He identifies five stages: preparation, challenge, conflict, crisis and confrontation, and communication. He also discusses the changing ideology of nonviolence in the movement and the effectiveness of nonviolent methods.

108   WOFFORD, HARRIS. "Gandhi the Civil Rights Lawyer." In *We Shall Overcome*, edited by David J. Garrow, vol. 3, 1151–62. Brooklyn, NY: Carlson Publishing, 1989. Speech delivered at Hampton Institute, 10 November 1955.

Wofford advocates using Gandhian principles of nonviolent civil disobedience in the coming civil rights struggle.

109   WOODWARD, C. VANN. "What happened to the Civil Rights Movement?" *Harper's*, January 1967, 29–37.

Noted historian Woodward compares the civil rights movement with the Reconstruction period. Although there are some striking similarities between the two eras, he points out that the civil rights movement was black-initiated and black-led, unlike the Reconstruction. He concludes that the gains of the movement are too strongly institutionalized to permit a retreat from civil rights similar to the Compromise of 1876 which ended the Reconstruction.

110   WYNN, DANIEL W. *The Black Protest Movement.* New York: Philosophical Library, 1974. 258 pages.

Wynn examines the historical development of five major black protest movements: (1) "legal action" of the NAACP, (2) "revolutionary protest antagonism" of leftist groups allied with the Communist party, (3) "nonviolent direct action" of Martin Luther King, (4) "militant direct action" of the Black Muslims, Malcolm X, and the Black Panther party, and (5) the Black Power movement.

111   X, MALCOLM. "Black Muslims and Civil Rights." In *Freedom Now! The Civil Rights Struggle in America*, edited by Alan F. Westin, 52–60. New York: Basic Books, 1964. Orig. pub. in *Playboy*, May 1963, 53–63.

Malcolm X presents the Black Muslim perspective on race relations in the United States.

112   X, MALCOLM, and JAMES FARMER. "Separation vs. Integration." In *Black Protest Thought in the Twentieth Century*, edited by August Meier, Elliot Rudwick, and Francis L. Broderick, 387–412. Indianapolis: Bobbs-Merrill, 1971. Orig. pub. in *Dialogue* 2 (May 1962): 14–18.

The leading spokesman for separatism (Malcolm X) debates a prominent advocate of integration (James Farmer) over the goals and methods of the civil rights movement.

113   YOUNG, WHITNEY M., JR. *To Be Equal.* New York: McGraw-Hill, 1964. 254 pages.

Young sets forth an agenda for social changes in areas such as employment, education, housing, and health care that he feels is needed if the goal of racial equality is to be reached.

114   ZANGRANDO, ROBERT L. "From Civil Rights to Black Liberation: The Unsettled 1960's." *Current History* 56, no. 7 (1969): 281–99.

Zangrando reviews changes in American race relations during the 1960s. He views the summer of 1964 as the critical moment in the shift from civil rights to black liberation. The refusal to seat the Mississippi Freedom Democratic party delegates at the Democratic convention, he argues, convinced militants within SNCC "that there was no longer any reason to adhere

to the integrationist, nonviolent, direct-action tactics" that they had previously advocated.

115   ZINN, HOWARD. "The Double Job in Civil Rights." In *We Shall Over-
      come*, edited by David J. Garrow, vol. 3, 1163–68. Brooklyn, NY:
      Carlson Publishing, 1989. Orig. pub. in *New Politics* 3 (Winter 1964):
      29–34.

Zinn discusses the challenges facing the civil rights movement. He
stresses the need to look beyond the issue of racial segregation and to focus
on the economic arrangements which produce racial inequality.

3

Collected Works

116 BARBOUR, FLOYD B., ed. *The Black Power Revolt: A Collection of Essays.* Boston: Porter Sargent Publisher, 1968. 287 pages.

A collection of thirty-seven essays dealing with Black Power. The first section consists of documents related to the history of blacks in America. The second section discusses the concept of Black Power, with contributions from Stokely Carmichael, Vincent Harding, LeRoi Jones, and others. The third section gives examples of Black Power in action, with contributions from Robert F. Williams, Ron Karenga, and Nathan Hare, among others. The final section includes six personal reactions to Black Power. Eleven of the essays in this book appear in print for the first time.

117 BARDOLPH, RICHARD A., ed. *The Civil Rights Record: Black Americans and the Law, 1840–1970.* New York: Thomas Y. Crowell & Co., 1970. 558 pages.

This valuable work consists of exerpts from judicial rulings, federal and state laws, presidential statements, political platforms, and comments by contemporary observers on the subject of black civil rights. The last and most extensive section of this book covers the period from the 1954 *Brown* decision to 1970. Bardolph provides a narrative which brings together information from a wide range of legal and judical sources.

118 BLAUSTEIN, ALBERT P., and ROBERT L. ZANGRANDO, eds. *Civil Rights and the American Negro: A Documentary History.* New York: Trident Press, 1968. 671 pages.

This collection documents the legal status of African Americans from their arrival at Jamestown in 1619. Section 8 covers the period from 1957 to 1968. It includes information on legislation, court decisions, and reports of government commissions.

119   BRACEY, JOHN H., JR., AUGUST MEIER, and ELLIOT RUDWICK, eds. *Conflict and Competition: Studies in the Recent Black Protest Movement.* Belmont, CA: Wadsworth Publishing, 1971. 239 pages.

This book contains fourteen articles previously published in social science journals. Half deal with the nonviolent civil rights movement of the early 1960s, and the rest discuss Black Power and the urban riots of the late 1960s.

120   BRODERICK, FRANCIS L., and AUGUST MEIER, eds. *Negro Protest Thought in the Twentieth Century.* New York: Bobbs-Merrill, 1965. 443 pages.

A collection of primary documents dealing with the black protest movement in the United States. Part 4 covers the modern civil rights movement and includes statements and articles reflecting the positions of the major civil rights leaders and organizations.

121   CARSON, CLAYBORNE, DAVID J. GARROW, VINCENT HARDING, and DIANE CLARK HINE, eds. *Eyes On the Prize: A Reader and Guide.* New York: Penguin, 1987. 355 pages.

A collection of primary source material and original essays compiled as a study guide to accompany the PBS television series "Eyes On the Prize."

122   COLES, ROBERT. *Farewell to the South.* Boston: Little, Brown & Co., 1972. 258 pages.

This collection of Coles's essays from the 1960s includes his conversations with civil rights activists and segregationists. As a humanistic psychiatrist, he views both groups with sympathy and understanding.

123   CRAWFORD, VICKI L., JACQUELINE ANNE ROUSE, and BARBARA WOODS, eds. *Women in the Civil Rights Movement: Trailblazers and Torchbearers, 1941–1965.* Vol 16, *Black Women in United States History*, edited by Darlene Clark Hine. Brooklyn, NY: Carlson Publishing, 1990. 290 pages.

This volume consists of seventeen original essays about women in the civil rights movement. Seven of the essays profile specific individuals such as Fannie Lou Hamer, Ella Baker, and Gloria Richardson. Others focus on the roles of women within the movement, or on specific organizations. (Each essay is listed individually in this bibliography.)

124   CRUSE, HAROLD. *Rebellion or Revolution?* New York: William Morrow & Co., 1968. 272 pages.

This collection of essays includes Cruse's criticism of the integrationist goals of the civil rights movements, and a presentation of his own nationalist views.

125   EAGLES, CHARLES W., ed. *The Civil Rights Movement in America.* Jackson: University Press of Mississippi, 1986. 188 pages.

This book consists of six essays on various aspects of the civil rights movement that were originally presented during a symposium at the University of Mississippi from Oct. 2–4, 1985. Each of the articles is accompanied by a short response by a prominent scholar. (Each essay is listed individually in this bibliography.)

126 FORMAN, JAMES. *The Political Thought of James Forman.* Detroit: Black Star Publishing, 1970. 190 pages.

Speeches and articles by SNCC leader Forman from 1966 to 1969—a time when he advanced a revolutionary nationalist position and SNCC formed an alliance with the Black Panther party.

127 FRANKLIN, JOHN HOPE, and ISIDORE STARR, eds. *The Negro in Twentieth Century America: A Reader on the Struggle for Civil Rights.* New York: Vintage Books, 1967. 542 pages.

This collection of primary source material includes statements by civil rights leaders, white reactions to black protest, and sections dealing with specific issues such as education, voting rights, justice, employment, and housing.

128 FRIEDMAN, LEON, ed. *The Civil Rights Reader: Basic Documents of the Civil Rights Movement.* New York: Walker & Co., 1968. 382 pages.

This is a compilation of primary source material on the civil rights movement from 1954 to 1968. It includes excerpts from journalistic accounts, popular books, court decisions, reports by governmental and private agencies, legislation, and presidential speeches.

129 _____. *Southern Justice.* New York: Pantheon Books, 1965. 306 pages.

This is a collection of essays dealing with legal obstacles faced by the civil rights movement in Mississippi. Most of the authors were involved with the 1964 Mississippi Summer Project. (Each essay is listed individually in this bibliography.)

130 GARROW, DAVID J., ed. *Atlanta, Georgia, 1960–1961: Sit-ins and Student Activism.* Brooklyn, NY: Carlson Publishing, 1989. 195 pages.

This volume is a collection of articles dealing with the civil rights movement in Atlanta. (Each article is listed individually in this bibliography.)

131 _____. *Birmingham, Alabama, 1956–1963: The Black Struggle for Civil Rights.* Brooklyn, NY: Carlson Publishing, 1989. 299 pages.

This work includes three previously unpublished studies of the civil rights movement in Birmingham. (Each study is listed individually in this bibliography.)

132 _____. *Chicago 1966: Open Housing Marches, Summit Negotiations and Operation Breadbasket.* Brooklyn, NY: Carlson Publishing, 1989. 359 pages.

This collection consists of five previously unpublished studies and three documents all dealing with the civil rights campaign in the city of Chicago in 1966. (Each study is listed individually in this bibliography.)

133 _____. *St. Augustine, Florida, 1963–1964: Mass Protest and Racial Violence.* Brooklyn, NY: Carlson Publishing, 1989. 364 pages.

This volume contains three studies and one government document, all dealing with desegregation protests led by Martin Luther King in St. Augustine during 1963 and 1964. (Each study is listed individually in this bibliography.)

134 _____. *The Walking City: The Montgomery Bus Boycott, 1955–1956.* Brooklyn, NY: Carlson Publishing, 1989. 636 pages.

This volume assembles eleven previously published articles and unpublished studies, including Ralph Abernathy's M.A. thesis, all dealing with the Montgomery bus boycott. (Each article is listed individually in this bibliography.)

135 _____. *We Shall Overcome: The Civil Rights Movement in the United States in the 1950's and the 1960's.* 3 vols. Brooklyn, NY: Carlson Publishing, 1989. 1201 pages.

This work is a collection of fifty-two articles and papers, most of which were previously published, on various aspects of the civil rights movement. (Each article is listed individually in this bibliography.)

136 GESCHWENDER, JAMES, ed. *The Black Revolt: The Civil Rights Movement, Ghetto Uprisings, and Separatism.* Englewood Cliffs, NJ: Prentice Hall Press, 1971. 483 pages.

Sixteen of the previously published essays in this volume deal with various aspects of the civil rights movement, all are by social scientists. Topics covered include conditions contributing to the protests, civil rights organizations, leadership, tactics, and characteristics of participants.

137 GRANT, JOANNE, ed. *Black Protest: History, Documents, and Analyses.* Greenwich, CT: Fawcett World Library, 1968. 505 pages.

This collection of primary source material on black protest in America ranges from slavery to Black Power, but the majority of the book covers the civil rights movement and its consequences. Nearly all of the selections included in this book are written by eyewitnesses or by movement participants such as Rosa Parks, James Forman, Robert Moses, and John Lewis. Much of the material found here is not available elsewhere.

138 HAMPTON, HENRY, STEVE FAGER, and SARAH FLYNN. *Voices of Freedom: An Oral History of the Civil Rights Movement from the 1950's Through the 1980's.* New York: Bantam Books, 1990. 692 pages.

A collection of interviews with participants in the civil rights movement that was compiled during the production of the PBS television series, "Eyes On the Prize."

139 HARE, A. PAUL, and HERBERT H. BLUMBERG. *Nonviolent Direct Action: American Cases: Social-Psychological Analyses.* Washington, DC: Corpus Books, 1968. 575 pages.

This collection of material on nonviolence includes six case studies of civil rights protests and nine social-psychological analyses of nonviolent protests.

140   JACOWAY, ELIZABETH, and DAVID R. COLBURN, eds. *Southern Business-men and Desegregation.* Baton Rouge: Louisiana State University Press, 1982. 324 pages.

This collection of original articles describes the desegregation process in fourteen southern cities. Some are well-known scenes of racial conflict (Little Rock, Birmingham, St. Augustine). Other received relatively little national publicity (Augusta, Louisville, Columbia). The emphasis in all of these case histories is on the role of white business leaders in response to the desegregation crises in their cities. Some studies focus on a single year (e.g., New Orleans in 1960), while others cover a broader time span (e.g., Birmingham 1950–1963). (Each article is listed individually in this bibliography.)

141   KING, DONALD B., and CHARLES W. QUICK, eds. *Legal Aspects of the Civil Rights Movement.* Detroit: Wayne State University Press, 1965. 447 pages.

This volume contains fourteen articles dealing with legal issues raised by the civil rights movement. It includes chapters dealing with specific areas such as education, voting, housing, transportation, employment, and public accommodations.

142   LINCOLN, C. ERIC. *Sounds of the Struggle: Persons and Perspectives in Civil Rights.* New York: William Morrow & Co., 1967. 252 pages.

This collection of previously pubished essays covers various questions facing African Americans during the 1960s. Several discuss the Black Muslims and black religion; only one deals directly with the civil rights movement.

143   LYND, STAUGHTON, ed. *Nonviolence in America: A Documentary History.* Indianapolis: Bobbs-Merrill, 1966. 535 pages.

This collection of documents deals with nonviolence in America. The last section covers the civil rights movement and includes several valuable reports from civil rights activists covering the period of 1961 to 1964.

144   MCCORD, JOHN H., ed. *With All Deliberate Speed: Civil Rights Theory and Reality.* Urbana: University of Illinois Press, 1969. 205 pages.

The six articles in this collection deal with legal issues concerning civil rights in various fields, including education, housing, employment, and public accommodations.

145   MARX, GARY T., ed. *Racial Conflict: Tension and Change in American Society.* Boston: Little, Brown & Co., 1971. 489 pages.

This volume contains fifty-four articles previously published in social science journals. Fourteen deal specifically with various aspects of the civil rights movement.

146   MEIER, AUGUST, ed. *The Transformation of Activism: Black Experience.* Chicago: Aldine Publishing Co., 1970. 178 pages.

This collection contains nine articles on various aspects of race relations and civil rights published in *Trans-action* magazine between 1967 and 1969.

147   MEIER, AUGUST, and ELLIOT RUDWICK, eds. *Black Protest in the Sixties.* Chicago: Quadrangle Books, 1970. 355 pages.

This book consists of twenty-seven articles which appeared in *The New York Times* between 1960 and 1969. Some are straight news stories, while others are in-depth analyses and profiles by free-lance writers and prominent authorities such as Kenneth Clark, Charles V. Hamilton, and C. Vann Woodward.

148   MEIER, AUGUST, ELLIOT RUDWICK, and FRANCIS L. BRODERICK, eds. *Black Protest Thought in the Twentieth Century.* 2d ed. Indianapolis: Bobbs-Merrill, 1971. Orig. pub. as *Negro Protest Thought in the Twentieth Century.*

This excellent collection of source materials consists primarily of speeches, reports, and articles in obscure journals which are not widely available elsewhere. The first two sections focus on the period before the Montgomery bus boycott. Section 3 covers "The Era of Nonviolent Direct Action," while section 4 discusses "The Era of Black Power."

149   MITCHELL, GLENFORD E., and WILLIAM H. PEACE III, eds. *The Angry Black South: Southern Negroes Tell Their Own Story.* New York: Corinth Books, 1962. 159 pages.

This is a collection of essays by young, college-educated blacks who were involved in the leadership of the civil rights movement in their communities. Five of the six authors are graduates of or are affiliated with North Carolina colleges.

150   MURPHY, RAYMOND J., and HOWARD ELINSON, eds. *Problems and Prospects of the Negro Movement.* Belmont, CA: Wadsworth, 1966. 440 pages.

Section 3, "Prospects and Strategies," contains eight previously published articles dealing with the civil rights movement.

151   NAMORATO, MICHAEL V., ed. *Have We Overcome? Race Relations Since Brown.* Jackson: University Press of Mississippi, 1979. 232 pages.

This volume contains seven articles by scholars and journalists presented at a 1978 symposium assessing the state of race relations in the United States in the quarter century since the *Brown* decision. Most of them deal, directly or indirectly, with the consequences of the civil rights movement.

152   PARSONS, TALCOTT, and KENNETH B. CLARK, eds. *The Negro American.* Boston: Beacon Press, 1966. 781 pages.

This collection of twenty-seven articles by prominent scholars deals with many issues affecting African Americans. Four deal directly with the civil rights movement.

153   PRICE, STEVEN D., comp. *Civil Rights.* Vol. 2, *1967–68.* New York: Facts on File, 1973. 437 pages.

This reference work contains a chronology and brief descriptions of news events related to civil rights in 1967 and 1968.

154   RAINES, HOWELL. *My Soul Is Rested: Movement Days in the Deep South Remembered.* New York: G. P. Putnam's Sons, 1977. 472 pages.

This is a collection of interviews with people directly involved in the southern civil rights movement from 1955 to 1968. Raines has captured the spirit of the times by speaking not only with the recognized leaders of the movement, but also by interviewing "foot soldiers" who risked their lives on the "front lines" of movement action. Major sections of the book include: the Montgomery bus boycott, the student sit-ins, the Freedom Rides, Birmingham, Selma, and Mississippi. He also includes interviews with segregationists, lawyers and lawmen, and reporters.

155   RECORD, WILSON, and JANE C. RECORD, eds. *Little Rock, U.S.A.: Materials for Analysis.* San Francisco: Chandler Publishing Co., 1960. 338 pages.

This volume is a collection of documentary source material dealing with the 1957 desegregation crisis in Little Rock, Arkansas.

156   ROSE, ARNOLD M., ed. *The Negro Protest.* Philadelphia: American Academy of Political and Social Sciences, 1965. 214 pages.

Originally published in the *Annals of the American Academy of Political & Social Sciences* in 1965, these academic essays deal with various aspects of blacks' social and economic conditions as well as the civil rights movement.

157   RUSTIN, BAYARD. *Down the Line: Collected Writings of Bayard Rustin.* Chicago: Quadrangle Books, 1971. 355 pages.

Rustin was one of the most influential thinkers and organizers in the movement. This volume contains his writings from 1942 to 1971, but a majority date from 1966 and later. Of particular interest are his accounts of the 1947 Journey of Reconciliation and the white reaction against desegregation in the Mississippi Delta in 1956. Also included are two of his most influential essays: "From Protest to Politics: The Future of the Civil Rights Movement," and "Black Power and Coalition Politics." Included is a brief biographical introduction by C. Vann Woodward.

158   SMITH, CHARLES U., ed. *The Civil Rights Movement in Florida and the United States: Historical and Contemporary Perspectives.* Tallahassee, FL: Father & Son Press, 1989. 326 pages.

Six of the essays in this collection deal with the civil rights movement in Tallahassee and Florida A & M, one covers school desegregation in Florida, and three address civil rights issues at the national level.

159   SOBEL, LESTER A., ed. *Civil Rights, 1960–1966.* New York: Facts on File, 1967. 504 pages.

This reference work contains a chronology and brief accounts of news events related to civil rights from 1960 to 1966.

160   SUTHERLAND, ELIZABETH, ed. *Letters from Mississippi.* New York: McGraw-Hill, 1965. 234 pages.

This collection of letters written by civil rights volunteers captures the exhilaration and fear they experienced while working in the Mississippi Summer Project of 1964.

161   SWIFT, JEANNINE, ed. *Dream and Reality: The Modern Black Struggle for Freedom and Equality.* Westport, CT: Greenwood Press, 1991. 155 pages.

This book consists of thirteen papers presented at a 1988 conference of the same name. Three deal particularly with the civil rights movement. (Each paper is listed individually in this bibliography.)

162   WARREN, ROBERT PENN. *Who Speaks for the Negro?* New York: Random House, 1965. 454 pages.

Warren traveled the country speaking with a variety of prominent blacks on their views of the civil rights movement and race relations in America. This book contains lengthy quotes from the civil rights leaders he interviewed including Aaron Henry, Robert Moses, Charles Evers, Stokely Carmichael, Roy Wilkins, Whitney Young, Martin Luther King, Wyatt T. Walker, James Forman, James Farmer, and Bayard Rustin.

163   WESTIN, ALAN F., ed. *Freedom Now! The Civil Rights Struggle in America.* New York: Basic Books, 1964. 346 pages.

The fifty-one articles dealing with various aspects of civil rights and racial discrimination in this volume are taken from scholarly journals, the popular press, and government documents. A majority of the articles discuss racial inequality and efforts to combat it in the North.

164   YOUNG, RICHARD P., ed. *Roots of Rebellion: The Evolution of Black Politics and Protest Since World War II.* New York: Harper & Row, 1970. 482 pages.

This collection of twenty-five previously published articles on American race relations since 1945 includes several works that discuss in whole or in part the civil rights movement.

165   ZINN, HOWARD. *The Southern Mystique.* New York: Alfred A. Knopf, 1964. 267 pages.

This book consists of four essays on various aspects of the civil rights movement and the South. In the first two Zinn writes about southern whites and blacks, drawing upon his experiences as a white professor at Spellman College in Atlanta. The third is an account of the Albany movement of 1961 to 1962 with emphasis on the work of SNCC organizers there. The final essay discusses the relationship between the South and the rest of the United States. He argues that the entire United States possesses all of the negative characteristics that are commonly attributed solely to the South.

4

States

Alabama

166   ABERNATHY, RALPH D. "The Natural History of a Social Movement: The Montgomery Improvement Association." In *The Walking City: The Montgomery Bus Boycott, 1955–1956*, edited by David J. Garrow, 99–172. Brooklyn, NY: Carlson Publishing, 1989. M.A. thesis, Atlanta University, 1958.

Abernathy's study of the Montgomery Improvement Association contains his personal insights as a man who was directly involved with the bus boycott from its earliest stages.

167   ADLER, RENATA. "Letter from Selma." *New Yorker*, 10 April 1965, 121–57.

Adler gives a day-by-day account of the Selma to Montgomery march. She dwells on the disorganization and disagreements among the marchers. She claims they lacked "a sharply defined sense of purpose" and that events "had made the march itself ceremonial—almost redundant."

168   AMMERMAN, NANCY T. "The Civil Rights Movement and the Clergy in a Southern Community." *Sociological Analysis* 41, no. 4 (1981): 339–50.

Ammerman interviewed seventy-two white clergymen in Tuscaloosa, Alabama, regarding their involvement in the civil rights movement. She found that affiliation with a "mainline" denomination, an urban childhood, and perceived support from fellow clergy were the strongest indicators of civil rights activism.

169   AUSTIN, ALEINE. "Behind the Montgomery Bus Boycott." *Monthly Review* 8 (September 1956): 163–67.

Austin attempts to identify the "factors which account for the occurrence of organized resistance in Montgomery." She identifies three main factors: (1) a history of protest activities, (2) favorable decisions by federal courts, and (3) the emergence of new, highly educated leaders. These, she argues, are all "by-products of the economic development of the South."

170 BAINS, LEE E., JR. "Birmingham, 1963: Confrontation over Civil Rights." In *Birmingham, Alabama, 1956–1963: The Black Struggle for Civil Rights*, edited by David J. Garrow, 151–289. Brooklyn, NY: Carlson Publishing, 1989. B.A. honors essay at Harvard University, 1977.

Bains's account of the 1963 Birmingham demonstrations concentrates on the responses of seven nonblack participants to the black protests. Among those he cites as exacerbating the problem were the city commission, especially Eugene "Bull" Connor, the newly-elected mayor and members of the city council, the state government of Alabama, and the hard-core white racists. According to Bains, those working to solve the city's racial problems were liberal white activists, white business leaders, and the federal government, especially Assistant Attorney General Burke Marshall.

171 BLASI, ANTHONY J. *Segregationist Violence and Civil Rights Movements in Tuscaloosa*. Washington, DC: University Press of America, 1980. 168 pages.

Blasi compares the civil rights movement of the 1950s and 1960s in Tuscaloosa, Alabama, with segregationist violence in the same city during the 1920s and 1930s. He points out that unlike in the earlier period, moderate white business leaders intervened in the later years to deflect the threats of Ku Klux Klan attacks on integrationists. The local black movement is portrayed as remaining independent of both national civil rights organizations and local political associations.

172 BOYNTON, AMELIA P. *Bridge Across Jordan*. New York: Carlton Press, 1979. 190 pages.

Amelia Boynton was a grass-roots leader of the civil rights movement in Selma, Alabama. As head of the Dallas County Voters League, she worked against great odds to promote black voter registration. Because of Boynton's efforts, Martin Luther King, Jr., chose Selma as the site of one of the major confrontations of the civil rights movement. Boynton's autobiography contributes to a greater understanding of the forces at work in Selma in 1965.

173 BRADEN, ANNE. "Birmingham, 1956–1979: The History That We Made." *Southern Exposure* 8 (Summer 1979): 48–54.

Braden interviews Rev. Fred Shuttlesworth, a leader of the civil rights movement in Birmingham, and describes his efforts to desegregate public schools and buses in the 1950s.

174 BURKS, MARY FAIR. "Trailblazers: Women in the Montgomery Bus Boycott." In *Women in the Civil Rights Movement*, edited by Vicki L. Crawford, Jacqueline Anne Rouse, and Barbara Woods, 71–83. Brooklyn, NY: Carlson Publishing, 1990.

Mary Fair Burks was a leader of the Women's Political Council (WPC) in Montgomery, Alabama. This organization had been protesting segregated transportation and official mistreatment of black citizens for many years prior to the Montgomery bus boycott. She describes in this essay her own involvement with the WPC, as well as the contributions of Rosa Parks and Jo Ann Gibson Robinson to the organization. Her account supplements Robinson's memoir, *The Montgomery Bus Boycott and the Women Who Started It* (1987, see entry 227).

175 CAMPBELL, DAVID. "The Lowndes County Freedom Organization: An appraisal." *New South* 37 (Winter 1972): 37–42.

In assessing the impact of the Lowndes County Freedom Organization (LCFO), Campbell finds that it had important effects at local, state, and national levels. It was responsible for organizing black political power in Lowndes County and for electing local officials, most notably the sheriff. It brought legal suits that changed Alabama law in areas such as jury selection and the justice of the peace system. Campbell also states that the LCFO served as a predecessor for the Black Panther party and helped set "the tone of American black-white race relations during the middle 1960's."

176 CAPECI, DOMINIC J., JR. "From Harlem to Montgomery: The Bus Boycott and Leadership of Adam Clayton Powell, Jr., and Martin Luther King, Jr." In *The Walking City*, edited by David J. Garrow, 303–22. Brooklyn, NY: Carlson Publishing, 1989. Orig. Pub. in *Historian* 41 (August 1979): 721–37.

Capeci finds many similarities between King's role in the Montgomery bus boycott and Powell's leadership in a similar protest in Harlem in 1941.

177 CHESTNUT, J. L., JR., and JULIA CASS. *Black in Selma: The Uncommon Life of J. L. Chestnut, Jr.* New York: Farrar, Straus & Giroux, 1990. 432 pages.

As the first black attorney in Selma, Alabama, J. L. Chestnut was in the midst of one of the most bitter and prolonged struggles of the civil rights movement. His insider's perspective adds valuable insights to the workings of the movement.

178 CLARK, JAMES G., JR. *The Jim Clark Story—"I Saw Selma Raped".* Birmingham: Selma Enterprises, 1966. 114 pages.

Clark, the sheriff of Dallas County, Alabama, defends his handling of the Selma protests in this work, and denounces the Selma to Montgomery march.

179 COOMBS, DAVID, M. H. ALSIKAFI, C. HOBSON BRYAN, and IRVING WEBBER. "Black Political Control in Greene County, Alabama." *Rural Sociology* 42, no. 3 (1977): 398–406.

Coombs et al. compare Greene County, where blacks had gained control of all elective offices, with neighboring Wilcox and Bullock Counties. They found that Green County had experienced: (1) a more rapid increase in governmental employment, (2) a greater flow of external public and private resources, (3) a greater improvement in black living standards, and (4) a higher degree of agreement between black and white leadership.

180 CORLEY, ROBERT. "In Search of Racial Harmony: Birmingham Business Leaders and Desegregation, 1950–1963." In *Southern Businessmen and Desegregation*, edited by Elizabeth Jacoway and David R. Colburn, 170–90. Baton Rouge: Louisiana State University Press, 1982.

Corley examines the role of white businessmen in Birmingham's racial crisis of 1950 to 1963. In 1950 moderate leaders formed the Interracial Committee, which won a few gains for blacks until it was forced to disband in the worsening atmosphere of 1956. Corley writes of this atmosphere: "The silence of moderate voices after 1956 permitted Birmingham to become the scene of some of the most violent episodes of the desegregation crisis." He points out that business leaders began to reclaim civil leadership in 1962 when they led the drive to replace Eugene "Bull" Connor and the commission form of government. He also states that it was these same leaders who negotiated with Martin Luther King, Jr., and SCLC in 1963 to end segregation in downtown stores and halt the mass demonstrations.

181 CORRY, JOHN. "A Visit to Lowndes County, Alabama." *New South* 27 (Winter 1972): 28–36.

Lowndes County, Alabama, had the reputation of being the "meanest" county in the South for civil rights workers. In 1965, two activists were killed and another was seriously wounded. Also in 1965, the Lowndes County Freedom Organization (LCFO) was established with the black panther as its symbol. In 1970 John Hulett, the leader of the LCFO, was elected sheriff of Lowndes County. Corry describes the considerable progress toward greater racial equality in this predominately black rural county and the lingering resentment of its white citizens towards that equality.

182 CUMMING, JOSEPH B. "Slumbering Greene County, a Remote Sliver of Alabama, Where Blacks and Whites May Realize the Highest Hope for the South and America." *Southern Voices*, March 1974, 22–30.

In 1970, voters in Greene County elected black candidates to five seats on the local school board, in addition to four black county commissioners and a black probate judge and sheriff. Cumming describes the adjustment of local whites to their loss of power and their few tentative steps to build interracial alliances.

183 DEMUTH, JERRY. "Black Belt, Alabama." In *We Shall Overcome*, edited by David J. Garrow, vol. 1, 181–88. Brooklyn, NY: Carlson Publishing, 1989. Orig. pub. in *Commonweal* 80 (7 August 1964): 536–39.

DeMuth describes the efforts of the civil rights movement in working for desegregation in Selma and in Dallas County against the determined opposition of Sheriff Jim Clark and his posse of deputies.

184 DURR, CLIFFORD. "Sociology and the Law: A Field Trip to Montgomery, Alabama." In *Southern Justice*, edited by Leon Friedman, 43–56. New York: Pantheon Books, 1965.

Durr describes the experiences of ten white students from McMurray College in Illinois who were arrested for attending a meeting at a black cafe in Montgomery, Alabama, while participating in a sociological field trip in 1960.

185 DURR, VIRGINIA FOSTER. *Outside the Magic Circle: The Autobiography of Virginia Foster Durr.* Edited by Hollinger F. Barnard. Tuscaloosa: University of Alabama Press, 1985. 360 pages.

Virginia Durr belonged to a socially prominent white family in Montgomery, Alabama, at the time of the Montgomery bus boycott. She had befriended Rosa Parks and it was her husband, attorney Clifford Durr, who bailed Parks out of jail following her arrest in 1955. Virginia Durr was an eyewitness to many of the events of the civil rights movement, and was a personal friend to many of its leading figures. The last four chapters of this autobiography contain her observations of the movement. Especially interesting is her assessment of several prominent white Alabamians such as Judge Frank Johnson ("tense" and "extremely strict"), George Wallace ("extremely smart as a politician," but "a little off-base"), and her cousin, Governor John Patterson ("just one long stream of racist insults").

186 DYKEMAN, WILMA, and JAMES STOKELY. "Montgomery Morning." *The Nation* (5 January 1957): 11–14.

Dykeman and Stokely credit the success of the Montgomery bus boycott to its ability to bridge the "great gap between the really learned and the desperately illiterate" in the black community. This happened "because from first to last the movement worked through the churches."

187 ESKEW, GLENN T. "The Alabama Christian Movement for Human Rights and the Birmingham Struggle for Civil Rights, 1956–1963." In *Birmingham*, edited by David J. Garrow, 3–114. Brooklyn, NY: Carlson Publishing, 1989. M.A. thesis, University of Georgia, 1987.

Eskew traces the history of the Alabama Christian Movement for Human Rights (ACMHR) from its creation in 1956 through its work until 1963. His chronicle of the civil rights movement in Birmingham is largely the story of the ACMHR's fiery, charismatic leader, the Rev. Fred Shuttlesworth. Eskew describes Shuttlesworth's efforts to desegregate public parks, transportation, schools, and employment. He views the 1963 demonstrations as the "culmination of the goals Shuttlesworth and the ACMHR had fought for since 1956," but he does not consider the resulting agreement with the white leadership an unqualified victory for the movement. He writes: "Instead of reforms from below, an alignment of the city's black and white upper classes limited the success of the local movement. In effect, King disarmed a struggle by the people, replaced their leader with his friends, and left town with the national victory."

188   FAGER, CHARLES. *Selma 1965: The March that Changed the South*. 2d
      ed. Boston: Beacon Press, 1985. 257 pages.
Fager describes the 1965 civil rights campaign in Selma which led to the
Selma to Montgomery march and, ultimately, to the passage of the Voting
Rights Act. His vivid account relates the events leading to the fateful con-
frontation on the Edmund Pettus Bridge. A major theme of Fager's chronicle
is the continuing tension between Selma's "moderate" police chief, Wilson
Baker, and his rabid segregationist counterpart, Dallas County Sheriff Jim
Clark.

189   FIELDS, URIAH J. *The Montgomery Story: The Unhappy Effects of the
      Montgomery Bus Boycott*. New York: Exposition Press, 1959. 87
      pages.
Rev. Fields was a Montgomery minister and secretary of the Montgomery Improvement Association (MIA) at the time of the bus boycott. He broke
with the MIA over charges of mismanagement and misappropriation of
funds. In this book he criticizes the boycott, claiming that it created "extreme
ill will, disharmony and discord" between blacks and whites, and did nothing to "gain the compasssionate interest of the reasonable, progressive and
community-minded people of both races."

190   FORMAN, JAMES. *Sammy Younge, Jr.: The First Black College Student
      to Die in the Black Liberation Movement*. New York: Grove Press,
      1968. 282 pages.
Sammy Younge was a student at Tuskegee Institute and a civil rights
worker with SNCC when he was shot while attempting to use a white rest
room at a local gas station. Forman tells the story of Younge's life, the cir-
cumstances of his death, and the trial of the white man accused of killing
him (he was found not guilty). He also describes the subsequent growing
impatience and militance of young black college students.

191   FRENCH, EDGAR N. "The Beginning of a New Age." In *The Walking
      City*, edited by David J. Garrow, 173–90. Brooklyn, NY: Carlson Pub-
      lishing, 1989. Orig. pub. in *The Angry Black South*, edited by
      Glenford E. Mitchell and William H. Peace, 30–51. New York: Corinth
      Books, 1962.
Edgar N. French was one of the leaders of the Montgomery Improvement Association. He describes here the origins of the Montgomery bus
boycott and credits the Supreme Court's *Brown* decision with helping to
launch the protest.

192   FRY, JOHN R. "The Voter Registration Drive in Selma, Alabama." In *We
      Shall Overcome*, edited by David J. Garrow, vol. 1, 249–69. Brooklyn,
      NY: Carlson Publishing, 1989. Orig. pub. in *Presbyterian Life*, 15 Jan-
      uary 1964, 12–22.
Fry describes the voter registration efforts of SNCC workers in Selma
during 1963.

193 GARDNER, TOM. "The Montgomery Bus Boycott: Interviews with Rosa Parks, E. D. Nixon, Johnny Carr, and Virginia Durr." *Southern Exposure* 9, no. 1 (1981): 13–21.

This article consists of interviews with four key figures in the Montgomery bus boycott. Rosa Parks was the seamstress whose arrest launched the boycott. E. D. Nixon was the NAACP leader who bailed Rosa Parks out of jail and helped organize the boycott. Virginia Durr was a liberal white who supported the boycott and whose husband, Clifford Durr, defended Mrs. Parks. Johnny Carr was active in the boycott and became president of the Montgomery Improvement Association in later years.

194 GARROW, DAVID J. "The Origins of the Montgomery Bus Boycott." In *The Walking City*, edited by David J. Garrow, 607–20. Brooklyn, NY: Carlson Publishing, 1989. Orig. pub. in *Southern Changes* 7 (1985): 21–27.

Garrow emphasizes the role of Jo Ann Gibson Robinson and the Women's Political Council in launching the Montgomery bus boycott.

195 _____. *Protest at Selma: Martin Luther King and the Voting Rights Act of 1965.* New Haven: Yale University Press, 1978. 346 pages.

Garrow describes how the strategy of protest employed by Martin Luther King, Jr. and SCLC at Selma influenced the emergence of the Voting Rights Act of 1965. He contends that the choice of Selma as a site for civil rights protests and the specific tactics that SCLC adopted in Selma were part of a plan to force the introduction and passage of national voting rights legislation. The foremost consideration in this campaign was the need to elicit "unprovoked white violence aimed at peaceful and unresisting civil rights demonstrators." Garrow argues that at Selma "a strategy that bordered on nonviolent provocation supplanted the earlier belief in nonviolent persuasion." SCLC correctly assumed that police violence would generate national media coverage and this, in turn, would stimulate reactions "throughout the country, and especially in Washington," leading to pressure for federal voting rights legislation.

196 GARROW, DAVID J., ed. *Birmingham, Alabama, 1956–1963: The Black Struggle for Civil Rights.* Brooklyn, NY: Carlson Publishing, 1989. 299 pages.
See entry 131.

197 _____. *The Walking City: The Montgomery Bus Boycott, 1955–1956.* Brooklyn, NY: Carlson Publishing, 1989. 636 pages.
See entry 134.

198 GILLIAM, THOMAS J. "The Montgomery Bus Boycott of 1955–56." In *The Walking City*, edited by David J. Garrow, 191–302. Brooklyn, NY: Carlson Publishing, 1989. M.A. thesis, Auburn University, 1968.

Gilliam examines the organization and strategy of the Montgomery Improvement Association during the bus boycott of 1955 to 1956. Although the subsequent desegregation was the result of a federal court ruling and not the boycott itself, he finds the significance of the protest in the ability of southern Negroes to organize and maintain unity in the face of powerful white opposition.

199   GORDON, BUD. *Nightriders: The Inside Story of the Liuzzo Killing.* Birmingham: BRALGO Publications, 1966. 64 pages.

Gordon describes the 1965 Selma to Montgomery march and the murder of Viola Liuzzo, a volunteer marcher, who was shot by Klansmen in Lowndes County. Gordon claims that the march was filled with "debauchery and indecency," and offers numerous photos of interracial couples among the marchers to prove his point. Liuzzo is described as "an overweight, unkept and homely, middle aged woman." He suggests that FBI informant Gary Thomas Rowe was responsible for her murder. Gordon gathered his infomation while working as public relations assistant to Col. Al Lingo, director of the Alabama State Troopers.

200   GRAETZ, ROBERT. "They're Still Walking in Montgomery." *Economic Justice* 24 (March 1956): 1–3.

Graetz, a white Lutheran minister serving a black parish in Montgomery, describes the origins and organization of the bus boycott. He refers to the protest as a "spontaneous, grass-roots movement."

201   GREGG, RICHARD B. *The Power of Nonviolence.* Nyack, NY: Fellowship Publications, 1959. 192 pages.

The Montgomery bus boycott is used as an example of nonviolent protest, which Gregg feels could be applied to the area of international relations.

202   HAMILTON, CHARLES V. *Minority Politics in Black Belt Alabama.* Eagleton Institute: Cases in Practical Politics, no. 19. New York: McGraw-Hill, 1962. 32 pages.

Hamilton chronicles the efforts of the Tuskegee Civic Association (TCA) between 1958 and 1960 to force the appointment of new members of the Macon County Board of Registrars as replacements for members who had resigned in order to avoid lawsuits for failing to register black voters. Hamilton faults the TCA for not following a more aggressive mass-oriented political strategy but credits the organization for helping to develop national awareness of voting discrimination. The same subject is covered in Norrell's *Reaping the Whirlwind* (1985, see entry 221).

203   HARDING, VINCENT. "A Beginning in Birmingham." *The Reporter,* 6 June 1963, 13–19.

Harding describes the behind-the-scenes negotiations between civil rights leaders and members of Birmingham's white power structure, which resulted in an agreement to end the demonstrations and desegregate city facilities. He emphasizes how blacks and whites grew to respect and trust each other during the course of their negotiations.

204 HINCKLE, WARREN, and DAVID WELCH. "Five Battles of Selma." In *We Shall Overcome*, edited by David J. Garrow, vol. 2, 419–54. Brooklyn, NY: Carlson Publishing, 1989. Orig. pub. in *Ramparts* 4 (June 1965): 19–52.

This special report describes the confrontation in Selma between segregationists and civil rights workers as being akin to a Civil War battle. The strategies of the "Union" and "Confederate" forces are examined. The federal government is depicted as a "'friendly power' observing the battle from a distance."

205 HINES, RALPH H., and JAMES E. PIERCE. "Negro Leadership after the Social Crisis: An Analysis of Leadership Changes in Montgomery, Alabama." *Phylon* 26, no. 2 (1965): 162–72.

Hines and Pierce use a reputational approach to identify the most prominent black leaders in Montgomery during three periods: before the bus boycott, during the protest, and following the protest. They report that the old accommodating leaders were replaced during the protest period, but within eighteen months leadership had returned to "those who tacitly or explicitly subscribe to the theory of accommodation."

206 HOWARD, JAN. "The Provocation of Violence: A Civil Rights Tactic?" In *We Shall Overcome*, edited by David J. Garrow, vol. 2, 455–60. Brooklyn, NY: Carlson Publishing, 1989. Orig. pub. in *Dissent* 13, no. 1 (1966): 94–99.

Howard argues that despite its official pledge of nonviolence, the civil rights movement has begun to use the provocation of violence as a latent tactic. The demonstrations at Selma are cited as an example of protestors attempting to provoke a violent response from white law enforcement forces.

207 HUBBARD, HOWARD. "From Failure to Success—Albany to Birmingham." In *Racial Conflict: Tension and Change in American Society*, edited by Gary T. Marx, 335–38. Boston: Little, Brown & Co., 1971. Orig. pub. in *Public Interest* 12 (Summer 1968): 4–8.

Hubbard compares the civil rights protests in Albany, Georgia, and Birmingham, Alabama, and advances three propositions: "(1) King's skill consisted mainly in his ability to contrive a situation . . . in which he was the injured party . . . (2) Such a strategy depends for its success on certain gaps and discontinuities in communication. (3) Where public opinion arbitrates, sentiment rallies to the victims."

208 JENKINS, RAY. "Majority Rule in the Black Belt: Greene County, Alabama." *New South* 24 (Fall 1969): 60–67.

Jenkins describes the efforts to elect black candidates to local office in Greene County, which eventually resulted in blacks winning four of five seats on the county commission and three of five seats on the county school board.

209   JOHNSON, WALTER. "Historians Join the March on Montgomery." *South Atlantic Quarterly* 79, no. 2 (1980): 158–74.

Johnson describes the participation of forty-three prominent historians, including C. Vann Woodward, Richard Hofstadter, and John Hope Franklin, in the Selma to Montgomery march.

210   JONES, LEWIS W. "Fred L. Shuttlesworth, Indigenous Leader." In *Birmingham*, edited by David J. Garrow, 115–50. Brooklyn, NY: Carlson Publishing, 1989.

This admiring profile of Rev. Fred Shuttlesworth, the leader of Birmingham's Alabama Christian Movement for Human Rights, is based on the author's personal interviews with him. Jones describes Shuttlesworth's early career and his crusade against segregation in Birmingham.

211   KEECH, WILLIAM R. *The Impact of Negro Voting: The Role of the Vote in the Quest for Equality.* Chicago: Rand McNally & Co., 1968. 113 pages.

Keech asks the question: "What impact does voting have on Negro social and economic status?" He examines Durham, North Carolina, and Tuskegee, Alabama, in an attempt to answer it. In Tuskegee he finds that "Negro votes brought about a radical change in the distribution of public services." In Durham, however, "Negro voting is not the clear, direct and unambigious cause of anything in the sense that it is in Tuskegee." Keech's study is helpful in pointing out the limited benefits that electoral reforms may bring.

212   KOPKIND, ANDREW. "In the Lair of the Black Panther." *New Republic*, 13 August 1966, 10–13.

Kopkind describes the efforts of the Lowndes County Freedom Organization to build black power in this Alabama Black Belt county. He documents both the need for an independent political organization to represent the needs of poor blacks and the serious difficulty of organizing a third party.

213   ———. "Lowndes County, Alabama: The Great Fear is Gone." *Ramparts*, April 1975.

Kopkind recounts here the history of the civil rights movement in Lowndes County and assesses the changes that took place since the formation of the Lowndes County Freedom Organization in 1965. In 1970 black voters were able to elect a black sheriff and two other county officials. Kopkind feels that whites have begun "to accommodate themselves to the new reality of black voting power," although they still control the board of education and the county commission. Rather than through revolution, Lowndes County's blacks have gained "incremental improvements based on interim tactics of accommodation and challenge to powerful white institutions."

214   LONGENECKER, STEPHEN L. *Selma's Peacemaker: Ralph Smeltzer and Civil Rights Mediation.* Philadelphia: Temple University Press, 1987. 273 pages.

Ralph Smeltzer was a white minister in the Church of the Brethren. In

November 1963 he came to Selma to aid black women who had been fired from their jobs for attempting to register to vote. He subsequently returned to work as a self-appointed mediator between the black and white communities. He worked quietly and shunned publicity, but Longenecker credits him with contributing to "the unification and emergence of Selma's black leadership" and with warning "Selma's white establishment that unless changes were made, [Martin Luther] King would come to Selma and significantly increase the city's crisis in human relations." Although the whites failed to heed his warnings, he remained in Selma until May 1965 and continued his mediation efforts.

215 MARABLE, MANNING. "Tuskegee and the Politics of Illusion in the New South." *Black Scholar* (May 1977): 13–24.

Marable describes political developments in Tuskegee following the civil rights movement as an example of the "politics of illusion." The retreat of the white business elite left control of local government in the hands of Tuskegee's black "petty bourgeoisie." Marable contends that the elected black leaders are unable to address the fundamental economic problems of the black masses in Macon County, in which Tuskegee is the seat.

216 MILLNER, STEVEN M. "The Montgomery Bus Boycott: A Case Study in the Emergence and Career of a Social Movement." In *The Walking City*, edited by David J. Garrow, 318–518. Brooklyn, NY: Carlson Publishing, 1989. Ph.D. dissertation, University of California at Berkeley, 1981.

Millner explains "from the point of view of the insider" how the Montgomery bus boycott unfolded. He identifies six factors which contributed to the success of the movement: (1) Montgomery's symbolic importance as the first capital of the Confederacy, (2) the presence of a substantial and organizable black population, (3) a moderately militant black middle class, (4) the numerous black voluntary organizations, (5) a small group of activist religious leaders, and (6) the relatively nonthreatening form of the protest. Appended to this work are transcripts of interviews with eight influential boycott leaders.

217 MORGAN, CHARLES, JR. *One Man, One Voice.* New York: Holt, Rinehart and Winston, 1979. 348 pages.

Morgan describes his work as the head of the ACLU's southern regional office between 1964 to 1972. Many of his cases involved civil rights, including the case of *White v. Crook*, which challenged the exclusion of black jurors in Lowndes County, Alabama.

218 _____. *A Time to Speak.* New York: Harper & Row, 1964. 177 pages.

Morgan was raised in Birmingham and practiced law there until 1964. His outspoken attacks on segregation and defense of the civil rights movement attracted threats against himself and his family. This book is a personal narrative that describes his growing disenchantment with the racial status quo in his home state, which led him to openly challenge "the southern way of life."

219 MURRAY, PAUL T. The Struggle for Political Power in a Black Belt County." *Humanity and Society* 12 (August 1988): 239–53.

Murray describes the electoral experiences of black candidates in Marengo County, Alabama, following the Voting Rights Act of 1965. Bloc voting on the basis of race by whites prevented the election of black candidates until litigation overturned the results of the at-large election of county supervisors and the Board of Education.

220 NIXON, E. D. "How It All Started." *Liberation* 1 (December 1956): 10.

Nixon describes how he originated the Montgomery Improvement Association and the bus boycott. He also claims to have selected Martin Luther King, Jr., to lead the movement.

221 NORRELL, ROBERT J. *Reaping the Whirlwind: The Civil Rights Movement in Tuskegee.* New York: Alfred A. Knopf, 1985. 254 pages.

In this excellent case study, Norrell traces the origins of "civic democracy" in Tuskegee and Macon County, Alabama. He maintains that the presence of many black professionals employed by Tuskegee Institute and the Veterans Administration hospital caused the civil rights movement to begin at an earlier date and follow a more moderate path than elsewhere in the South. Norrell identifies Charles G. Gomillion, a sociology professor and founder of the Tuskegee Civic Association, as the leading figure in this struggle. Gomillion encouraged his fellow blacks to concentrate on securing the right to vote, and eventually his name was attached to the landmark Supreme Court decision, *Gomillion v. Lightfoot,* which overturned Tuskegee's practice of gerrymandering the city limits to diminish black voting strength. Norrell recounts the growth of black political power in Tuskegee that culminated in the election of three black candidates to the city council in 1964.

222 OATES, STEPHEN B. "The Week the World Watched Selma." *American Heritage* 33, no. 4 (1982): 48–63.

Oates offers a popularized account of the civil rights protests in Selma from January to March of 1965, and the subsequent Selma to Montgomery march. Many excellent photographs accompany the text.

223 REDDICK, L. D. "The Bus Boycott in Montgomery." In *The Walking City,* edited by David J. Garrow, 69–82. Brooklyn, NY: Carlson Publishing, 1989. Orig. pub. in *Dissent* 3, no. 2 (1956): 107–17.

Reddick's account stresses the discipline of Montgomery's black community and "the intelligence and organization with which the boycott has been maintained."

224 ———. "The State vs. the Student." *Dissent* 7, no. 3 (1960): 219–28.

Reddick describes the campaign of official repression directed against black students at Alabama State College in Montgomery when they joined the sit-in movement by attempting to integrate a snack bar at the county court house.

225 ROBERTS, GENE. "A Kind of Black Power in Macon County, Alabama." *New York Times Magazine,* 26 February 1967, 32–88.

Roberts reports on the adjustment of whites in Macon County following the election of a black sheriff. He finds deep divisions between the moderates who support the sheriff and public education and the segregationists who attempt to retain their "way of life" in the face of growing black power.

226 _____. "A Remarkable Thing is Happening in Wilcox County, Alabama." *New York Times Magazine,* 17 April 1966.

Roberts describes the changes in Wilcox County, Alabama, following the registration of 3,600 black voters. These changes included, for example, the announcement of Walter J. Calhoun, a black store owner, as a candidate for sheriff, and the beginning of solicitation of support for white incumbents from black voters.

227 ROBINSON, JO ANN GIBSON. *The Montgomery Bus Boycott and the Women Who Started It: The Memoir of Jo Ann Gibson Robinson.* Edited by David J. Garrow. Knoxville: University of Tennessee Press, 1987. 190 pages.

One of the true unsung heroes of the civil rights movement is Jo Ann Gibson Robinson. In this autobiography Robinson provides an engrossing first-hand behind-the-scenes look at the people and events that launched the Montgomery gus boycott. When Rosa Parks was arrested on 1 December 1955, Robinson was president of the Montgomery Women's Political Council and an assistant professor of English at Alabama State College. She describes how her organization sprang into action when the news of Park's arrest reached them. Robinson worked all night to make 10,000 copies of a flyer calling for a one-day boycott of the city's buses. This successful protest led to the founding of the Montgomery Improvement Association and the historic ten-month long boycott. Gibson reminds the reader that Martin Luther King, Jr. did not start the Montgomery bus boycott but joined a movement well under way.

228 ROSE, STEPHEN C. "Test for Nonviolence." *Christian Century,* 29 May 1963, 714–16.

Rose examines conditions in Birmingham following the 12 May 1963 announcement of an agreement between the civil rights movement and white business leaders.

229 RUSTIN, BAYARD. "The Meaning of Birmingham." *Liberation* 8 (June 1963): 7–9. Reprinted in *Black Protest Thought in the Twentieth Century,* edited by August Meier, Elliot Rudwick, and Francis L. Broderick, 332–40. Indianapolis: Bobbs-Merrill, 1971.

Rustin describes the new, more militant mood of the black community, as shown in the Birmingham demonstrations. He presents his opinion of the rationale for mass protests: "Black people see that the white community would rather yield to the threats of the segregationist than change the social system. And so Negroes conclude that they must upset the social equilibrium more drastically than the opposition can."

230 _____. "Montgomery Diary." *Liberation* 1 (April 1956): 7–10. Reprinted in *Down the Line*, by Bayard Rustin, 255–61. Chicago: Quadrangle Books, 1971.

Rustin describes one week in February 1956 that he spent in Montgomery, meeting with movement leaders and observing the boycott in action. Despite the movement's commitment to nonviolence, he describes the great polarization between blacks and whites: "There is little middle ground on which to maneuver and few compromises that are possible."

231 SHUTTLESWORTH, FRED. 1971. "Birmingham Revisited." *Ebony*, August 1971, 114–18.

Shuttlesworth reviews the events of the civil rights movement in Birmingham beginning with the formation of the Alabama Christian Movement for Human Rights in 1956, and continuing with the attempt to desegregate public schools in 1957, the attack on the Freedom Riders in 1961, and the climactic demonstrations in the spring of 1963. He also comments on the progress made in Birmingham since 1963.

232 _____. "Birmingham Shall Be Free Some Day." *Freedomways* 4, no. 1 (1964): 16–19.

Shuttlesworth contends that the violent resistance encountered by the civil rights movement in Birmingham did not "deter us from our goal," but rather "laid the basis for the massive assault" against segregation in the spring of 1963.

233 SIKORA, FRANK. *Until Justice Rolls Down: The Birmingham Church Bombing Case.* Tuscaloosa: University of Alabama Press, 1991. 192 pages.

Sikora traces the case of the 1963 Birmingham church bombing, which took the lives of four girls attending Sunday school there. He describes the investigation, trial, and conviction of Robert Chambliss to life in prison for his role in the bombing. The heroes of this account are Alabama Attorney General Bill Baxley, who reopened the case, and Bob Eddy, the investigator who uncovered the evidence that resulted in the conviction.

234 STEVENSON, JANET. "Rosa Parks Wouldn't Budge." *American Heritage* 23, no. 2 (1972): 56–64.

In this popular account of the Montgomery bus boycott, Stevenson focuses on the roles of E. D. Nixon and Clifford Durr. Nixon is portrayed as the man who originated the idea of a boycott and suggested Martin Luther King, Jr., as the movement's leader. Durr is seen as the mastermind of the legal strategy. Little mention is made of Fred Gray's role in the legal battles, and there is no mention at all of Jo Ann Gibson Robinson and the Women's

Political Council. A different view of the boycott's origins is presented by Robinson herself (1987, see entry 227).

235 THORNTON, J. MILLS, III. "Challenge and Response in the Montgomery Bus Boycott of 1955–1956." In *The Walking City*, edited by David J. Garrow, 323–80. Brooklyn, NY: Carlson Publishing, 1989. Orig. pub. in *The Alabama Review* 33 (July 1980): 163–235.

Thornton's carefully researched study of the developments leading up to the Montgomery bus boycott and events during the boycott focuses on changes in Montgomery's politics in the post-World War II era. He maintains that the "growing independence of the white lower middle class" caused the demise of Mayor Gunter's political machine, which had represented the interests of Montgomery's upper class. This led to the election of politicians who were staunch segregationists in contrast to the more moderate, paternalistic whites who previously ruled. According to Thornton, the new leadership's unwillingness to compromise on the original demands of the Montgomery Improvement Association resulted in the year-long boycott and the eventual demise of segregated transportation. This account is particularly valuable for its insights into the response of white leaders to the boycott.

236 THRASHER, THOMAS R. "Alabama's Bus Boycott." In *The Walking City*, edited by David J. Garrow, 59–68. Brooklyn, NY: Carlson Publishing, 1989. Orig. pub. in *The Reporter* (8 March 1956): 13–16.

This account from the early months of the bus boycott sees the growth of the White Citizens' Council as one unintended consequence of the protest.

237 VALIEN, PRESTON. "The Montgomery Bus Protest as a Social Movement." In *The Walking City*, edited by David J. Garrow, 83–98. Brooklyn, NY: Carlson Publishing, 1989. Orig. pub. in *Race Relations*, edited by Jitsuichi Masuoka and Preston Valien, 112–127. Chapel Hill: University of North Carolina Press, 1961.

Valien examines the Montgomery bus boycott from a sociological perspective and offers four propositions that illustrate the common features this protest shares with other social movements.

238 WALTON, NORMAN W. "The Walking City: A History of the Montgomery Bus Boycott." In *The Walking City*, edited by David J. Garrow, 1–58. Brooklyn, NY: Carlson Publishing, 1989. Orig. pub. in five issues of the *Negro History Bulletin* from October 1956 to January 1958.

Walton describes events in Montgomery from 1 December 1955 to May of 1957.

239 WATTERS, PAT. "Why the Negro Children March." *New York Times Magazine*, 21 March 1965. Reprinted in *Black Protest in the Sixties*, edited by August Meier and Elliot Rudwick. Chicago: Aldine Publishing Co., 1970.

After conducting interviews with young blacks active in the protests at

Selma, Watters is impressed by "the miracle of their generally nonviolent, mainly constructive, responses" to "the injustices and inequities of their lives."

240 WEBB, SHEYANN, and RACHEL WEST NELSON. *Selma, Lord, Selma: Girlhood Memories of the Civil Rights Days.* Tuscaloosa: University of Alabama Press, 1980. 146 pages.

Two young women who were involved in the Selma demonstrations as children share in this book their recollections of those experiences.

241 WOFFORD, HARRIS. "A Preliminary Report on the Status of the Negro in Dallas County, Alabama." In *We Shall Overcome*, edited by David J. Garrow, vol. 3, 1063–1150. Brooklyn, NY: Carlson Publishing, 1989. Paper originally presented at Yale Law School, January 1953.

Wofford presents a comprehensive study of racial segregation in Dallas County, Alabama, in 1952.

242 WRIGHT, ROBERTA HUGHES. *The Birth of the Montgomery Bus Boycott.* Southfield, MI: Charro Press, 1991. 156 pages.

Wright's account of the Montgomery bus boycott concentrates on the five days from the arrest of Rosa Parks on 1 December 1955 to the first day of the protest and the formation of the Montgomery Improvement Association on December 5. She also includes a review of earlier protests against segregated transportation in New Orleans and other cities.

243 YOUNG, ANDREW. "Dynamics of a Birmingham Movement in the Sixties." In *Nonviolence in the 70s*, edited by Andrew Levinson, 9–15. Atlanta: Institute for Nonviolent Social Change, 1972. Orig. pub. in *Drum Major* 1 (1971): 21–27.

Young, a key aide to Martin Luther King, describes the strategy and organization behind the 1963 Birmingham campaign. He emphasizes the importance of the boycott of downtown merchants, which became effective following the mass arrests of demonstrators, and which he credits with pressuring the "power structure" to accept the movement's demands.

Arkansas

244 BATES, DAISY. *The Long Shadow of Little Rock.* New York: David McKay Co., 1962. 234 pages.

Daisy Bates was the NAACP leader in Little Rock, Arkansas, in 1958 when Central High School was desegregated by federal troops. She played a key role in supporting the nine black students who entered Central High School and helping them deal with the hostility and publicity they encountered.

245 BLOSSOM, VIRGIL T. *It Has Happened Here.* New York: Harper & Row, 1959. 209 pages.

Blossom was superintendent of schools in Little Rock from 1953 to

1958. After the Supreme Court's *Brown* decision, he began to prepare a plan for the gradual desegregation of public schools. His careful plans were ignored, however, when Governor Orville Faubus challenged the authority of the federal courts and ordered the Arkansas National Guard to prevent Negro children from enrolling at Central High School. By 1958 segregationists had gained control of the school board and fired Blossom as superintendent. In this book, he blames the failure of school desegregation in Little Rock on "the vacillation of political leaders at state and federal levels—all tried to avoid responsibility for enforcement—and a deliberate plot by segregationists all over the South to force a finish fight in Little Rock in an effort to delay or prevent a showdown on their home grounds."

246 CAMPBELL, ERNEST Q., and THOMAS F. PETTIGREW. *Christians in Racial Crisis: A Study of Little Rock's Ministry.* Washington, DC: Public Affairs Press, 1959. 196 pages.

Campbell and Pettigrew report on their study of white Protestant ministers during the Little Rock desegregation crisis. They found little evidence of the "united and forceful leadership many expected." Although most ministers supported their denominations' public positions favoring racial integration, they faced hostility from a laity that did not share their beliefs and threatened to disrupt their smoothly functioning parishes.

247 _____. "Men of God in Racial Crisis." *Christian Century,* 4 June 1958, 663–65.

Campbell and Pettigrew studied the activities of white Little Rock clergymen during the school desegregation crisis of 1957. In this article, they identify four types of ministers by their responses: the "Silent," the "Segregationist," the "Prudent Integrationist," and the "Avowed Integrationist."

248 _____. "Racial and Moral Crisis: The Role of Little Rock Ministers." *American Journal of Sociology* 64, no. 5 (1959): 509–16.

Campbell and Pettigrew studied the behavior of twenty-nine white clergymen during the school desegregation crisis of 1957, and report their findings here. Five are classified as segregationists, eight are designated as active integrationists, and the remaining sixteen are described as "inactive integrationists" who agreed that integration was morally right, but "were generally silent" during the crisis. Their inaction is explained by citing conflicting demands of the ministers' membership reference system, the professional reference system, and the self-reference system.

249 _____. "Vignettes from Little Rock." *Christianity and Crisis,* 29 September 1958, 128–36.

Campbell and Pettigrew offer composite portraits of five white Protestant ministers who adopted various positions in response to the Little Rock school desegregation crisis. They range from "hard core resistance" to outspoken support for integration.

250 FREYER, TONY. *The Little Rock Crisis: A Constitutional Interpretation.* Westport, CT.: Greenwood Press, 1984. 186 pages.

Freyer examines the Little Rock school desegregation from a legal and political perspective, drawing upon FBI and NAACP files. He argues that at Little Rock the legal and political issue of the supremacy of federal power overshadowed the moral issue of racial justice. The eventual desegregation of Little Rock's public schools was a victory for judicial activism "in which moderate conservatism triumphed over moral principle."

251 HAYS, BROOKS. *A Southern Moderate Speaks.* Chapel Hill: University of North Carolina Press, 1959. 231 pages.

A former Arkansas member of Congress describes his behind-the-scenes efforts to resolve the Little Rock school desegregation crisis of 1957.

252 HUCKABY, ELIZABETH. *Crisis at Central High: Little Rock, 1957–58.* Baton Rouge: Louisiana State University Press, 1980. 222 pages.

Huckaby was assistant principal of Little Rock's Central High School at the time of the school desegregation crisis. She describes the events from 2 September 1957 to 3 June 1958 from an insider's perspective. Her account emphasizes the actions of students and teachers rather than the politicians who created the crisis.

253 JACOWAY, ELIZABETH. "Taken by Surprise: Little Rock Business Leaders and Desegregation." In *Southern Businessmen and Desegregation,* edited by Elizabeth Jacoway and David R. Colburn, 15–41. Baton Rouge: Louisiana State University Press, 1982.

From September 1957 to May 1959, Little Rock's traditional business leaders were silent on the issue of school desegregation. Superintendent Virgil Blossom had carefully prepared for integration and he and other moderate white leaders were taken by surprise when Governor Faubus intervened to prevent black students from attending Central High School. Jacoway outlines four stages of the business leaders response to the crisis: (1) they tried to arrange a delay of the integration order, (2) they tried to elect moderate candidates to the school board, but were only partly successful, (3) they elected new school board members dedicated to reopening the schools, and (4) they worked with black leaders to desegregate all public facilities.

254 MCMILLEN, NEIL R. "White Citizens' Council and Resistance to School Desegregation in Arkansas." *Arkansas Historical Quarterly* 30 (Spring 1971): 95–122.

McMillen traces the activities of the White Citizens' Council in Arkansas during the late 1950s. He writes that most of its activities were centered in Little Rock and focused on the opposition to the desegregation of Central High School. One major success was the opening of an all-white private high school in 1958, but by 1960 the Council had lost most of its influence in the state.

255 PHILLIPS, WILLIAM M., JR. "The Boycott: A Negro Community in Conflict." *Phylon* 22 (Spring 1961): 24–30.

A case study of a boycott of two variety stores organized in 1960 by the NAACP in Pine Bluff, Arkansas.

256 RECORD, WILSON, and JANE C. RECORD, eds. *Little Rock, U.S.A.: Materials for Analysis.* San Francisco: Chandler Publishing Co., 1960. 338 pages.

See entry 155.

Florida

257 BUTTON, JAMES W. *Blacks and Social Change: Impact of the Civil Rights Movement in Southern Communities.* Princeton: Princeton University Press, 1989. 326 pages.

Button studied six Florida communities to determine the extent to which blacks benefitted from the civil rights movement. He found that at the local level the movement varied considerably in the way it began and the form it took. He concludes that "southern blacks have achieved marked gains in the political arena in most communities, but improvements in the economic and social sectors have been more difficult and less apparent. Nevertheless some economic change has occurred, even in the most traditional settings, and political forces, especially black activism, have often been important in forging gains in various aspects of society."

258 COLBURN, DAVID R. *Racial Change and Community Crisis: St. Augustine, Florida, 1877–1980.* New York: Columbia University Press, 1985. 258 pages.

Colburn examines the forces that led to the racial crisis in St. Augustine in 1963 to 1964 and its aftermath. The city's "civil" relationship between black and white residents began to deteriorate in 1963 when Dr. Robert Hayling organized younger blacks in militant protests against segregation. The conservative white leadership viewed civil rights as a communist plot and made little effort to restrain militant white racists. When Hayling was unable to gain concessions from local leaders he called on SCLC for assistance. Colburn criticizes SCLC's efforts in St. Augustine for being more interested in passing national legislation than in solving local problems, and for its failure to "develop or encourage a grass-roots movement which would provide the black community with leadership and direction following their departure." When moderate whites began to assume positions of influence following 1965, blacks witnessed a number of significant changes including school desegregation, access to public accommodations, and improved city services. The city's continuing reliance on tourism and its reluctance to recruit new industry, however, "effectively impeded black chances for social and economic advancement."

259 _____. "The Saint Augustine Business Community: Desegregation, 1963–1964." In *Southern Businessmen and Desegregation*, edited by Elizabeth Jacoway and David R. Colburn, 211–35. Baton Rouge: Louisiana State University Press, 1982.

Colburn portrays St. Augustine as an "Old South" city with a conservative white elite closely tied to the John Birch Society. Faced with protests organized by SCLC in 1964, business leaders became even more adamant in their opposition to integration. Law enforcement officials even allowed Klansmen to attack and intimidate demonstrators. Finally, Colburn describes how the active intervention of federal judge Bryan Simpson was necessary to restore order.

260 FENDRICH, JAMES M., and CHARLES U. SMITH. "Florida A & M Civil Rights Activists: A Partial Legacy." In *The Civil Rights Movement in Florida and the United States*, edited by Charles U. Smith, 292–310. Tallahassee, FL: Father & Son Press, 1989.

Fendrich and Smith examine the adult political attitudes and protest behavior of former Florida A & M students. Former student activists were found to have higher social status, more education at the graduate level, and more involvement in protest behavior.

261 FLORIDA LEGISLATIVE INVESTIGATION COMMITTEE. "Racial and Civil Disorders in St. Augustine."Published originally by the State of Florida, 1965. 147 pages. Reprinted in *St. Augustine*, edited by David J. Garrow, 177–326. Brooklyn, NY: Carlson Publishing, 1989.

This report of a state legislative committee's investigation of the St. Augustine civil rights protests of 1964 is heavily weighted against the civil rights movement as a whole. It accuses Martin Luther King and his associates of being fellow travelers of the communist conspiracy, and blames them for disrupting the harmonious race relations which had existed in the city. The report concludes that the racial problems facing the city "very probably could have been amicably solved by the Negro and white citizens of St. Augustine had they been free from outside agitation. The intrusion of King and his trained army of provocateurs with ample financial resources destroyed interracial relations." Curiously, the report makes no mention of several white racists who traveled to St. Augustine from around the country to battle against the civil rights forces.

262 FRIEDMAN, LEON. "Federal Courts of the South: Judge Bryan Simpson and His Reluctant Brethren." In *Southern Justice*, edited by Leon Friedman, 187–213, New York: Random House, 1965.

Friedman examines the performance of southern federal district court judges in civil rights cases and finds some of them "astonishingly bad." One exception he finds is Judge Bryan Simpson of the Middle District of Florida. Friedman praises his handling of cases that that came to his court as a result of civil rights demonstrations in St. Augustine, Florida, in 1963 and 1964.

263 GARROW, DAVID J., ed. *St. Augustine, Florida, 1963–1964: Mass Protest and Racial Violence.* Brooklyn, NY: Carlson Publishing, 1989. 364 pages.
See entry 133.

264 HARTLEY, ROBERT W. "A Long Hot Summer: The St. Augustine Racial Disorders of 1964." In *St. Augustine*, edited by David J. Garrow, 3–92. Brooklyn, NY: Carlson Publishing, 1989. M.A. thesis, Stetson University, 1972.
In his study of the civil rights demonstrations in St. Augustine, Hartley concentrates on the response of various segments of the white community and the differences among these segments. The reader learns that internal divisions crippled the white power structure and "in the absence of a unified power structure that spoke forcefully for the city," white racists assumed leadership roles. One learns relatively little, however, of any divisions within the black community, and there is not much discussion of SCLC and its role in this confrontation.

265 HERBERS, JOHN. "Critical Test for the Nonviolent Way." *New York Times Magazine*, 5 July 1964.
Herbers describes the confrontation between civil rights forces led by Martin Luther King and white segregationist vigilantes. He observes that "further racial progress is blocked—not so much by local law and massive resistance as by terror."

266 KALLAL, EDWARD W., JR. "St. Augustine and the Ku Klux Klan: 1963 and 1964." In *St. Augustine*, edited by David J. Garrow, 93–176. Brooklyn, NY: Carlson Publishing, 1989. Senior thesis, University of Florida, 1976.
Kallal examines the role of the Klan and "quasi-Klan" organizations in the St. Augustine civil rights campaign. In explaining how the Klan could assume such a dominant position in this community, he stresses their essential Americanism: "Klansmen reflect and magnify attitudes and dispositions found throughout American society." According to Kallal, these include violence, nativism, fraternalism, anticommunism, and racism.

267 KILLIAN, LEWIS M. "Organization, Rationality and Spontaneity in the Civil Rights Movement." In *We Shall Overcome*, edited by David J. Garrow, vol. 2, 503–16. Brooklyn, NY: Carlson Publishing, 1989. Orig. pub. in *American Sociological Review* 49 (December 1984): 770–83.
Killian examines the 1956 Tallahassee bus boycott and the 1960 sit-ins to determine the relative importance of spontaneity and prior organization in launching these protests. He concludes: "While organization and rational planning are key variables, social movement theory must take into account spontaneity and emergence and the forces which generate them."

268   KILLIAN, LEWIS M., and CHARLES M. GRIGG. *Racial Crisis in America: Leadership in Conflict.* Englewood Cliffs, NJ: Prentice Hall Press, 1964. 144 pages.

Killian and Grigg studied a biracial committee in an unnamed Florida city. They found that serving on the committee placed black leaders in a contradictory position, as they were expected to preserve racial peace in the community and could no longer act as advocates for changes that would benefit blacks. They also examined changes in leadership in Tallahassee during its bus boycott. They found that the "old" accommodating leaders had been replaced by "new" protest leaders. They conclude that conflict is a necessary precondition for racial progress because only through conflict can the black community demonstrate enough power to force whites to negotiate.

269   KILLIAN, LEWIS M., and CHARLES U. SMITH. "Negro Protest Leaders in a Southern Community." *Social Forces* 38 (March 1960): 253–57. Reprinted in *Conflict and Competition: Studies in the Recent Black Protest Movement*, edited by John Bracey, August Meier, and Elliot Rudwick, 34–41. Belmont, CA: Wadsworth, 1970.

Killian and Smith studied Negro leadership in Tallahassee, Florida, before and after that city's bus boycott. They report a complete change afterward, with the old accommodating leaders being replaced by a new group of protest leaders. They found that white leaders, however, were unwilling to deal with the new black leaders because they "refused to negotiate with whites in the circumscribed, accommodating fashion of yesterday."

270   LAWSON, STEVEN F. "From Sit-In to Race Riot: Businessmen, Blacks, and Pursuit of Moderation in Tampa, 1960–1967." In *Southern Businessmen and Desegregation*, edited by Elizabeth Jacoway and David R. Colburn, 257–81. Baton Rouge: Louisiana State University Press, 1982.

Lawson examines the involvement of white business leaders in Tampa's desegregation between 1960 and 1967. He views Tampa as an example of the "New South," where the business elite took an active role in promoting racial change in the name of economic growth. "Community leaders prescribed cooperation and the soothing power of rational persuasion to check extremism and end discrimination," he argues. He believes that the efforts of Tampa's white leaders were stimulated and aided by black leaders who "blended militancy with restraint." In Lawson's view, a twelve-member biracial committee established by the mayor in 1959 was the primary vehicle for promoting peaceful integration and interracial communication.

271   NEYLAND, LEEDELL W. "The Tallahassee Bus Boycott in Historical Perspective: Changes and Trends." In *The Civil Rights Movement in Florida and the United States*, edited by Charles U. Smith, 29–59. Tallahassee, FL: Father & Son Press, 1989.

Neyland finds that the success of the bus boycott was due to "the acquisition of new attitudes, the development of greater social consciousness, and the positive self-esteem of students, faculty, and community residents of Tallahassee.

272 RICHARDSON, H. NEIL. "Pilgrimage of Reconciliation: A Trip to St. Augustine." *Nexus* 8 (November 1964): 31–34.

Richardson describes the efforts of four Boston University professors to initiate communication between black and white leaders in St. Augustine in the spring of 1964.

273 SMITH, CHARLES U. "The Sit-Ins and the New Negro Student." *Journal of Intergroup Relations* 2 (1961): 223–29. Reprinted in *American Race Relations Today,* edited by Earl Raab, 69–75. Garden City, NY: Anchor Books, 1962.

Smith describes the growing activism of students at Florida A & M in Tallahassee and the development of a new self-image as a result of their participation in the civil rights movement.

274 SMITH, CHARLES U., ed. *The Civil Rights Movement in Florida and the United States: Historical and Contemporary Perspectives.* Tallahassee, FL: Father & Son Press, 1989. 326 pages.

See entry 158.

275 SMITH, CHARLES U., and LEWIS M. KILLIAN. "The Tallahassee Bus Protest." In *We Shall Overcome,* edited by David J. Garrow, vol. 3, 1017–40. Brooklyn, NY: Carlson Publishing, 1989. Orig. pub. as a pamphlet. New York: The Anti-Defamation League of B'nai B'rith, February 1958.

Smith and Killian describe the protest against segregated buses in Tallahassee during 1956 and 1957.

276 WATTERS, PAT. "The American Middle Ground in St. Augustine." *New South* 19 (September 1964): 3–20.

Watters describes the confrontations between civil rights demonstrators and segregationists during the 1964 protests in St. Augustine. He emphasizes the "failure of law enforcement" to control segregationist violence and the tacit complicity of law enforcement personnel with the Klan's efforts to intimidate and attack civil rights demonstrators.

Georgia

277 ANDERSON, WILLIAM G. "The Spirit of Albany." *Labor Today* 3 (Winter 1962): 11–14.

Anderson, the leader of the Albany movement, describes the fight against segregation in this small Georgia city during 1961 and 1962.

278 CARSON, CLAYBORNE. "SNCC and the Albany Movement." *Journal of Southwest Georgia History* 2 (Fall 1984): 15–25.

Carson describes the work of SNCC organizers in Albany, Georgia, from October 1961 to the fall of 1962 and discusses the significance of the Albany movement in SNCC's development. He claims that Albany was "a training ground for many SNCC workers who learned new techniques for sustaining mass militancy." He also feels that Albany "convinced SNCC workers that their distinctive organizing strategy . . . had broad support among blacks in the deep South."

279 CLEGHORN, REESE. "Epilogue in Albany: Were the Mass Marches Worthwhile?" *New Republic*, 20 July 1963, 15–18.

Cleghorn reviews the mass demonstrations in Albany and concludes they were a failure. He points out that with the exception of interstate transportation terminals, the city remains segregated and the police have increased their arrests of demonstrators. He concludes that the main reasons for the failure of the Albany movement were "a diffusion of goals" and "the lack of clear thinking about tactics."

280 CLUSTER, DICK. "The Borning Struggle: An Interview with Bernice Johnson Reagon." *Radical America* 12 (November/December 1978): 8–25.

Bernice Johnson Reagon discusses in this interview the Albany movement, the importance of singing in the movement, the social and personal changes which have occurred as a result of the movement, and the central role of the civil rights movement in other social movements of the 1960s.

281 COBB, JAMES C. "Yesterday's Liberalism: Business Boosters and Civil Rights in Augusta, Georgia." In *Southern Businessmen and Desegregation*, edited by Elizabeth Jacoway and David R. Colburn, 151–69. Baton Rouge: Louisiana State University Press, 1982.

In 1954 Augusta "appeared to be a citadel of defiance" to the Supreme Court's school desegregation order, but less than a decade later most of the city's businesses were peacefully integrated. Cobb claims that this about-face "was largely attributable to the influence of growth-minded civic and business leaders who feared that continued refusal to desegregate would undermine their efforts to lure new industries to the area." Cobbs believes that after 1962, however, "city officials used tokenism and ballyhoo to create an illusion of cooperation and harmony" without further addressing the demands of black citizens.

282 FORT, VINCENT D. "The Atlanta Sit-In Movement 1960–61: An Oral Study." In *Atlanta*, edited by David J. Garrow, 113–80. Brooklyn, NY: Carlson Publishers, 1989. M.A. thesis, Atlanta University, 1980.

Fort's history of the Atlanta sit-in movement is based on interviews with many of the participants. It focuses on "how the movement was organized, the effect it had on the students, and on their relations with other groups in the Atlanta University Center."

283 GALPHIN, BRUCE M. "Judge Pye and the Hundred Sit-Ins." *New Republic* 30 May 1964, 8–9.

Galphin describes the efforts of segregationist Atlanta Judge Durwood Pye to make life difficult for civil rights demonstrators appearing in his court.

284 GARROW, DAVID J., ed. *Atlanta, Georgia, 1960–1961: Sit-Ins and Student Activism.* Brooklyn, NY: Carlson Publishing, 1989. 195 pages. See entry 130.

285 GREENE, MELISSA FAY. *Praying for Sheetrock.* Reading, MA: Addison-Wesley Publishing Co., 1991. 337 pages.

Greene describes the social and political changes resulting from the civil rights movement in McIntosh County, Georgia. She focuses on the story of Thurnell Alston who emerged as the spokesman for the black community of McIntosh County and leader of the movement to oust the corrupt white sherrif who dominated the local political organization. Alston was elected to the county commission in 1978, but civil rights militancy in the county ebbed after his election. Alston gradually lost his crusading zeal and in 1988 was convicted on a drug charge. Greene offers a sad but compelling picture of the rise and eventual decline of grass roots activism and idealism.

286 HANKS, LAWRENCE J. *The Struggle for Black Political Empowerment in Three Georgia Counties.* Knoxville: University of Tennessee Press, 1987. 227 pages.

Hanks examines the impact of the civil rights movement on the political participation of blacks in three Georgia counties—Hancock, Peach, and Clay. He finds three very different patterns depending upon the size of the black population in the county, the degree of white resistance, and the nature of the black political organization.

287 HARDING, VINCENT, and STAUGHTON LYND. "Albany, Georgia." In *We Shall Overcome*, edited by David J. Garrow, vol. 1, 313–22. Brooklyn, NY: Carlson Publishing, 1989. Orig. pub. in *The Crisis* 70 (February 1963): 69–78.

Harding and Lynd review in this essay the efforts of the Albany movement as mass protests are becoming replaced by "more conventional tactics." They conclude that the "federal government has miserably and disgracefully failed in its duty of protecting the elementary civil rights of the Negro citizens of Albany."

288 HORNSBY, ALTON, JR. "A City That Was Too Busy to Hate: Atlanta Businessmen and Desegregation." In *Southern Businessmen and Desegregation*, edited by Elizabeth Jacoway and David R. Colburn, 120–36. Baton Rouge: Louisiana State University Press, 1982.

In 1961 Atlanta's peaceful desegregation of public schools earned it the title, "the city too busy to hate." Hornsby credits Atlanta's successful desegregation to the city's large black middle class and the close alliance between its white business and political leaders. He describes the efforts of the business elite to build support for integrated public schools. Curiously, Hornsby makes only passing reference to the two-year struggle by black college students to desegregate lunch counters and restaurants in Atlanta.

289   HUBBARD, HOWARD. "From Failure to Success—Albany to Birmingham." In *Racial Conflict: Tension and Change in American Society,* edited by Gary T. Marx, 335–38. Boston: Little, Brown & Co., 1971. Orig. pub. in *Public Interest* 12 (Summer 1968): 4–8.
See entry 207.

290   KING, SLATER. "The Bloody Battleground of Albany." *Freedomways* 4, no. 1 (1964): 93–101.
King assesses the impact of the Albany movement. He finds few gains other than the development of a strong sense of community and identity among Albany's blacks and the growth of self-help organizations. The main failing of the movement, in his opinion, was that it "attacked segregation too broadly," rather than focusing on one project at a time. A major source of disillusionment in King's view has been the Justice Department's indictment of local civil rights leaders on conspiracy and perjury charges while not taking any action against whites accused of violating blacks' rights.

291   _____. "Our Main Battle in Albany." *Freedomways* 5, no. 3 (1965): 417–23.
King counts gains for the civil rights movement in Albany with the hiring of six black policemen and the increased number of registered black voters. The closing of all public recreational facilities to avoid desegregation he sees as a setback for the movement, and believes that the major problem facing the black community is the lack of jobs and economic power.

292   LINCOLN, C. ERIC. "The Strategy of a Sit-In." In *Atlanta*, edited by David J. Garrow, 95–103. Brooklyn, NY: Carlson Publishing, 1989. Orig. pub. in *The Reporter*, 5 January 1961, 20–23.
Lincoln provides an eyewitness account of sit-ins in Atlanta during November of 1960.

293   NEWSOME, LIONEL, and WILLIAM GORDEN. "A Stormy Rally in Atlanta." In *Atlanta*, edited by David J. Garrow, 105–12. Brooklyn, NY: Carlson Publishing, 1989. Orig. pub. in *Today's Speech* 11 (April 1963): 18–21.
Newsome and Gorden describe a 10 March 1961 mass meeting called to gain support for an agreement ending the Atlanta sit-in demonstrations.

294   PAGE, MARION S. "Report from Albany, Georgia." *Liberation* 10 (February 1966): 46.
Page describes progress toward integration in Albany, including the desegregation of hotels, motels, theaters and eating places; increased hiring of black bus drivers; and employment of six black police officers.

295 PFISTER, JOE. "Twenty Years and Still Marching." *Southern Exposure* 10 (January 1982): 20–27.

Pfister describes the Albany movement of 1961 to 1962. He states that the Albany protests "showed the world that it was possible to break through the bonds of class differences and band together to take direct action on a massive scale." He includes interviews with Albany movement participants Reverend Samuel Wells and Annette Jones White.

296 RICKS, JOHN A. "'De Lawd' Descends and Is Crucified: Martin Luther King, Jr., in Albany, Georgia." In *We Shall Overcome*, edited by David J. Garrow, vol. 3, 985–96. Brooklyn, NY: Carlson Publishing, 1989. Orig. pub. in *Journal of Southwest Georgia History* 2 (Fall 1984): 3–14.

Ricks describes events in Albany, Georgia in 1961 to 1962 with emphasis in the conflicts within the movement between SCLC and SNCC. He attributes the "failure" of the Albany movement to the "amazing cohesiveness of the white community," as well as to the absence of violence against civil rights protestors, dissenters within the black community, lack of complete commitment to the Albany struggle by SCLC, and an overly broad agenda for sudden and total change.

297 ROZIER, JOHN. *Black Boss: Political Revolution in a Georgia County.* Athens: University of Georgia Press, 1982. 220 pages.

Rozier traces the career of John McCown, who came to Hancock County in 1967 and rapidly became the most powerful person in the county. Rozier describes how the former civil rights activist "built a small empire atop a growing base of government and foundation funds."

298 SHIPP, BILL. *Murder at Broad River Bridge: The Slaying of Lemuel Penn by Members of the Ku Klux Klan.* Atlanta: Peachtree Publishers, 1981. 91 pages.

In this brief book Shipp presents a vivid, journalistic account of the 1964 murder of Washington, D.C. educator Lemuel Penn, and the trials of the Klansmen responsible for his death.

299 CLARK, BENJAMIN VAN. "Siege at Savannah." *Freedomways* 4, no. 1 (1964): 131–35.

Clark describes the efforts of SCLC and Hosea Williams to organize the Chatham County Crusade for Voters, in an attempt to increase black political power in Savannah and address the needs of the black community.

300 WALKER, JACK L. "The Functions of Disunity: Negro Leadership in a Southern City." In *Racial Conflict*, edited by Gary T. Marx, 379–87. Boston: Little, Brown & Co., 1971. Orig. pub. in *Journal of Negro Education* 32 (Summer 1963), 227–36.

Walker examines changes in Atlanta's black leadership during the 1960 to 1961 sit-ins. He finds a "tactical balance" between conservative and protest leaders. Because he sees the conservative leaders as more acceptable to powerful whites, Walker suggests that they can serve a valuable role as bargaining agents for the black community. He concludes: "A Negro community in a southern city is likely to be more effective if it has both conservative and protest elements within its leadership."

301   _____. "Protest and Negotiation: A Case Study of Negro Leadership in Atlanta, Georgia." In *Atlanta,* edited by David J. Garrow, 31–58. Brooklyn, NY: Carlson Publishing, 1989. Orig. pub. in *Midwest Journal of Political Science* 7 (May 1963): 99–124.

Walker examines differences between younger and older black leaders in Atlanta. He finds general agreement on goals, with an increased number of job opportunities having the highest priority. Although both groups emphasize voting as the most important tactic of their struggle, the younger leaders place greater emphasis on economic boycotts while the older leaders prefer negotiations and legal suits.

302   _____. "Sit-Ins in Atlanta: A Study in the Negro Revolt." In *Atlanta,* edited by David J. Garrow, 59–93. Brooklyn, NY: Carlson Publishing, 1989. Orig. pub. as *Eagleton Institute Cases in Practical Politics no. 34.* New York: McGraw-Hill, 1964.

Walker's analysis of the 1960 to 1961 Atlanta sit-ins focuses on the differences between the militant young protest leaders and the older representatives of the black establishment. Because white civic and political leaders were unaware of this development, according to Walker, they made "serious miscalculations several times during the controversy over the sit-ins."

303   WALKER, WYATT T. "Albany, Failure or First Step?" *New South* 18 (June 1963): 3–8.

Walker, an organizer for SCLC, replies to critics who charge that the Albany demonstrations were a "failure." He insists that "the ordeal and effort of Albany is an historic high point" in the Negro revolution. He praises the Albany movement for its united assault on the entire system of segregation and blames the "unjust use of just laws by police" and the "do-nothing posture of the federal government" for keeping the movement from attaining all its objectives.

304   WATTERS, PAT. *Down to Now: Reflections on the Southern Civil Rights Movement.* New York: Pantheon Books, 1971. 426 pages.
       See entry 100.

305   ZINN, HOWARD. *Albany: A Study in National Responsibility.* Atlanta: Southern Regional Council, 1962. 35 pages.

Zinn examines the civil rights protests in Albany during 1962 and presents the case for federal intervention on behalf of the black demonstrators.

306   _____. *The Southern Mystique.* New York: Alfred A. Knopf, 1964. 267 pages.
       See entry 165.

Louisiana

307 COLLINS, ROBERT F., NILS R. DOUGLAS, and LOLIS E. ELIE. "Clinton, Louisiana." In *Southern Justice*, edited by Leon Friedman, 112–26. New York: Pantheon Books, 1965.

These lawyers describe their work defending civil rights workers in East Feliciana Parish during 1963.

308 FARMER, JAMES. *Freedom—When?* New York: Random House, 1965. 197 pages.

Farmer describes CORE's voter registration campaign in Plaquemine, Louisiana, in the summer of 1963, and the evolution of CORE as a civil rights organization. He addresses the need to go "beyond civil rights" and work for political participation and community development.

309 INGER, MORTON. "The New Orleans School Crisis of 1960." In *Southern Businessmen and Desegregation*, edited by Elizabeth Jacoway and David R. Colburn, 82–97. Baton Rouge: Louisiana State University Press, 1982.

Inger attributes New Orleans's school desegregation crisis of November 1960 to a failure of the city's business and political leaders who "did nothing to prepare the community for a peaceful transition" to integrated education. He points out that although some white moderates began to encourage support for public education, their efforts were to little avail following protracted legal battles with the state government and poor planning by the board of education. He also describes how after weeks of street battles, a group of business and professional leaders appealed for an end to the conflict, and by September of 1961 civic and political leaders finally lined up solidly in favor of desegregation.

310 _____. *Politics and Reality in an American City: The New Orleans School Crisis of 1960.* New York: Center for Urban Education, 1969. 114 pages.

Inger presents a case study of the crisis that occurred during the desegregation of public schools in New Orleans in 1960. Much of this material is also included in Crain's *The Politics of School Desegregation* (1968, see entry 1266).

311 LIPSITZ, GEORGE. *A Life In the Struggle: Ivory Perry and the Culture of Opposition.* Philadelphia: Temple University Press, 1988. 292 pages.

Lipsitz tells the story of Ivory Perry, a rank and file activist in the civil rights movement in St. Louis during the 1950s and 1960s, who also volunteered to work for CORE in Bogalousa, Louisiana. He describes Perry as an "organic intellectual"—a person who directs "the ideas and aspirations" of his class even though he holds no formal status or employment as an intellectual.

312   MOORE, RONNIE M. "We Are Catching Hell Down Here." In *Black Protest Thought in the Twentieth Century*, edited by August Meier, Elliot Rudwick, and Francis L. Broderick, 340–46. Indianapolis: Bobbs-Merrill, 1971. Memorandum to Richard Haley, Marvin Rich, and Jim McCain, 6 September 1963.

Moore describes CORE's organizing efforts in Plaquemine Parish, Louisiana.

313   ROGERS, KIM LACY. "Decoding a City of Words: Fantasy Theme Analysis and the Interpretation of Oral Interviews." *International Journal of Oral History* 7 no. 1 (1986): 43–56.

Rogers describes her interviews with civil rights leaders and activists in New Orleans. She found that the personal histories "often contradicted the public and archival record," which did not reveal "the process of negotiation, the degree of white hostility and sometimes outright terrorism . . . and the intensity of personal bonds that developed among several groups of activists."

314   _____. "Organizational Experience and Personal Narrative: Stories of New Orleans' Civil Rights Leadership." *Oral History Review* 13 (1985): 23–54.

Rogers's interviews with leaders of the civil rights movement in New Orleans reveal a wide gulf separating two distinct groups of black activists. They show that the more moderate members of the NAACP and the National Urban League "tended to see their experiences as cumulative. . . . Their lives had an evolutionary positive shape . . . and the eventual triumph of law reinforced their beliefs in the essential soundness of American institutions." The younger members of CORE and the Free Southern Theater described their experiences as both rewarding and disillusioning. Their stories outlined "an exuberant struggle and climb upward in the transcendent years of movement experience, followed by a sudden plunge downward when they realized the personal costs of their crusade and the limitations of the political changes won by the civil rights movement." Rogers relates the different quality of their experiences to differences in the organizational structures in which they worked.

315   TEACHOUT, PETER R. "Louisiana Under Law." In *Southern Justice*, edited by Leon Friedman, 57–79. New York: Pantheon Books, 1965.

Using both historical and contemporary examples, Teachout describes how the law has been used to repress the black citizens of Louisiana. In this essay he documents the police harassment resulting from a voter registration campaign in West Monroe in 1964.

Mississippi

316   ABNEY, GLENN F. "Factors Related to Negro Voter Turnout in Mississippi." *Journal of Politics* 36 (November 1974): 1057–63.

Abney examines black voter turnout during Mississippi's 1971 gubernatorial election. He finds that turnout was high in rural counties, in counties with higher black educational levels, and where there were several black candidates running for local office.

317   ADLER, RENATA. "The Meredith Mississippi March." In *The Civil Rights Reader*, edited by Leon Friedman, 96–106. New York: Walker & Co., 1966. Orig. pub. in *New Yorker*, 16 July 1966, 21–24.

Adler describes the events and issues involved in the 1966 Meredith march through Mississippi. She writes, that "the Negro leaders required the government of Mississippi to deal with them—for the first time—as men. For this reason, if for no other, the march marked a turning point in the Negro's relationship to the white community, North and South."

318   ALVIS, JOEL L. "Racial Turmoil and Religious Reaction: The Rt. Rev. John M. Allin." *Historical Magazine of the Protestant Episcopal Church* 50 (March 1981): 83–96.

John M. Allin was Episcopal Bishop of Mississippi during the 1960s and 1970s. Alvis uses the example of Allin to interpret the "role of the Southern 'moderate' in the civil rights crisis." He focuses on two areas: Allin's participation in the Committee of Concern, a group of white churchmen who raised money to rebuild black churches burned during the summer of 1964; and his criticism of the National Council of Churches for its failure to consult with local white churchmen when establishing the Delta Ministry. For more on the Delta Ministry see Hilton (1969, see entry 364).

319   BELFRAGE, SALLY. *Freedom Summer.* New York: Viking, 1965. 246 pages.

Belfrage spent July and August of 1964 in Greenwood, Mississippi, where she was a volunteer worker in a Freedom School that was part of the Mississippi Summer Project. *Freedom Summer* is her personal account of her experiences, which included being arrested for picketing the courthouse on Greenwood's Freedom Day and traveling to the Democratic National Convention with the Freedom Democratic party delegation. Most of the book, however, describes her day-to-day experiences as an "outside agitator", working with children in the Freedom School, getting to know the black family she lived with, discussing politics with other volunteers, and learning to live with the fear of violence that saturated the Mississippi air.

320   BERRY, JASON. *Amazing Grace: With Charles Evers in Mississippi.* New York: Saturday Review Press, 1973. 370 pages.

Shortly after graduating from Georgetown University in 1971, Berry traveled south to work on Charles Evers's Mississippi gubernatorial campaign. This sympathetic insider's view describes the transition from working in the civil rights movement to becoming a part of partisan politics, and Evers's role as both a politician and a civil rights leader.

321   BRADEN, WALDO W. "The Rhetoric of a Closed Society." *Southern Speech Communication Journal* 45 (Summer 1980): 333–51.

Braden examines the persuasive strategies utilized in Mississippi between 1954 and 1964 to defend white supremacy, to resist integration, to suppress internal opposition, and to thwart efforts of the federal government to end segregation.

322   BRAITERMAN, MARVIN. "Harold and the Highwaymen." In *Southern Justice*, edited by Leon Friedman, 88–102. New York: Pantheon Books, 1965.

Braiterman describes his experiences in defending a white civil rights worker charged with a traffic offense in Madison County in 1964.

323   BRAVERMAN, MIRIAM. "Mississippi Summer." *Library Journal* 90 (15 November 1965): 5045–47.

Braverman reports on the condition and the needs of Freedom Libraries, which were established in several Mississippi communities during the Freedom Summer of 1964. She views these libraries as an important alternative to local publc libraries that do not welcome or meet the needs of the black population.

324   BRENNER, JESSE H. "The Case of the Disappearing Docket." In *Southern Justice*, edited by Leon Friedman, 103–6. New York: Pantheon Books, 1965.

Brenner describes his experiences in Madison County as a lawyer for two civil rights workers who attempted to bring charges against a gas station owner who had beaten them.

325   CAGIN, SETH, and PHILIP DRAY. *We Are Not Afraid.* New York: Macmillan Publishing Co., 1988. 613 pages.

This is the definitive account of the murders of James Chaney, Andrew Goodman, and Michael Schwerner in Neshoba County, Mississippi, in the summer of 1964. Cagin and Dray include extensive biographical portraits of the three young activists, a detailed account of the investigation of their deaths, and a full description of the trials of the men accused of their murders.

326   CANZONERI, ROBERT. *"I Do So Politely": A Voice from the South.* Boston: Houghton Mifflin Co., 1965. 182 pages.

Canzoneri shares his personal reflections on race relations in Mississippi from his vantage point as an "enlightened" native teaching at the University of Mississippi during the Meredith crisis of 1962.

327   CARTER, HODDING. *So the Heffners Left McComb.* Garden City, NY: Doubleday, 1965. 142 pages.

Red and Malva Heffner were a typical middle-class couple living in an affluent subdivision of McComb, Mississippi, in the summer of 1964. Red was a successful insurance salesman. Malva's daughter, Jan (Red's stepdaughter), was the reigning Miss Mississippi. Then they committed the unpardonable "sin" of inviting two white civil rights workers to their home for dinner and conversation. Almost immediately the Heffners began receiving death threats, old friends stopped talking to them, Red's business evaporated, and their pet dachshund was killed. By the end of the summer they had put their home up for sale and moved out of the state—victims of the fear that gripped "the closed society" in the summer of 1964. Carter provides in this book a sympathetic portrait of the Heffner's tribulations, but has remarkably little sympathy for the black Mississippians who were being bombed and beaten at the same time for trying to exercise their constitutional rights.

328 CHATFIELD, JACK. "Port Gibson, Mississippi: A People of the Future." *New South* 24 (Summer 1969): 45–55.

Little civil rights acitivity occurred in Port Gibson or Claiborne County until December of 1965 when Charles Evers revived the NAACP and launched a highly successful boycott of local merchants. Chatfield describes the techniques used to sustain the boycott, including "the threat of public shame and . . . small acts of physical intimidation."

329 CHEVIGNY, PAUL G. "A Busy Spring in the Magnolia State." In *Southern Justice*, edited by Leon Friedman, 13–34. New York: Pantheon Books, 1965.

Chevigny describes legislation passed by the Mississippi legislature in the spring of 1964 in anticipation of the Mississippi Summer Project. He points out that most of the laws were passed without any public discussion so there could be no record of "legislative intent," and that the majority of these laws granted greater powers to law enforcement officers in controlling public demonstrations.

330 COLBY, DAVID C. "Black Power, White Resistance, and Public Policy: Political Power and Poverty Program Grants in Mississippi." *Journal of Politics* 47, no. 2 (1985): 579–95.

Colby examines the distribution of poverty grant monies to Mississippi counties in 1968 and 1972. He reports that "black electoral power contributes to larger poverty program grants," and that protest activity has an inverse effect on funding.

331 _____. The Voting Rights Act and Black Registration in Mississippi." *Publius* 16 (Fall 1986): 123–37.

In this article, Colby documents the impact of the 1965 Voting Rights Act on black voter registration in Mississippi. The number of registered blacks went from 28,000 in 1965 to 406,000 in 1984. He shows that the impact of the law was greatest in counties with a large number of unregistered blacks, because these counties were the scene of more civil rights activity, which provoked the intervention of federal examiners.

332 _____. "White Violence and the Civil Rights Movement." In *Blacks in Southern Politics*, edited by Laurence W. Moreland, Robert P. Steed, and Tod A. Baker, 31–48. New York: Praeger Publishers, 1987.

Colby reports his analysis of more than 1,000 violent acts during the civil rights movement in Mississippi from 1960 to 1969. He found that the best indicator of white violence is black electoral strength. The second best indicator is the level of black protest activity. He concludes that there were more attacks on blacks in areas where the movement was active as "whites utilized violence in an attempt to retain political control."

333   COLES, ROBERT, and JOSEPH BRENNER. "American Youth in a Social Struggle: The Mississippi Summer Project." *American Journal of Orthopsychiatry* 35 (October 1965): 907–26.

Coles and Brenner discuss their work as psychiatrists with the 1964 Mississippi Summer Project. They describe the project volunteers as "uniformly intelligent, determined youth, willfully desirous of ending what to most of them was a deeply felt state of injustice in their country." They outline four psychological stages the volunteers experienced as they adjusted to their work: (1) the "naive and awkward" period, (2) a period of "isolated, determined sophistication," (3) a period of self-examination, followed by (4) a stage of "effective confidence."

334   COUNCIL of FEDERATED ORGANIZATIONS. *Mississippi Black Paper.* New York: Random House, 1965. 92 pages.

This book consists of statements and affidavits by fifty-seven individuals involved in the civil rights movement regarding illegal acts of Mississippi law enforcement officers, their failure to protect civil rights workers and black citizens attempting to exercise their consitutional rights, and their refusal to prosecute persons known to be responsible for violence against people involved in the movement. These documents were gathered as part of a law suit against Sheriff Rainey of Neshoba County and other state officials.

335   CRAWFORD, VICKI L. "Beyond the Human Self: Grassroots Activists in the Mississippi Civil Rights Movement." In *Women in the Civil Rights Movement,* edited by Vicki L. Crawford, Jacqueline Anne Rouse, and Barbara Woods, 13–26. Brooklyn, NY: Carlson Publishing, 1990.

Crawford describes the work of three black women who were active in different areas of Mississippi: Winson Hudson of Harmony, Annie Devine of Canton, and Unita Blackwell of Mayersville.

336   CUMMINGS, RICHARD. *The Pied Piper: Allard K. Lowenstein and the Liberal Dream.* New York: Grove Press, 1985. 569 pages.

Allard Lowenstein worked with SNCC in Mississippi during 1963 and 1964. He was responsible for recruiting outside college students to work on the 1963 Freedom Vote and is sometimes credited with suggesting the Mississippi Summer Project of 1964. In the aftermath of the Democratic convention, Lowenstein was vilified by many civil rights workers for "selling out" the MFDP. Cummings devotes one section of this biography to Lowenstein's Mississippi exploits.

337   DEMUTH, JERRY. "Summer in Mississippi: Freedom Moves in to Stay." *The Nation,* 14 September 1964, 104–10.

DeMuth outlines the goals of the Mississippi Summer Project and its continuing programs including Freedom Schools, community centers, and voter registration. He describes the efforts of volunteer workers in several communities across the state.

338 _____. "Tired of Being Sick and Tired." *The Nation*, 1 June 1964, 548–51.

DeMuth profiles Mississippi civil rights organizer, Fannie Lou Hamer, and her race for Congress to represent the Second Congressional District. He also describes her attempt to register to vote in 1962, her arrest and beating in 1963, and her organizing efforts in the Mississippi Delta.

339 DITTMER, JOHN. "The Politics of the Mississippi Movement, 1954–1964." In *The Civil Rights Movement in America*, edited by Charles W. Eagles, 65–96. Jackson: University Press of Mississippi, 1986.

Dittmer outlines what he sees as three distinct phases of the civil rights movement in Mississippi. The first phase began with the 1954 *Brown* decision and was dominated by the NAACP's efforts to desegregate school and register voters. He describes how the rise of white fanatical resistance defeated these initiatives and left the NAACP without a program. The second phase began with the arrival of the freedom riders in Jackson in 1961. He points out that older, middle-class leaders were replaced by younger activists, many from outside Mississippi, who forged an alliance with the majority of poor blacks in the state. This stage culminated in the MFDP challenge at the 1964 Democratic convention. The third phase began following the convention as many of the young radical organizers withdrew from Mississippi and the NAACP regained its dominant position by joining with moderate white Democrats to defeat the MFDP.

340 DORSEY, L. C. *Freedom Came to Mississippi.* New York: Field Foundation, 1977. 44 pages.

Dorsey gives an autobiographical perspective on the social changes that happened in Mississippi as a result of the civil rights movement. She concludes that the differences before and after the movement are "gigantic," but that much remains to be done and that the "concern and commitment of outsiders" are essential if the changes are to continue.

341 EAST, P. D. *The Magnolia Jungle: The Life, Times and Education of a Southern Editor.* New York: Simon and Schuster, 1960. 243 pages.

East was the editor of a small Mississippi weekly, *The Petal Paper*. His autobiography describes his efforts to ridicule the White Citizens' Council and advocate better treatment for blacks at a time when these were not popular or profitable positions.

342 EMMERICH, J. OLIVER. *Two Faces of Janus: The Saga of Deep South Change.* Jackson: University and College Press of Mississippi, 1973. 163 pages.

Oliver Emmerich was editor of the McComb *Enterprise-Journal* during the 1950s and 1960s. He was branded a racial "moderate" for editorially urging adherence to Supreme Court rulings and the restoration of law and order. He describes in this work the climate of terror that gripped his town during the civil rights era.

343 EVERS, CHARLES. *Evers*, edited by Grace Halsell. New York: World Publishing, 1971. 196 pages.

Charles Evers returned to Mississippi in 1963 when his brother Medgar was murdered, and continued his work as the state NAACP organizer. Subsequently, he was elected mayor of Fayette, and was a candidate for Congress and governor of Mississippi. The second half of the book describes his activities after 1963.

344 EVERS, MYRLIE B., and WILLIAM PETERS. *For Us, the Living*. Garden City, NY: Doubleday, 1967. 378 pages.

Myrlie Evers was the wife of Mississippi NAACP leader Medgar Evers, who was murdered in 1963. This is her story of his life and death and their life together.

345 FERNANDEZ, ROBERTO M., and DOUG MCADAM. "Multi-Organizational Fields and Recruitment to Social Movements." In *Organizing for Social Change: Social Movement Organizations Across Cultures*, edited by Bert Klandermas, 315–43. Greenwich, CT: JAI Press, 1987.

Fernandez and McAdam use data from their study of Mississippi Summer Project volunteers from the University of Wisconsin to examine the ways in which linkages among social movement organizations facilitated recruitment to the civil rights movement. They report that an individual's structural position in the network of campus organizations was an important determinant of participation in the Summer Project. They conclude that organizational memberships "serve to channel individuals whose personal biographies predispose them to protest activity into participation in the Freedom Summer campaign."

346 FINDLAY, JAMES. "In Keeping with the Prophets: The Mississippi Summer of 1964." *Christian Century*, 8–15 June 1988, 574–76.

Findlay reports the memories of some of the 300 ministers recruited by the National Council of Churches to participate in the 1964 Mississippi Summer Project. Most recalled their brief stays in the state as being one of their most powerful experiences, and several claimed that it had transformed their lives.

347 FOSTER, E. C. "A Time of Challenge: Afro-Mississippi Political Developments since 1965." *Journal of Negro History* 68 (Spring 1983): 185–200.

Foster traces the political impact of the 1965 Voting Rights Act in Mississippi. He finds that there were 432 black, elected officials as of early 1983, but that there were few in positions to exercise meaningful power. He points out that no blacks had been elected to statewide office, none were mayors of large cities, and none were members of Congress (this has since changed). He concludes that the election of blacks has been largely of symbolic value.

348 FRIEDMAN, LEON, ed. *Southern Justice.* New York: Pantheon Books, 1965. 306 pages.
See entry 128.

349 FRUCHTER, NORM. "Mississippi: Notes on SNCC." *Studies on the Left* (Winter 1965): 74–80.

Fruchter blasts the federal government for helping perpetuate "institutionalized racism in Mississippi" and praises the SNCC for realizing this occurrence and "working to develop alternative organizations and institutions which are responsive to what local Negroes need and want."

350 FUSCO, LIZ. "Deeper Than Politics: The Mississippi Freedom Schools." *Liberation* (November 1964): 17–19.

Fusco describes the objectives of the Freedom Schools, which were organized by civil rights workers during the Mississippi Summer Project of 1964, and gives examples of their unique approach. She claims that Freedom Schools were a success because "the people trying to change Mississippi were asking themselves real questions about what is wrong with Mississippi" and that they encouraged students in their schools to raise similar questions.

351 GOOD, PAUL. "The Meredith March." *New South* 21 (Summer 1966): 2–16.

Good describes the atmosphere and events of the 1966 Meredith march. He finds that despite much-publicized disagreements among participants, the march "achieved many things, tangible and subtle."

352 GREENBERG, POLLY. *The Devil Has Slippery Shoes: A Biased Biography of the Child Development Group of Mississippi.* New York: Macmillan Publishing Co., 1969. 704 pages.

The Child Development Group of Mississippi (CDGM) was created in early 1965 when a group of civil rights activists decided to bring the newly created Head Start program to Mississippi's poorest children. They were determined to create an independent organization that took seriously the Office of Economic Opportunity's injunction to enlist "the maximum feasible participation" of the poor. Under the leadership of Dr. Tom Levin, they convinced the federal government to fund their project and, for a few years, used anti-poverty money to build an organization that would be directly responsive to the needs of the black community. Since its funding was not controlled by local white politicians and its leaders were closely allied with the movement, CDGM was under attack from its inception. Greenberg's book is an eloquent defense of CDGM by one of its founders.

353 GUTMAN, JEREMIAH S. "Oktibbeha County, Mississippi." In *Southern Justice*, edited by Leon Friedman, 80–87. New York: Pantheon Books, 1965.

Gutman describes his experiences defending a black civil rights worker before a justice of the peace in rural Mississippi.

354 GUYOT, LAWRENCE, and MIKE THELWELL. "The Politics of Necessity and Survival in Mississippi." *Freedomways* 6, no. 2 (1966): 120–32.

Guyot and Thelwell explain the Mississippi Freedom Democratic Party's challenge to Mississippi's political structure in light of the state's history of racial oppression and the continuing efforts by white politicians to keep blacks in a powerless position. They contend that there has been "no effective change . . . in the policy of tolerance on the part of those who hold national power, towards the systematized degradation of the black population in Mississippi by the State."

355 ———. "Toward Independent Political Power." *Freedomways* 6, no. 3 (1966): 246–54.

Guyot and Thelwell explain the program of the Mississippi Freedom Democratic Party to challenge the election of Mississippi members of Congress and to build a "state-wide network of precinct and county organizations." According to the authors, the primary task is to "continue organizing these black voters into an independent political organ capable of unified action on the state level."

356 HALBERSTAM, DAVID. "A County Divided Against Itself." *The Reporter*, 15 December 1955, 30–32.

Halberstam describes the reaction in Yazoo County, Mississippi, to a petition filed by the NAACP calling for the desegregation of the local school system. Of the fifty-three black parents who signed the petition, all but two had withdrawn their names. Opposition to integration was led by the White Citizens' Council, which published the names of all signers in the local newspaper. Halbertstam writes that workers whose names appeared on the list were fired from their jobs and found it impossible to find other work in the area. He shows how, although there was no physical violence, the economic reprisals were sufficient to discourage further attempts at school desegregation and to weaken the local NAACP chapter.

357 HAMER, FANNIE LOU. "It's in Your Hands." In *Black Women in White America: A Documentary History*, edited by Gerda Lerner, 609–14. New York: Pantheon Books, 1972. Speech given at NAACP Legal Defense Fund Institute, 7 May 1971.

Hamer discusses civil rights, women's rights, and poverty in the context of her work for poor blacks in Mississippi.

358 ———. "Sick and Tired of Being Sick and Tired." *Katallagete*, Fall 1968, 19–26.

Mississippi civil rights organizer Fannie Lou Hamer voices her opinion on the need for black political involvement in the context of the 1968 presidential election. She recounts the story of her political education, including her experience with the MFDP delegation at the 1964 Democratic convention.

359 HAMMER, RICHARD. "Yankee Lawyers in Mississippi Courts." *Harper's*, November 1966, 79–88.

Hammer describes the work of two organizations of civil rights lawyers working in Mississippi—the Lawyers' Committee for Civil Rights Under Law, and the Lawyers' Constitutional Defense Committee. He compares the sponsorship and orientation of the two organizations. He concludes that the presence of outside lawyers has forced Mississippi courts and law enforcement personnel to be more cautious in their treatment of civil rights workers.

360 HARKEY, IRA B., JR. *The Smell of Burning Crosses: An Autobiography of a Mississippi Newspaperman.* Jacksonville, IL: Harris, Wolfe & Co., 1967. 207 pages.

Harkey was editor and publisher of the Pascagoula *Chronicle* during the early 1960s. He recounts here his journalistic crusade to promote reason and moderation in the face of the steadily worsening racial climate in Mississippi. For these efforts he was awarded the Pulitzer Prize, and was forced to sell his paper and move out of the state.

361 HAYDEN, TOM. "SNCC in Action: Dignity for the Enslaved and for All of Us." In *The New Student Left*, edited by Mitchell Cohen and Dennis Hale, 75–86. Boston: Beacon Press, 1966. Orig. pub. as the pamphlet "Revolution in Mississippi," 1961.

Hayden describes the SNCC's organizing efforts in McComb, Mississippi, in September and October of 1961.

362 HECK, EDWARD V., and JOSEPH STEWART, JR. 1982. "Ensuring Access to Justice: the Role of Interest Group Lawyers in the 60s Campaign for Civil Rights." *Judicature* 66, no. 2 (1982): 84–94.

Heck and Stewart analyzed the records of 1,583 cases handled in Mississippi between 1964 and 1971 by three civil rights agencies: the NAACP Legal Defense Fund (LDF), the Lawyers' Committee for Civil Rights Under Law (LCCRUL), and the Lawyers' Constitutional Defense Committee (LCDC). He reports a pattern of specialization with regard to the kind of cases handled by each group. LDF lawyers specialized in school desegregation cases and "other cases litigated in federal court with the expectation of an appeal to higher courts." LCCRUL and LCDC handled "relatively routine cases" defending civil rights workers against traffic violations and criminal charges in state and local courts.

363 HEINZE, FREDERICK. "The Freedom Libraries." *Library Journal* 90 (15 April 1965): 37–39.

Heinze describes the objective of the Freedom Libraries as an attempt to bring Mississippi blacks into contact with the world outside the "closed society."

364 HILTON, BRUCE. *The Delta Ministry.* New York: Macmillan Publishing Co., 1969. 240 pages.

When the efforts of the major civil rights organizations in Mississippi began to dwindle, the Delta Ministry was organized by the National Council of Churches to continue working for social change and black advancement.

365   HOLT, LEN. *The Summer That Didn't End.* New York: William Morrow
         & Co., 1965. 351 pages.

Holt is a movement lawyer who spent much of the summer of 1964 in Mississippi defending civil rights workers. His book offers an insider's view of the Mississippi Summer Project with special emphasis on four areas: Freedom Schools, the "white folks" project, the Mississippi Freedom Democratic party, and the Democratic National Convention. His seven appendices provide valuable documentation on the summer project. Especially valuable is the daily summary of incidents from June 16 to August 26.

366   HONNOLD, JOHN. "The Bourgeois Bar and the Mississippi Movement."
         American Bar Association Journal 52 (March 1966): 228–32.

Honnold describes his experiences defending jailed civil rights demonstrators as a lawyer for the Lawyers' Committee for Civil Rights Under Law. He discusses the conflict between the lawyer's responsibility to free his clients and the movement's need to keep demonstrators in jail to increase pressure on local officials.

367   HOWE, FLORENCE. "Mississippi's Freedom Schools: The Politics of Education." *Harvard Educational Review* 34 (Spring 1965): 144–60.

Howe describes her work in a Jackson, Mississippi, Freedom School during the summer of 1964 and discusses the objectives of the schools and teaching methods they employed. She explains how the staff tried to redefine the role of the teacher and replace the traditional authoritarian approach with more egalitarian methods. She also notes that the citizenship curriculum the schools employed was designed to develop self-respect and critical awareness among the students so they could continue the work of the freedom movement.

368   HUEY, GARY. *Rebel with a Cause: P. D. East, Southern Liberalism,
         and the Civil Rights Movement, 1953–1971.* Wilmington, DE: Scholarly Resources, 1985. 232 pages.

Huey tells the story of P. D. East, a liberal white Mississippi editor who made the "mistake" of favoring justice for blacks, and was ostracized by his community as a result. See East's autobiography, *The Magnolia Jungle* (1960, see entry 341).

369   HUIE, WILLIAM BRADFORD. *Three Lives for Mississippi.* New York: WCC
         Books, 1965. 254 pages.

Huie is a white Southern journalist who investigated the death of Emmett Till and other racial atrocities. In 1963 he went to Neshoba County, Mississippi in hopes of locating the killers of Michael Schwerner, Andrew Goodman, and James Chaney. The FBI eventually identified the men responsible for the murders. Huie's book describes both the civil rights work that Schwerner and Chaney were conducting in Meredian and surrounding counties, and the mentality of the Klansmen who were determined to stop them. Huie maintains that Schwerner was the Klan's principal target and that Chaney and Goodman were killed because they accompanied Schwerner. The book includes memos that Schwerner and his wife Rita sent to CORE headquarters detailing their work in Meridian. Huie also interviews local blacks and visitors who describe the personal courage and humor of the young civil rights workers and the climate of fear and intimidation in which they lived and died.

370 JAFFEE, ANDREW. "Grenada, Mississippi: Perspective on the Backlash." *New South* 21 (Fall 1966): 15–27.

Jaffee describes developments in Grenada, Mississippi, after the 1966 Meredith march. He recounts the efforts of eight SCLC staffers who stayed in the town to work on voter registration projects. They encountered stiff resistance including a police tear gas attack on a mass meeting and mob violence when black children attempted to integrate local public schools. Jaffee observes that white moderates are unable to wrest control of the city government from racist elements.

371 JOUBERT, PAUL E., and BEN M. CROUCH. "Mississippi Blacks and the Voting Rights Act of 1965." *Journal of Negro Education* 46 (Spring 1977): 157–67.

Joubert and Crouch document the gains in black voter registration in Mississippi following the passage of the 1965 Voting Rights Act. They show that black registration, which numbered 35,000 on 1 August 1965, had increased to 286,000 by December 1970. The greatest gains, they indicate, happened in counties where federal examiners were present.

372 KEATING, EDWARD M., ed. *Mississippi Notebook: The Three Civil Rights Workers—How They were Murdered.* Menlo Park, CA: Layman's Press, 1964. 63 pages.

This special report on the 1964 murders in Neshoba County was compiled by a team of investigators, including Louis Lomax, William Kunstler, and Dick Gregory. It includes an eyewitness account of the killings, but does not reveal the identities of the members of the lynch mob.

373 KERNELL, SAM. "Comment: A Re-Evaluation of Black Voting in Mississippi." *American Political Science Review* 67, no. 4 (1973): 1307–18.

Kernell examines data on black political participation in Mississippi counties, but reaches different conclusions than Salamon and van Evera (1973, see entry 405). He contends that fear "does not appear to have much independent importance in explaining county-to-county variations in black turnout." He emphasizes education as "a powerful and stable factor in black political participation."

374 KLEIN, JOE. "The Emancipation of Bolton, Mississippi." *Esquire*, December 1985, 258–62.

Klein tells the story of Bennie Thompson, a former civil rights worker

for SNCC, who was elected mayor of Bolton, Mississippi, in 1973 and subsequently elected to the Hinds County Board of Supervisors. Klein profiles
here the man he calls "perhaps the most powerful black man in the state of
Mississippi."

375   KLING, SUSAN. "Fannie Lou Hamer: Baptism by Fire." In *Reweaving
      the Web of Life*, edited by Pam McAllister, 106–11. Philadelphia: New
      Society Publishers, 1982.

Kling describes Hamer's initial involvement with SNCC during 1962 and
1963, and includes an account of her arrest and beating in the Winona,
Mississippi, jail. This is a chapter from Kling's book, *Fannie Lou Hamer*
(1979, see entry 376).

376   _____. *Fannie Lou Hamer: A Biography*. Chicago: Women for Racial
      and Economic Equality, 1979. 56 pages.

This brief tribute to Fannie Lou Hamer reviews her life and work in the
Mississippi civil rights movement. It is based largely on published interviews
and articles about Hamer.

377   LADNER, JOYCE. "What 'Black Power' means to Negroes in Missis-
      sippi." *Trans-action* 5 (November 1967): 7–15.

Ladner reports her research in Mississippi during the summer of 1966.
She distinguishes between "locals" and "cosmopolitans" among Mississippi
Black Power advocates. The cosmopolitans she describes as well-educated,
often not Mississippi natives, who are more interested in developing black
consciousness. The locals she sees as less-educated Mississippi natives who
are more "committed to concrete economic and political programs." Ladner
views the development of black power as "an inevitable outgrowth of the
disillusionment that black people have experienced in their intense efforts
to become integrated into the mainstream of American society."

378   LAWRENCE, KEN. "Mississippi Spies." *Southern Exposure* 9 (Fall 1981):
      82–86.

The Mississippi State Sovereignty Commission operated between 1956
and 1973 as an arm of the state government to preserve segregation and
combat efforts to promote integration. Its functions included spreading pro-
segregation propaganda across the country and lobbying against civil rights
legislation, but its most important activity was surveillance and political intelligence gathering. Lawrence documents how the Sovereignty Commission
spied on civil rights workers and then used the information it gathered in
attempts to discredit the civil rights movement and create internal discord
within the movement.

379   LOCKE, MAMIE E. "Is This America? Fannie Lou Hamer and the Missis-
      sippi Freedom Democratic Party." In *Women in the Civil Rights Move-
      ment*, edited by Vicki L. Crawford, Jacqueline Anne Rouse, and Bar-
      bara Woods, 27–37. Brooklyn, NY: Carlson Publishing, 1990.

Locke presents a brief biography of Fannie Lou Hamer, the influential

Mississippi civil rights organizer. This account focuses primarily on Hamer's involvement with the MFDP.

380 LORD, WALTER. *The Past That Would Not Die.* New York: Harper & Row, 1965. 275 pages.

Lord approaches the struggle for civil rights in Mississippi by emphasizing the state's memories of the Civil War and suspicions of the federal government. He tells the story of the 1962 desegregation of the University of Mississippi with sympathy for, but no approval of, the segregationists' position.

381 LYND, STOUGHTON. "Freedom Schools." *Freedomways* 5, no. 2 (1965): 302–9.

Lynd was director of the Freedom Schools for the 1964 Mississippi Summer Project. He describes the philosophy and operation of the schools as well as the convention of Freedom School students held in Meridian on 8–9 August 1964.

382 MCADAM, DOUG. *Freedom Summer.* New York: Oxford University Press, 1988. 322 pages.

McAdam relates the history of the Mississippi Summer Project, but the most original portion of this work is his in-depth analysis of the volunteers for the summer project, their social background, and their motivations for participating. Follow-up interviews with former volunteers twenty years after their summer in Mississippi reveal lives of continued activism and strong commitment to social change.

383 _____. "Recruitment to High Risk Activism: The Case of Freedom Summer." *American Journal of Sociology* 92, no. 1 (1986): 64–90.

McAdam studied applicants for the 1964 Mississippi Summer Project. Comparing 720 project participants with 241 people who applied but did not join the project, he found three major differences between the two groups. The participants were distinguished from the withdrawals on the basis of their (1) greater number of organizational affiliations, (2) higher levels of prior civil rights activity, and (3) stronger and more extensive ties to other participants.

384 MCCORD, WILLIAM. *Mississippi: The Long Hot Summer.* New York: W. W. Norton & Co., 1965. 222 pages.

McCord is a sociologist who came to Mississippi in 1964 to participate in the Mississippi Summer Project. He describes the events and personalities of the summer. He offers portraits of black and white Mississippians and their reactions to the civil rights movement. He reports from remote spots such as Carthage, Ruleville, Moss Point, and Clarksdale. His book combines history, social science, and current events.

385 MCMILLEN, NEIL R. "Black Enfranchisement in Mississippi: Federal Enforcement and Black Protest in the 1960's." *Journal of Southern History* 43, no. 3 (1977): 351–72. Reprinted in *We Shall Overcome,* edited

by David J. Garrow, vol. 2, 679–700. Brooklyn, NY: Carlson Publishing, 1989.

McMillen argues that the denial of black voting rights in Mississippi was so blatant and extreme that the federal government was provoked to intervene after the passage of the Voting Rights Act of 1965. He reviews the legal and extralegal measures that were used to limit black voter registration and examines the efforts of the Eisenhower and Kennedy administrations to remedy this denial of civil rights. McMillen contends that the actions of the Justice Department's civil rights division during the Kennedy years looked good only in comparison to the complete inaction during the Eisenhower years. Because both the Kennedy and Johnson administrations "construed their prosecutorial powers narrowly," relatively little action was taken against voting discrimination in Mississippi. The voter registration campaigns organized by SNCC between 1961 and 1963 were ineffective in increasing black registration in the face of overwhelming white resistance and federal reluctance to intervene. Greater federal involvement came about only when SNCC changed its strategy to what McMillen describes as a form of "guerrilla theater." He maintains that the 1963 Freedom Election, the 1964 Freedom Summer, the Mississippi Freedom Democratic Party challenge at the Democratic convention, and the 1965 effort to unseat Mississippi's congressional delegation were all designed to sway public opinion and force federal intervention. McMillen concludes that these protests led to the passage of the Voting Rights Act in 1965 and made possible a rapid increase in black voter registration in Mississippi, so that by 1970 two-thirds of the state's eligible blacks had been registered.

386   _____. "Development of Civil Rights, 1956–1970." In *A History of Mississippi*, edited by Richard Aubrey McLemore, vol. 2, 154–76. Hattiesburg: University and College Press of Mississippi, 1973.

McMillen reviews the civil rights movement in Mississippi from reaction to the 1954 *Brown* decision to the early 1970s. The main focus is on state government. He cites three major phases: (1) the control of state government by the segregationist White Citizens' Council during the administration of Governor Ross Barnett, (2) reaction against the Mississippi Summer Project of 1964 during the administration of Governor Paul Johnson, and (3) acceptance of some changes following the passage of the Voting Rights Act in 1965.

387   MARS, FLORENCE. *Witness in Philadelphia*. Baton Rouge: Louisiana State University Press, 1977. 296 pages.

Florence Mars was born to a prominent family in Philadelphia, Mississippi. When three civil rights workers were killed in the summer of 1964, she attempted to speak on behalf of moderation and racial understanding. As a result, she was virtually ostracized by the white community of Philadelphia. *Witness in Philadelphia* is her personal account of life in the segregated South during the civil rights movement.

388 MEREDITH, JAMES. *Three Years in Mississippi.* Bloomington: University of Indiana Press, 1966. 328 pages.

A personal account of the desegregation of the University of Mississippi by a man who lived it.

389 MILLER, CHAR. "The Mississippi Summer Project Remembered—the Stephen Mitchell Bingham Letter." *Journal of Mississippi History* 47, no. 4 (1985): 284–307.

Stephen Bingham was the son of a wealthy and influential Connecticut family who spent the summer of 1964 as a volunteer civil rights worker in Mississippi. In February of 1965 he sent a lengthy "letter" to politicians, civil rights activists, and leaders of Mississippi's "white power structure." He hoped that the letter would open "some minimal channel of communication" between the movement and "moderate" whites. In this letter he offers his own critical assessment of the Mississippi Summer Project and its political ramifications. Miller has edited Bingham's letter and provided an introduction that puts Bingham and his message in context.

390 MOODY, ANNE. *Coming of Age in Mississippi.* New York: Dell Publishing Co., 1968. 348 pages.

Anne Moody became involved in the civil rights movement while a student at Tougaloo College in Jackson. Soon she went to work full-time as a CORE organizer in Madison County. This book recounts her firsthand experiences on the front lines of the movement from 1963 to 1965.

391 MORRIS, WILLIE. *Yazoo: Integration in a Deep Southern Town.* New York: Harper's Magazine Press, 1971. 192 pages.

Morris describes the integration of public schools in his home town of Yazoo City during 1970.

392 MORRISON, MINION K. C. *Black Political Mobilization: Leadership, Power, and Mass Behavior.* Albany: State University of New York Press, 1987. 303 pages.

Morrison studied three small towns in Mississippi—Bolton, Mayersville and Tchula—each of which had elected black mayors following the passage of the Voting Rights Act. In this book, he examines the basis of support for the mayors and what they have been able to do for their towns since their elections.

393 MORRISON, [MINION] K. C., and JOE C. HUANG. "The Transfer of Power in a Mississippi Town." *Growth and Change* 4 (April 1973): 25–29.

Morrison and Huang report the results of a survey of black residents of Fayette, Mississippi, following the 1969 election of Charles Evers as mayor. Although most respondents endorsed the idea of Black Power, nearly all rejected the proposition that the town's government "be controlled by blacks only."

394 MOSES, BOB. "Mississippi: 1961–1962." *Liberation* 14 (January 1970): 7–17.

Moses was an influential figure within SNCC and was responsible for launching SNCC's first Mississippi voter registration project in Pike, Amite, and Walthall Counties in the summer of 1961. This campaign was met with intense resistance from local officials, resulting in the murder of Herbert Lee. This article is the transcript of a tape recording made in the fall of 1962 in which Moses describes these organizing efforts in southwest Mississippi and subsequent efforts in LeFlore and Sunflower Counties in the Delta. He provides a detailed description of the dangers faced by civil rights workers and their determination to continue in the face of formidable opposition. Howard Zinn relied on this account in *SNCC: The New Abolitionists* (1965, see entry 548).

395 NORTON, ELEANOR HOLMES. "The Woman Who Changed the South: A Memory of Fannie Lou Hamer." *MS*, July 1977, 51.
Norton remembers the contributions of Mississippi civil rights organizer Fannie Lou Hamer.

396 O'DELL, JACK H. "Life in Mississippi: An Interview with Fannie Lou Hamer." *Freedomways* 5, no. 2 (1965): 231–42.
O'Dell interviews Mississippi civil rights organizer Fannie Lou Hamer. He covers her early life, her trip to Africa, her involvement with the movement and the MFDP at the 1964 Democratic convention, and the violence directed at her and other movement participants.

397 OPPENHEIM, JACK. "The Abdication of the Southern Bar." In *Southern Justice*, edited by Leon Friedman, 127–35. New York: Pantheon Books, 1965.
Oppenheim describes his experiences defending civil rights workers in Sunflower County, Mississippi. He is especially critical of local members of the bar for their failure to represent civil rights workers.

398 PARKER, FRANK R. *Black Votes Count: Political Empowerment in Mississippi After 1965.* Chapel Hill: University of North Carolina Press, 1990. 254 pages.
After the passage of the 1965 Voting Rights Act, two of the largest obstacles to black political participation—literacy tests and the poll tax—were removed. But black voters in the South faced another set of disfranchising devices designed to nullify or dilute their votes. These included at-large elections, racial gerrymandering, abolishing elective offices, and increasing the qualifying requirements for office. Parker describes here the legal strategies that he and other civil rights lawyers used to attack the measures he calls "the second generation of massive resistance" and how this struggle changed Mississippi politics. This book is a pointed rejoinder to Thernstrom's *Whose Votes Count?* (1987, see entry 728).

399 PAYNE, BRUCE. "The Quiet War." In *The New Student Left*, edited by Mitchell Cohen and Dennis Hale, 50–58. Boston: Beacon Press, 1966. Orig. pub. in *The Activist* 4 (1964).
Payne relates his experiences around Natchez as a northern volunteer

in the 1963 Freedom Vote—the effort organized by SNCC to place on the ballot Aaron Henry and Ed King for governor and lieutenant governor, respectively. He describes the intimidation and harassment, including being arrested, beaten, and shot at, that was directed at civil rights workers in the state.

400 PAYNE, CHARLES. "Men Led, but Women Organized: Movement Participation of Women in the Mississippi Delta." In *Women in the Civil Rights Movement*, edited by Vicki L. Crawford, Jacqueline Anne Rouse, and Barbara Woods, 1–11. Brooklyn, NY: Carlson Publishing, 1990.

In his study of movement participation around Greenwood, Mississippi, Payne found a disproportionate number of women involved, especially between the ages of thirty and fifty. He suggests that the greater participation of women was due to their greater involvement in kin and communal networks, especially the church.

401 ROMAINE, ANNE. "Interview with Fannie Lou Hamer." *Southern Exposure* (Spring 1981): 47–48.

In this 1966 interview Hamer discusses her actions with the MFDP at the 1964 Democratic convention in Atlantic City and the decision to reject the compromise offered by the party leadership.

402 ROTHSCHILD, MARY AICKIN. *A Case of Black and White: Northern Volunteers and the Southern Freedom Summers, 1964–1965.* Westport, CT: Greenwood Press, 1982. 213 pages.

Rothschild examines the northern volunteers who worked with civil rights organizations in the Deep South during the summers of 1964 and 1965. The volunteers for SNCC's Mississippi Summer Project are well known and widely studied (see McAdam, *Freedom Summer* [1988, see entry 382]). Rothschild also includes a smaller number of volunteers who worked in the summer of 1965 with SNCC in Mississippi, and the SCOPE volunteers who worked with SCLC on voter registration projects in several states. (This group has been extensively studied by Demerath et al. in *Dynamics of Idealism* [1971, see entry 831]). Rothschild describes the social characteristics of the volunteers, their motivation for participating, their experiences in the South, the impact they had on the movement, and the impact their summer experience had on their subsequent lives. She is positive about their contributions to the movement, which included generating "enormous media attention," opening projects in "communities that the movement had previously never been able to reach," bringing "the first federal protection for civil rights workers," and contributing to the passage of two major civil rights bills.

403 RUGABER, WALTER. " 'We Can't Cuss White People Any More. It's in Our Hands Now.'" *New York Times Magazine*, 4 August 1968. Reprinted in *Black Protest in the Sixties*, edited by August Meier and Elliot Rudwick, 302–14. Chicago: Quadrangle Books, 1970.

Rugaber offers a portrait of Mississippi civil rights leader Charles Evers and his race in the 1968 Democratic primary for the U.S. Congress. He uses Evers's campaign to illustrate the progress made by Mississippi blacks as a result of the civil rights movement.

404 RUSTIN, BAYARD. "Fear in the Delta." In *Down the Line*, edited by Bayard Rustin, 62–87. Chicago: Quadrangle Books, 1971. Orig. pub. in *Liberation* 1 (December 1956): 17–19.

Rustin describes the growing pressure on outspoken and independent blacks in the Mississippi Delta following the formation of the White Citizens' Council. This article is based on his interviews with leaders of the NAACP and local businessmen.

405 SALAMON, LESTER, and STEPHEN VAN EVERA. "Fear, Apathy, and Discrimination: A Test of Three Explanations of Political Participation." *American Political Science Review* 67, no. 4 (1973): 1288–1306.

Salamon and Van Evera examine the characteristics of the potential black electorate in Mississippi's twenty-nine black majority counties to explain variations in black political participation for the years following the passage of the Voting Rights Act. They report that an "expanded fear" model that measures economic independence and local political organization best explains black participation. See Kernell (1973, entry 373).

406 SALLIS, CHARLES, and JOHN QUINCY ADAMS. "Desegregation in Jackson, Mississippi." In *Southern Businessmen and Desegregation*, edited by Elizabeth Jacoway and David R. Colburn, 236–56. Baton Rouge: Louisiana State University Press, 1982.

Sallis and Adams describe a change in Jackson's white leadership from militant rejection of any form of racial integration to a more moderate stance. They date this development from 1965 when "many businessmen realized that continued resistance, racial unrest, and violence projected the image of a lawless state and would retard economic development."

407 SALTER, JOHN R., JR. *Jackson, Mississippi: An American Chronicle of Struggle and Schism*. 1979. Reprint. Malabar, FL: R. E. Krieger Publishing Co., 1987. 248 pages.

Salter was a young sociologist who arrived in Mississippi in 1961 to teach at Tougaloo College. Before long he became involved as an advisor to the NAACP Youth Council. Within a year Salter was a leader of the movement to desegregate public facilities in Jackson, working closely with state NAACP leader Medgar Evers. The protestors met staunch resistance from the city police who even refused to let pickets walk on the street in front of segregated lunch counters. Despite this official harassment, the Jackson movement grew in size and militance and organized a boycott of downtown merchants. By the summer of 1963 the protests had escalated, but city officials appeared unwilling to make any concessions. When Medgar Evers was assassinated, the city of Jackson narrowly averted a major battle between police and angry blacks. *Jackson, Mississippi* is Salter's personal memoir of these turbulent years. Perhaps the most interesting aspect of the book is his account of the conflict between the local protest leaders and the national NAACP officials who struggled for control of the movement. Salter is critical of Roy Wilkins, Gloster Current, and other "outsiders" who attempted to dampen the militance of the NAACP Youth Council.

408   SCHULMAN, ROBERT P. "Clarksdale Customs." In *Southern Justice*, edited by Leon Friedman, 107–11. New York: Pantheon Books, 1965.

Schulman describes his experiences as a civil rights lawyer in Clarksdale.

409   SILVER, JAMES W. *Mississippi: The Closed Society.* 2d ed. New York: Harcourt, Brace and World, 1966. 375 pages.

Silver, a history professor at the University of Mississippi, wrote this book to explain how the crisis over the matriculation of James Meredith at the University of Mississippi in 1962 happened. Silver is critical of the white politicians in the state who encouraged mob violence in the hope that they could prevent desegregation. The 1966 edition contains a 120-page section, "Revolution Begins in the Closed Society," describing the events of 1964 and 1965 as the civil rights movement put Mississippi in the national spotlight.

410   SINSHEIMER, JOSEPH A. "The Freedom Vote of 1963: New Strategies of Racial Protest in Mississippi." *Journal of Southern History* 55, no. 2 (1989): 217–44.

Sinsheimer describes the Freedom Vote, a successful effort by SNCC to protest the 1963 Mississippi gubernatorial election. By collecting nearly 100,000 mock "freedom ballots," SNCC illustrated the extent of black disfranchisement. Sinsheimer contends that the project was valuable because it helped build an effective statewide organization, pumped "new blood into a movement badly in need of a transfusion," and "laid the groundwork for the formation of the Mississippi Freedom Democratic party six months later."

411   _____. "Never Turn Back: An Interview with Sam Block." *Southern Exposure* 15 (Summer 1987): 37–50.

Block was an SNCC organizer in Greenwood, Mississippi, in 1962 and 1963. During this time he helped coordinate a major voter registration campaign, which attracted considerable attention both for its success in mobilizing black residents and for the violent attacks directed against himself and other civil rights workers. In this interview he reflects on his experiences as a movement activist.

412   SITTON, CLAUDE. "Bullets and Ballots in Greenwood, Mississippi." In *Freedom Now! The Struggle for Civil Rights in America*, edited by Alan F. Westin, 87–94. New York: Basic Books, 1964. Orig. pub. in the *New York Times*, 6 April 1963, 20.

Sitton describes the shooting of Jimmy Travis on 28 February 1963 and other violence directed against civil rights workers and blacks attempting to register in the Mississippi Delta.

413   STERN, GERALD M. "Judge William Harold Cox and the Right to Vote
      in Clarke County, Mississippi." In *Southern Justice*, edited by Leon
      Friedman, 165–86. New York: Pantheon Books, 1965.

Judge Cox, of the Southern District of Mississippi, earned the reputation
as one of the most determined segregationists on the federal bench. Stern, a
former attorney for the Civil Rights Division of the Justice Department, traces
in this article the ways in which Cox frustrated voting rights litigation in
Clarke County, Mississippi.

414   STEWART, JOSEPH, JR., and JAMES F. SHEFFIELD, JR.. "Does Interest Group
      Litigation Matter? The Case of Black Political Mobilization in Missis-
      sippi." *Journal of Politics* 49 (August 1987): 780–98.

Stewart and Sheffield examine the impact of litigation by civil rights
groups on the political mobilization of Mississippi blacks. They report a
"close relationship between litigation and black voter registration and black
candidate recruitment." Litigation, however, does not appear to have any
direct effect on promoting black voter turnout or electing black candidates
to office.

415   SUGARMAN, TRACY. *Stranger at the Gates: A Summer in Mississippi.*
      New York: Hill & Wang, 1966. 240 pages.

Sugarman is a professional illustrator who spent the summer of 1964 as
an observer of the Mississippi Summer Project. He attended the project's
training session in Oxford, Ohio, and then lived in the mainly black community of Ruleville. He describes in this book the summer volunteers, their
work, the local blacks they worked with, and especially Charles McLaurin,
the SNCC worker who was the director of the Ruleville project. Sugarman
also recounts his contacts with a few of Ruleville's white residents.

416   SUTHERLAND, ELIZABETH. "The Cat and Mouse Game." *The Nation*, 14
      September 1964: 105–6.

Sutherland describes the relationship between civil rights workers and
Mississippi lawmen as a "cat and mouse game." She points out that attacks
on civil rights workers have declined, due largely to "the presence of so
many white volunteers." She also notes that at the same time, however,
police harassment is routine and the threat of violence remains constant.

417   SUTHERLAND, ELIZABETH, ed. *Letters from Mississippi.* New York:
      McGraw-Hill, 1965. 234 pages.
      See entry 160.

418   THELWELL, MICHAEL. "Fish are Jumping an' the Cotton is High: Notes
      from the Mississippi Delta." In *Duties, Pleasures, and Conflicts: Es-
      says in Struggle*, edited by Michael Thelwell, 74–86. Amherst: Univer-
      sity of Massachusetts Press, 1987. Orig. pub. in *Massachusetts Review*
      7, no. 2 (1966): 362–74.

Thelwell describes conditions in Sunflower County, Mississippi, following the passage of the 1965 Voting Rights Act. One of the effects, he notes,

is that black sharecroppers are being driven from their homes as plantations automate to cut costs and reduce the potential effect of a black voting majority.

419 TUCKER, SHIRLEY. *Mississippi from Within.* New York: Arco Publishing, 1965. 144 pages.

Tucker covers the period from July 1964 to June 1965. This book consists mainly of clippings from Mississippi newspapers, interspersed with photographs of civil rights activities in the state. It documents the curious ways that local news reporters interpreted events of the civil rights movement, and the pervasive climate of violence and intolerance that gripped the state.

420 U.S. COMMISSION on CIVIL RIGHTS. "Justice in These United States." In *The Great Society Reader,* edited by Marvin E. Gettleman and David Mermelstein, 306–32. New York: Random House, 1967.

The transcript of these hearings includes the testimony of Willie Dillon of McComb, Mississippi, whose home was bombed in the summer of 1964 because of his wife's participation in civil rights activities. When the bombing was investigated by the sheriff, Dillon was arrested and sent to jail for five months. The men responsible for the bombing were apprehended but let off with a verbal reprimand. Other witnesses in the hearings describe the racial climate and law enforcement practices in McComb during 1964.

421 VON HOFFMAN, NICHOLAS. *Mississippi Notebook.* Port Washington, NY: David White, 1964. 117 pages.

Von Hoffman came to Mississippi in the summer of 1964 as a correspondent for the *Chicago Daily News.* This book is a collection of his dispatches. He offers a sympathetic, yet critical view of the movement. He describes the terror and the courage he observed among civil rights activists. He also reports his contacts with local whites of various persuasions, from persecuted moderates to a paternalistic plantation owner.

422 WATTERS, PAT. "Their Text is a Civil Rights Primer." *New York Times Magazine,* 20 December 1964. Reprinted in *Black Protest in the Sixties,* edited by August Meier and Elliot Rudwick, 79–88. Chicago: Quadrangle Books, 1970.

Watters describes conditions in the Ruleville, Mississippi, Freedom School in the months following the Mississippi Summer Project.

423 WHITEHEAD, DON. *Attack on Terror: The FBI against the Ku Klux Klan in Mississippi.* New York: Funk & Wagnalls, 1970. 321 pages.

Whitehead tells the story of the FBI's investigation of the 1964 murder of three civil rights workers in Neshoba County, and the subsequent prosecution of the Klansmen responsible for the killings. Also mentioned are the FBI probes in the deaths of Viola Liuzzo and Vernon Dahmer and the 1968 bombing by Klansmen in Meridian, Mississippi. Whitehead praises the work of the FBI and blames the KKK for most of the anti-civil rights violence in

Mississippi. He claims that the FBI "provided the hard core of integrity around which the anti-Klan forces could rally and on which they could depend for support."

424 WILSON, JAMES B. "Municipal Ordinances, Mississippi Style." In *Southern Justice*, edited by Leon Friedman, 35–42. New York: Pantheon Books, 1965.

Wilson describes the legal maneuvering that followed his challenge of a Drew, Mississippi, ordinance which forbade civil rights workers to spend the night in that town.

425 WIRT, FREDERICK M. *The Politics of Southern Equality: Law and Change in a Mississippi County.* Westport, CT: Greenwood Press, 1970. 335 pages.

In this excellent case study, Wirt examines the impact of the civil rights movement on Panola County, Mississippi. He traces the consequences of the movement in three areas: voting, education, and economics. His purpose for conducting this study is to examine the relationship between the law and social change. Wirt has documented his study using interviews with participants in the movement and records of the Justice Department's Civil Rights Division that were opened to him. His in-depth analysis provides a valuable example of both historical documentation and sociological analysis.

426 YOUTH of the RURAL ORGANIZING and CULTURAL CENTER. *Minds Stayed on Freedom: The Civil Rights Struggle in the Rural South.* Edited by Jay MacLeod. Boulder: Westview Press, 1991. 189 pages.

This remarkable book consists of a series of interviews with participants in the civil rights movement in Holmes County, Mississippi. The interviewers were young people working at the Rural Organizing and Cultural Center. Unlike other oral histories of the movement, none of these subjects were well known beyond their own community. This book presents a view of the movement from the "grass roots." Holmes County is a particularly interesting case study because of its strong movement organization based on a nucleus of independent black farmers.

North Carolina

427 BARKSDALE, MARCELLUS C. "Civil Rights Organization and the Indigenous Movement in Chapel Hill, North Carolina, 1960–1965." *Phylon* 47 (March 1986): 29–42.

Barksdale traces efforts to desegregate public facilities in Chapel Hill from the first sit-in in 1960 to the passage of the 1964 Civil Rights Act. He covers the struggle to integrate restaurants, movie theatres, athletic teams, and businesses that continued throughout this period.

428 _____. "Robert F. Williams and the Indigenous Civil Rights Movement in Monroe, North Carolina, 1961." *Journal of Negro History* 69, no. 2 (1984): 73–89.

Barksdale describes the events of the summer of 1961 in Monroe, North Carolina, and the swimming pool protest led by Robert Williams which resulted in intense community conflict. This work is based on the author's interviews with several participants as well as published sources.

429 BLUMBERG, HERBERT H. "Accounting for a Nonviolent Mass Demonstration." In *Nonviolent Direct Action*, edited by A. Paul Hare and Herbert H. Blumberg, 475–91. Washington, DC: Corpus Books, 1968. Orig. pub. in *Sociological Inquiry* 38 (Winter 1968): 43–50.

Blumberg analyzes the organization, participation, and outcome of a nonviolent demonstration in Durham, North Carolina, during 1963.

430 CHAFE, WILLIAM H. *Civilities and Civil Rights: Greensboro, North Carolina, and the Black Struggle for Freedom.* New York: Oxford University Press, 1980. 436 pages.

Chafe chronicles the evolution of the civil rights movement in Greensboro, the site of the first student sit-in in 1960. He advances the thesis that North Carolina's committment to superficial racial tolerance created conditions in which protest could surface, but that this "civility" masked an underlying resistance to lasting change. Only after a violent confrontation at North Carolina A & T in 1971 did Greensboro's whites seriously begin to address the needs of the black community. He explains how the sit-ins grew out of the strength of the black community, and discusses the ways in which the white leadership sought to "contain and diffuse the many stages of black insurgency."

431 _____. "Greensboro, North Carolina: Perspectives on Progressivism." In *Southern Businessmen and Desegregation*, edited by Elizabeth Jacoway and David R. Colburn, 42–69. Baton Rouge: Louisiana State University Press, 1982.

In 1957, Greensboro was the first city in North Carolina to begin the token desegregation of its school system. Following the sit-ins of 1960, white leaders helped negotiate the desegregation of lunch counters. According to Chafe, however, after 1963 "white city leaders refused to promote further integration in jobs, government, or schools." He argues that "one of the South's most 'progressive' cities actually lagged behind more overtly bigoted areas in securing integration and racial justice."

432 _____. "The Greensboro Sit-Ins." *Southern Exposure* 6 (Fall 1978): 78–87.

Chafe examines the conditions in Greensboro that contributed to the 1960 sit-in demonstrations. He stresses two themes: that the sit-ins "continued a long tradition of protest in black Greensboro," and that white leaders believed that their style of moderation "could both preserve the progressive image of their city and meet the demands for some change." He concludes that the sit-ins were not "a radical departure from the black past of protest," but they provided "a transition to a new language of self-expression which broke through white patterns of self-deception and control." He pursues these themes in greater depth in *Civilities and Civil Rights* (1980, see entry 430).

433 EHLE, JOHN. *The Free Men.* New York: Harper & Row, 1965. 340 pages.

Despite its liberal reputation, Chapel Hill, North Carolina, was slow to desegregate public accommodations. Ehle relates the story of a series of futile protests during 1963 and early 1964 against segregated eating establishments. He focuses on white university students John Dunne and Pat Cusick and their black friend, Quinton Baker, who formed the nucleus of the local CORE chapter.

434 KEECH, WILLIAM R. *The Impact of Negro Voting: The Role of the Vote in the Quest for Equality.* Chicago: Rand McNally & Co., 1968. 113 pages.

See entry 211.

435 LADD, EVERETT CARLL, JR. *Negro Political Leadership in the South.* Ithaca, NY: Cornell University Press, 1966. 348 pages.

Ladd examines the meaning of leadership, styles of leadership, and race advancement organizations in Winston-Salem, North Carolina, and Greenville, South Carolina. Largely as a result of the civil rights movement, he found three changes in the structure of race leadership: (1) a marked increase in the number of Negro leaders, (2) "an increasing differentiation of the race leadership structure," and (3) a growing militance among Negro leaders.

436 WEHR, PAUL E. "A Southern Sit-In." In *Nonviolent Direct Action,* edited by A. Paul Hare and Herbert H. Blumberg, 100–106. Washington, DC: Corpus Books, 1968.

Wehr describes a 1960 sit-in in Durham, North Carolina, and discusses general characteristics of these nonviolent protests.

437 WILLIAMS, ROBERT F. *Negroes With Guns.* New York: Marzani & Munsell, 1962. 128 pages.

An early advocate of armed self-defense for blacks, Williams was president of the NAACP chapter in Monroe, North Carolina. He describes how his group's protest activities led to conflict with local police. Williams was later charged with kidnapping a white couple and eventually fled to Cuba.

438 _____. "The Swimming Pool Showdown." *Southern Exposure* 8 (Summer 1980): 22–24.

In this selection from *Negroes With Guns* (1962, see entry 437), Williams describes his organization of an NAACP chapter in Monroe, North Carolina, and its efforts to integrate the local swimming pool. This led to an armed clash with the Ku Klux Klan in 1957.

439 WOLFF, MILES. *Lunch at the 5 & 10: The Greensboro Sit-Ins, A Contemporary History.* 1970. Reprint. Chicago: Elephant Paperbacks, 1990. 204 pages.

Wolff offers a detailed account of the first student sit-in demonstrations in Greensboro, North Carolina, in February of 1960 and describes the four young men who began the sit-in movement. His epilogue profiles the four men thirty years after their historic protest.

Tennessee

440 ANDERSON, MARGARET. *The Children of the South.* New York: Farrar, Straus & Giroux, 1966. 208 pages.

Anderson, a teacher in the Clinton, Tennessee, public schools, describes the desegregation of that city's school system. She focuses especially on its effect on the black school children.

441 BEIFUSS, JOAN TURNER. *At the River I Stand: Memphis, the 1968 Strike, and Martin Luther King.* Brooklyn, NY: Carlson Publishing, 1989. 370 pages. Orig. pub. privately, 1985.

This study of the 1968 Memphis sanitation workers' strike is based on interviews with 364 participants in the strike and subsequent protests. The focus is primarily on the workers and their cause. The involvement and killing of Martin Luther King, Jr. are seen as important but secondary elements in this story.

442 COLLINS, THOMAS W. "An Analysis of the Memphis Garbage Strike of 1968." *Public Affairs Forum* 3 (April 1974): 1–6.

Collins examines the 1968 strike by Memphis sanitation workers that led to the assassination of Martin Luther King, Jr.

443 DYKEMAN, WILMA, and JAMES STOKELY. "Courage in Action in Clinton, Tennessee." *The Nation,* 22 December 1956, 531–33.

Dykeman and Stokely describe the courage of Rev. Paul Turner, a white Baptist pastor in Clinton who was beaten by segregationists after escorting Negro children to the local public school.

444 LENTZ, RICHARD. "Sixty-five Days in Memphis: A Study of Culture, Symbols, and the Press." In *We Shall Overcome,* edited by David J. Garrow, vol. 2, 547–88. Brooklyn, NY: Carlson Publishing, 1989. Orig. pub. in *Journalism Monographs* 98 (August 1986): whole issue.

Lentz reviews press coverage of the 1968 Memphis sanitation workers' strike. He examines the newspapers' use of cultural symbols to portray Mayor Henry Leob as a paternalistic defender of black workers and as a protector of public order. Lentz contends that the effect of these images was opposite of that intended by the papers, as the black community was "moved by the power of culturally significant themes" to unite behind the striking black workers.

445 MCKNIGHT, GERALD D. "A Harvest of Hate: The FBI's War against Black Youth—Domestic Intelligence in Memphis, Tennessee." In *We Shall Overcome,* edited by David J. Garrow, vol. 2, 657–78. Brooklyn, NY: Carlson Publishing, 1989. Orig. pub. in *South Atlantic Quarterly* 86 (Winter 1987): 1–21.

McKnight documents the campaign of surveillance, harassment, and disruption directed against the Invaders, an organization of militant young blacks working for black advancement in Memphis during and following the sanitation workers strike of 1968. His analysis of FBI files reveals the extent to which the bureau waged "a relentless campaign against a small and ineffective group of young black militants." This case study of the FBI's COINTELPRO efforts should be viewed in the national context provided by O'Reilly's *Racial Matters* (1989, see entry 696).

446 _____. "The 1968 Memphis Sanitation Strike and the FBI: A Case Study in Urban Surveillance." In *We Shall Overcome,* edited by David J. Garrow, vol. 2, 637–56. Brooklyn, NY: Carlson Publishing, 1989. Orig. pub. in *South Atlantic Quarterly* 83 (Spring 1984): 138–56.

McKnight describes the FBI's domestic surveillance program against the striking Memphis sanitation workers and their allies in the black community. He argues that this is a single front in J. Edgar Hoover's "campaign to contain the rising tide of black militancy."

447 MCMILLEN, NEIL R. "Organized Resistance to School Desegregation in Tennessee." *Tennessee Historical Quarterly* 30 (Fall 1971): 315–28.

Although school desegregation resulted in violence in Clinton and Nashville during 1956, segregationists enjoyed relatively little success in Tennessee. McMillen focuses on the efforts of Frederick John Kasper, a racist demagogue who was active in the state during the late 1950s, and on the more dignified Tennessee Federation for Constitutional Government. He concludes: "Organized resistance (to integration) found the racial climate of Tennessee singularly inhospitable."

448 NASH, DIANE. "Inside the Sit-Ins and Freedom Rides: Testimony of a Southern Student." In *We Shall Overcome,* edited by David J. Garrow, vol. 3, 955–74. Brooklyn, NY: Carlson Publishing, 1989. Orig. pub. in *The New Negro,* edited by Matthew Ahmann, 43–60. Notre Dame, IN: Fides Publishers, 1961.

Nash was a leader of the student sit-ins in Nashville and a key figure in the early years of SNCC. When the original Freedom Riders were attacked in Birmingham, she was instrumental in recruiting a group of Nashville students to continue the rides. In this article she describes her experiences in the sit-ins and the Freedom Rides.

449 PROUDFOOT, MERRILL. *Diary of a Sit-In*. New Haven: College and University Press, 1962. 204 pages.

Proudfoot was a professor at Knoxville College in 1960 when his students began planning lunch counter sit-in demonstrations similar to those occurring across the South following the initial sit-in in Greensboro, North Carolina. Proudfoot participated in the planning and demonstrations during June and July in Knoxville. This book is his personal account of these events.

450 SUGARMON, RUSSELL, JR. "Breaking the Color Line in Memphis, Tennessee." In *Freedom Now! The Civil Rights Struggle in America,* edited by Alan F. Westin, 164–68. New York: Basic Books, 1964.

Sugarmon describes desegregation protests in Memphis during 1960 and 1961.

451 TROTTER, ANNE. "The Memphis Business Community and Integration." In *Southern Businessmen and Desegregation,* edited by Elizabeth Jacoway and David R. Colburn, 282–300. Baton Rouge: Louisiana State University Press, 1982.

Trotter chronicles the failure of Memphis business leaders to take an active role in dealing with the city's racial problems. "Integration in Memphis," she concludes, "has been accomplished by pressure from the federal government and the growing cohesion of blacks." Most of this study focuses on the 1968 sanitation workers' strike, when most business leaders supported Mayor Henry Leob's hard-line stance in refusing to negotiate with the strikers. Only after Martin Luther King, Jr.'s assassination did the Chamber of Commerce begin to deal with the city's racial problems.

Virginia

452 ABBOTT, CARL. "The Norfolk Business Community: The Crisis of Massive Resistance." In *Southern Businessmen and Desegregation,* edited by Elizabeth Jacoway and David R. Colburn, 98–119. Baton Rouge: Louisiana State University Press, 1982.

Abbott describes the reaction of Norfolk business leaders to the school desegregation crisis of 1958 to 1959. He examines the official "mythology" that the Committee of 100 played the decisive role in the acceptance of integrated schools and finds that it did not initiate change. Rather, it helped assure a peaceful transition. Abbott writes: "By openly ratifying the inevitable, the city's business leaders helped make desegregation respectable."

453 BELFRAGE, SALLY. "Danville on Trial." *New Republic* 2 November 1963, 11–12.

Belfrage describes the trials of civil rights demonstrators and the harassment of others active in the Danville movement.

454   CHARITY, RUTH HARVEY, CHRISTINA DAVIS, and ARTHUR KINOY. "Dan-
      ville Movement: The People's Law Takes Hold." *Southern Exposure*
      10, no. 4 (1982): 35–45.
      Davis interviewed movement attorneys Charity and Kinoy who de-
scribe the legal battles that grew out of desegregation protests in Danville in
1963. In a highly unusual maneuver, the lawyers successfully petitioned to
remove cases of arrested demonstrators from local courts to federal court.
This campaign is covered in more detail in Len Holt's *An Act of Conscience*
(1965, see entry 458).

455   ELY, JAMES W. "Negro Demonstrations and the Law: Danville as a Test
      Case." *Vanderbilt Law Review* 27 (October 1974): 927–68. Reprinted
      in *We Shall Overcome*, edited by David J. Garrow, vol. 1, 189–230.
      Brooklyn, NY: Carlson Publishing, 1989.
      Ely examines the role of the courts and the Kennedy administration
in responding to the 1963 civil rights protest movement in Danville, Virginia. He concludes that "the principal reason for the collapse of the
protests was the inability of Danville Negroes to enlist meaningful assistance from either the Kennedy administration or the federal courts." As a
result, "the city was able to harass and arrest the demonstrators at will."
For other accounts of the Danville demonstrations see Holt's *An Act of
Conscience* (1965, see entry 458) and Kunstler's *Deep In My Heart* (1966,
see entry 773).

456   FITZGERALD, CHARLOTTE D. "The Anatomy of a Movement: Danville,
      Virginia, as a Case History." *Humanity and Society* 12, no. 3 (1988):
      254–66.
      Fitzgerald analyzes the following components of social movements as
applied to the Danville protests of 1963: legitimate claims and claimants,
decisive leadership, a visible antagonist, media coverage, clearly defined
goals, and the personal growth of participants. She finds that the Danville
movement was not successful because it lacked several of these components.

457   GATES, ROBBINS L. *The Making of Massive Resistance: Virginia's Poli-
      tics of Public School Desegregation, 1954–1956.* Chapel Hill: Univer-
      sity of North Carolina Press, 1964. 224 pages.
      Gates analyzes the debate in the Virginia legislature on the plan pro-
posed by Governor Thomas B. Stanley, which would authorize the governor
to withhold state school funds from local communities where public schools
were threatened with desegregation.

458   HOLT, LEN. *An Act of Conscience.* Boston: Beacon Press, 1965. 236
      pages.
      Holt was closely involved in the 1963 civil rights protests in Danville,
Virginia. In this book he tells the story of Danville from his perspective as a
movement lawyer.

459 MUSE, BENJAMIN. *Virginia's Massive Resistance.* Bloomington: Indiana University Press, 1961. 184 pages.

Muse covers white reaction to the *Brown* decision from 1954 to 1959. Virginia was the first state to attempt "massive resistance" to school desegregation. In Prince Edward County public schools were closed, as people refused to comply with Federal Court orders to integrate. Muse's account focuses on Gov. Lindsay Almond and his ultimately futile campaign to defy federal authority.

460 SMITH, BOB. *They Closed Their Schools: Prince Edward County, Virginia, 1951–1964.* Chapel Hill: University of North Carolina Press, 1965. 281 pages.

Smith, a Norfolk newspaper editor, provides a journalistic account of the school desegregation crisis in Prince Edward County, Virginia. He begins with the 1951 strike by black high school students as protest against their inadequate facilities. The Prince Edward County school system was one of five named in the Supreme Court's *Brown* decision. In 1959, when white politicians were unable to further delay court-ordered desegregation, they decided to close all public schools in the county. It was not until 1964 that public education was resumed. Smith concludes that "reliance on the courts to settle any and all problems . . . can be as dangerous as the flouting of the courts in the nation's streets."

Washington, D.C.

461 BROOKS, MAXWELL R. "The March on Washington in Retrospect." *Journal of Human Relations* 12 (January 1964): 73–87.

Brooks argues that the March on Washington "served to unify these individualistic (civil rights) organizations into a popular front." While he does not find any immediate political gains arising from the March, he claims that it did succeed in dramatizing the plight of the Negro in America and "captured the imagination and sympathy of people around the world."

462 GENTILE, THOMAS. *March On Washington: August 28, 1963.* Washington, DC: New Day Publications, 1983. 301 pages.

A detailed account of the march, its origins and planning.

463 HEDGEMAN, ANNA ARNOLD. *The Trumpet Sounds: A Memoir of Negro Leadership.* New York: Holt, Rinehart and Winston, 1964. 202 pages.

In the last chapter of this autobiography Hedgeman describes her involvement in planning the 1963 March on Washington.

464 JONES, BEVERLY W. "Before Montgomery and Greensboro: The Desegregation Movement in the District of Columbia, 1950–1953." *Phylon* 43, no. 2 (1982): 144–54.

Jones describes direct action against segregated restaurants in Washington, D.C., organized by Mary Church Terrell.

465   LONG, MARGARET. "March on Washington." *New South* 18 (September
      1963): 3–19.

Long describes the events of the March on Washington as a demonstration of Negroes' "profound faith in the American promise."

466   RUSTIN, BAYARD. "The Meaning of the March on Washington." *Liber-
      ation* 8, no. 8 (1963): 11–13. Reprinted in *Black Protest Thought in
      the Twentieth Century*, edited by August Meier, Elliot Rudwick, and
      Francis L. Broderick, 381–86. Indianapolis: Bobbs-Merrill, 1971.

Rustin, a key organizer of the March on Washington, argues that if the
objectives of the march are to be realized, blacks must keep the support of
white allies and must resist the temptation to retaliate against racist violence
such as the church bombing in Birmingham.

467   _____. "The Washington March—a Ten-Year Perspective." *Crisis* 80
      (August 1973): 224–27.

In his assessment of the 1963 March on Washington, Rustin maintains
that the march was successful in accomplishing its moral objective of winning civil rights for African Americans, that it but failed to attain far-reaching
economic changes. The reasons for the failure, he claims, are the "fragmen-
tation of black leadership" and a "failure of will among certain elements of
liberalism."

468   THELWELL, MICHAEL. "The August 28th March on Washington." In *Du-
      ties, Pleasures, and Conflicts: Essays in Struggle*, edited by Michael
      Thelwell, 57–73. Amherst: University of Massachusetts Press, 1987.
      Orig. pub. in *Presence Africaine* 21, no. 49 (1964).

Thelwell describes the March on Washington as "a subtle and terrible
betrayal." He explains how the original plan to use aggressive civil disobedience to protest the federal government's inaction on civil rights was abandoned to enlist the cooperation of the NAACP, the National Urban League,
the AFL-CIO, and the Kennedy administration.

469   VANDER ZANDEN, JAMES W. "For Jobs and Freedom: Three Views of
      the Washington March." *Midwest Quarterly* 5, no. 2 (1964): 99–108.

Vander Zanden offers a sobering assessment of the likely consequences
of the March on Washington. Although the march may have bolstered black
self-esteem, he detects a growing resentment among whites toward civil
rights demonstrations. He agrees that the elimination of Jim Crow barriers
will probably be accomplished in "the foreseeable future," but feels that
genuine integration remains "at best an extremely distant goal." He believes
that due to technological advances, shifting patterns of employment, and the
consequences of generations of discrimination, it will be difficult for blacks
to make rapid gains in the area of employment. He concludes that "the
March on Washington raised many hopes among Negroes that are bound to
lead to disappointment."

Other States

470   ANDERSON, ALAN B., and GEORGE W. PICKERING. *Confronting the Color Line: The Broken Promise of the Civil Rights Movement in Chicago.* Athens: University of Georgia Press, 1986. 515 pages.

Anderson and Pickering describe the civil rights movement in Chicago as it confronted the issues of de facto segregation in schools and housing, and black poverty and unemployment between 1963 and 1967. Their account focuses on the Coordinating Council of Community Organizations and its role as a coalition of diverse organizations and personalities united around the issue of civil rights. They contrast two sets of values and beliefs—the "civic credo," which promised equality in the long run as the result of the workings of democratic institutions, and "racist realism" which claimed that blacks could never expect equality because white racism was too strong to overcome. By attacking issues of de facto segregation, they believe that the civil rights movement challenged the assumptions of the civic credo. The authors contend that the movement in Chicago was "defeated by the civic credo interpretation, and its demise was marked by a resurgence of racist realism."

471   BLUMBERG, RHODA L. "Careers of Women Civil Rights Activists." *Journal of Sociology and Social Welfare* 7 (1980): 708–29.

Blumberg studied the careers of forty-one white women who were active in civil rights organizations in New Jersey cities during the 1960s. She reports that many of the women continued their involvement during the Black Power phase of the late 1960s, although the nature of their participation changed. By the time of her interviews in 1976, few of the women were continuing their volunteer work, but most were employed in the human service professions working with clients or target groups who were poor, minority, elderly, or handicapped people.

472   ———. "White Mothers in the American Civil Rights Movement." In *Research in the Interweave of Social Roles: Women and Men,* edited by Helena A. Lopata, vol. 1, 33–50. Greenwich, CT: JAI Press, 1980.

Blumberg studied the activities of thirty-eight white women who were active in New Jersey civil rights organizations. She describes how they balanced their domestic responsibilities with their work in the movement. She reports that the women found that their civil rights activities satisfied a need for involvement in the larger community, and were ideologically compatible with their role as mothers. Time management was the most serious problem they encountered, she found, especially as their children grew older.

473   BROCK, ANNETTE K. "Gloria Richardson and the Cambridge Movement." In *Women in the Civil Rights Movement,* edited by Vicki L. Crawford, Jacqueline Anne Rouse, and Barbara Woods, 121–44. Brooklyn, NY: Carlson Publishing, 1990.

During 1963 Cambridge, Maryland, was the scene of tense confrontations between civil rights demonstrators organized into the Cambridge Nonviolent Action Committee (CNAC) and city officials. Gloria Richardson was the militant leader of the CNAC. Brock chronicles Richardson's role in these events.

474 BROPHY, WILLIAM. "Active Acceptance—Active Containment: The Dallas Story." In *Southern Businessmen and Desegregation*, edited by Elizabeth Jacoway and David R. Colburn, 137–50. Baton Rouge: Louisiana State University Press, 1982.

In September 1961, Dallas schools were desegregated without the scenes of violence that occurred in other southern cities due largely to the efforts of white business leaders in the Dallas Citizens Council. Downtown lunch counters were voluntarily desegregated in July 1961 after months of demonstrations, and a boycott led to successful negotiations between black and white leaders. These steps were soon followed by the desegregation of hotels and city parks. Brophy credits moderate leaders on both sides who were "able to convince whites that the old order had to be changed and blacks that it had to be changed gradually."

475 CHASTEEN, EDGAR. "Public Accommodations: Social Movements in Conflict." In *Social Movements and Social Change*, edited by Robert L. Lauer, 156–73. Carbondale: Southern Illinois University Press, 1976. Orig. pub. in *Phylon* 30, no. 3 (1969): 234–50.

Chasteen describes the changes in leadership, goals, membership, tactics, and strategy thtat occurred in the civil rights movement in Kansas City, Missouri, when the emergence of an anti-public accommodations movement created a crisis within the civil rights forces.

476 CONNOLLY, KATHLEEN. "The Chicago Open Housing Conference." In *Chicago 1966*, edited by David J. Garrow, 49–96. Brooklyn, NY: Carlson Publishing, 1989.

Connolly describes the negotiations that ended the Chicago open housing marches in the summer of 1966. She emphasizes that the resulting "summit agreement" between the civil rights forces and "the power structure" served the interests of both groups because both wanted to see the marches end quickly.

477 FINLEY, MARY LOU. "The Open Housing Marches: Chicago, Summer '66." In *Chicago 1966*, edited by David J. Garrow, 1–48. Brooklyn, NY: Carlson Publishing, 1989.

Finley describes the objectives and strategy of the Chicago open housing marches and provides a detailed chronology of events during July and August of 1966. She concludes that the major unresolved problem of the Chicago movement was leadership: "Key people were unable to agree on a structure of leadership for the organization."

478 GAITHER, TOM. "Jailed-In." In *Nonviolence in America*, edited by Staughton Lynd, 399–415. Indianapolis: Bobbs-Merrill, 1966. Orig. pub. by League for Industrial Democracy, New York, 1961.

Gaither describes the experiences of eight college students and himself who were arrested at a 1960 sit-in in Rock Hill, South Carolina, and subsequently served thirty days in the county jail when they refused to pay fines or accept bail.

479   GARROW, DAVID J., ed. *Chicago 1966: Open Housing Marches, Summit Negotiations and Operation Breadbasket.* Brooklyn, NY: Carlson Publishing, 1989. 359 pages.
See entry 132.

480   GRAVES, CARL R. "The Right to Be Served: Oklahoma City's Lunch Counter Sit-Ins, 1958–1964." In *We Shall Overcome*, edited by David J. Garrow, vol. 1, 283–97. Brooklyn, NY: Carlson Publishing, 1989. Orig. pub. in *Chronicles of Oklahoma* 59 (Summer 1981): 361–73.
Graves describes sit-in demonstrations organized by the NAACP Youth Council against segregated eating establishments in Oklahoma City, which began in 1958 and continued sporadically until 1964.

481   KEMPTON, MURRAY. "Gloria, Gloria." *New Republic,* 16 November 1963, 15–17.
Kempton profiles Cambridge's militant civil rights leader, Gloria Richardson. She is described as being disliked by white leaders because of her unwillingness to accept token victories. Kempton traces Richardson's uncompromising stance to her identification with the city's poor blacks, which caused her to fight relentlessly for economic improvement.

482   LADD, EVERETT CARLL, JR. *Negro Political Leadership in the South.* Ithaca, NY: Cornell University Press, 1966. 348 pages.
See entry 435.

483   LEVINE, RICHARD. "Jesse Jackson: Heir to Dr. King?" *Harper's,* March 1969, 58–70.
Levine describes the work of Operation Breadbasket in Chicago, the role of its leader, Jesse Jackson, and his attempt to "build consensus around his leadership in a black community plagued by factional rivalries and class antagonisms."

484   LIPSITZ, GEORGE. *A Life In the Struggle: Ivory Perry and the Culture of Opposition.* Philadelphia: Temple University Press, 1988. 292 pages.
See entry 311.

485   LOFTON, PAUL S., JR. "Calm and Exemplary: Desegregation in Columbia, South Carolina." In *Southern Businessmen and Desegregation,* edited by Elizabeth Jacoway and David R. Colburn, 70–81. Baton Rouge: Louisiana State University Press, 1982.
Lofton claims that desegregation occurred more quietly in Columbia than in other southern cities because its city fathers wanted to preserve their carefully cultivated image as a "peaceful, progressive community." In addition, he argues that Columbia's sit-in demonstrations were relatively "late, timid, and short lived." Lofton credits a group of fifteen prominent business

leaders with persuading their peers to accept voluntary integration. He also cites the mayor's appointment of a biracial committee as another reason for the uneventful desegregation of city facilities and public schools.

486   McKNIGHT, JOHN. "The Summit Negotiations: Chicago, August 17, 1966-August 26, 1966." In *Chicago 1966*, edited by David J. Garrow, 111–45. Brooklyn, NY: Carlson Publishing, 1989.

McKnight provides a detailed account of the meetings on 17 and 26 August 1966 between civil rights forces conducting open housing marches in Chicago and its suburbs, and representatives of the "white power structure" of the city. These meetings resulted in the "summit agreement" of August 26.

487   MASSONI, GARY. "Perspectives on Operation Breadbasket." In *Chicago 1966*, edited by David J. Garrow, 179–346. Brooklyn, NY: Carlson Publishing, 1989. M.A. thesis, Chicago Theological Seminary, 1971.

Massoni examines the history and functions of Operation Breadbasket in Chicago. He concludes that there are "at least three different 'subcommunities' with differing orientations within Breadbasket." These include people motivated by direct, personal loyalty to Jesse Jackson; people who participate primarily because of their enthusiasm for the black cultural heritage provided by Breadbasket's events; and people who are concerned about Breadbasket's programs in areas such as employment opportunities and business development.

488   MEIER, AUGUST. "The Successful Sit-Ins in a Border City: A Study in Social Causation." In *We Shall Overcome*, edited by David J. Garrow, vol. 2, 721–28. Brooklyn, NY: Carlson Publishing, 1989. Orig. pub. in *Journal of Intergroup Relations* 2 (Summer 1961): 230–37.

Meier describes successful sit-in demonstrations in Baltimore during the spring of 1960.

489   MEIER, AUGUST, THOMAS S. PLAUT, and CURTIS SMOTHERS. "Case Study in Nonviolent Direct Action." In *We Shall Overcome*, edited by David J. Garrow, vol. 2, 783–88. Brooklyn, NY: Carlson Publishing, 1989. Orig. pub. in *The Crisis* 71 (December 1964): 573–78.

The authors describe a successful 1963 protest against a segregated movie theater in Baltimore.

490   NELSON, JACK, and JACK BASS. *The Orangeburg Massacre*. New York: World Publishing, 1970. 272 pages.

Nelson and Bass describe the 1968 killings of three black students by South Carolina highway patrolmen during protests at a segregated bowling alley near the campus of South Carolina State University. They examine the events leading up to the shootings and the subsequent investigation and trial at which nine officers were acquitted.

491 OLDENDORF, SANDRA B. "The South Carolina Sea Islands Citizenship Schools, 1957–1961." In *Women in the Civil Rights Movement*, edited by Vicki L. Crawford, Jacqueline Anne Rouse, and Barbara Woods, 169–82. Brooklyn, NY: Carlson Publishing, 1990.

In 1957 under the guidance of Septima Clark, Myles Horton, Esau Jenkins, and Bernice Robinson, the Highlander Folk School established its first citizenship schools on the Sea Islands of South Carolina. Olderdorf describes the philosophy, organization, and impact of this remarkable civil rights project.

492 PITCHER, ALVIN. "The Chicago Freedom Movement: What Is It?" In *Chicago 1966*, edited by David J. Garrow, 155–78. Brooklyn, NY: Carlson Publishing, 1989.

Pitcher examines the structure of the Chicago freedom movement and examines the relationships among participating organizations. He describes the strains between "grass roots" organizations and "old line" organizations.

493 ROBBINS, JHAN, and JUNE ROBBINS. "'Why Didn't They Hit Back?'" In *Nonviolent Direct Action*, edited by A. Paul Hare and Herbert H. Blumberg, 107–27. Washington, DC: Corpus Books, 1968. Orig. pub. in *Redbook* 52 (July 1963): 110–15.

The Robbinses tell the story of Eddie Dickerson, a young Maryland white, who was converted to the cause of nonviolence after attacking civil rights demonstrators in Cambridge, Maryland, in 1962.

494 SILBERMAN, CHARLES. *Crisis in Black and White.* New York: Random House, 1964. 370 pages.

Silberman's analysis of the problems facing urban blacks in the North contains one chapter dealing with the civil rights movement. He maintains that the approach of traditional civil rights organizations is not adequate to solve the problems faced by urban blacks. He examines the appeal of black nationalism, especially as espoused by Malcolm X, as an alternative to the civil rights strategy.

495 VON ESCHEN, DONALD, JEROME KIRK, and MAURICE PINARD. "The Conditions of Direct Action in a Democratic Society." *Western Political Quarterly* 22 (June 1969): 309–25.

Von Eschen and associates draw upon their study of civil rights protestors in Maryland to construct a general model of the conditions necessary for successful direct action. They maintain that for a movement to be successful a moral dilemma must exist within the dominant group and an unincorporated group (a group that is excluded by the dominant group) must threaten to create disorder. They conclude that whether the elite reacts with capitulation or disorder depends on "whether the movement is regarded as more or less desirable and legitimate than its opposition."

496   WALLACE, DAVID M. "From the Fullness of the Earth: The Story of
      Chicago's Operation Breadbasket." *Chicago Theological Seminary
      Register*, 57 (November 1966): 16–20.
    Wallace describes the work of clergymen, including Rev. Jesse Jackson,
who organized Operation Breadbasket in Chicago, and the five-step proce-
dure they use to challenge job discrimination.

497   WOODS, BARBARA A. "Modjeska Simkins and the South Carolina Con-
      ference of the NAACP, 1939–1957." In *Women in the Civil Rights
      Movement*, edited by Vicki L. Crawford, Jacqueline Anne Rouse, and
      Barbara Woods, 99–120. Brooklyn, NY: Carlson Publishing, 1990.
    Woods describes Simpkins's work as secretary of the South Carolina
conference of the NAACP during the 1940s and 1950s. She notes that the
most important case to come out of the state was the Clarendon County suit,
which became part of the landmark *Brown* decision.

498   WRIGHT, GEORGE C. "Desegregation of Public Accommodations in
      Louisville: A Long and Difficult Struggle in a 'Liberal' Border City." In
      Southern Businessmen and Desegregation, edited by Elizabeth
      Jacoway and David R. Colburn, 191–210. Baton Rouge: Louisiana
      State University Press, 1982.
    Wright traces the long effort to desegregate businesses in downtown
Louisville. He describes how the first protests organized by the NAACP in
1957 were followed by a series of partial victories in dime stores and drug
stores. According to Wright, large-scale demonstrations in 1961 led to the
formation of an emergency committee of business leaders that gained voluntary desegregation of more restaurants. He explains that the black community then turned its attention to voter registration and in November 1961
elected a new mayor more favorable to desegregation. Wright credits the
city's business elite with securing the passage of a public accommodations
ordinance in May 1963.

499   YARBROUGH, TINSLEY E. *A Passion for Justice: J. Waties Waring and
      Civil Rights*. New York: Oxford University Press, 1987. 282 pages.
    Waring was a federal judge from South Carolina who was an outspoken
champion for racial equality. He angered his neighbors in Charleston by
ruling in favor of equal pay for black school teachers, by striking down
South Carolina's white primary, and by entertaining blacks in his home. His
most important judicial opinion was his 1952 dissent in the case of *Briggs v.
Elliot*, in which the NAACP attacked segregated schools in Clarendon
County. Waring anticipated the 1954 *Brown* decision when he wrote: "Segregation is per se inequality." Yarbrough tells Waring's life story with special
emphasis on his views on racial equality.

5

Civil Rights Organizations

SNCC

500   ALLEN, ARCHIE E. "John Lewis: Keeper of the Dream." *New South* 26, no. 2 (1971): 15–25.

Allen traces Lewis's youth and involvement in the civil rights movement between 1960 and 1966. He describes Lewis as "a typical product of the South" who is "the personification of the love, militance, vision, courage, and determination which characterized the civil rights movement from 1960 through 1966."

501   ANDERSON, S. E. "Black Students: Racial Consciousness and the Class Struggle, 1960–1976." *Black Scholar* 8 (January–February 1977): 35–43.

Anderson identifies three stages of the black student movement: (1) the civil rights movement of 1960 to 1966, (2) the black nationalist period of 1966 to 1972, and (3) the "dissipated" stage of 1972 to 1976. In his discussion of the first stage he emphasizes the role of SNCC in creating a radical social consciousness among black students.

502   BOND, JULIAN. "The Movement Then and Now." *Southern Exposure* 3 (1976): 5–16.

In this interview Bond describes his initial involvement with the sit-in movement as a college student in Atlanta and his role as director of publicity for SNCC. He tells of his initial venture into electoral politics in 1965 when he was elected to the Georgia House of Representatives, and shares his observations of the 1968 Democratic convention and presidential election. He also offers his comments on the shortcomings of the movement and SNCC.

503   BROWN, H. RAP. *Die Nigger Die!* New York: Dial Press, 1969. 145 pages.

H. Rap Brown was an organizer for SNCC in Alabama in 1966 and was elected its chairman in 1967. He was also involved with the Nonviolent Action Group (NAG) at Howard University in the early 1960s. In this book he relates his life story and articulates his militant philosophy. He is equally outspoken against white racists and "negroes" who do not support the cause of Black Power.

504   CARSON, CLAYBORNE, JR. "Blacks and Jews in the Civil Rights Movement. In *Jews in Black Perspective: A Dialogue*, edited by Joseph R. Washington, 113–31. Rutherford, NJ: Farleigh Dickinson University Press, 1984.

Carson discusses the relationships of black and Jewish activists within SNCC. He argues that "many of the Afro-American-Jewish conflicts of the period after 1966 were manifestations of internal conflicts and ambivalances within the Afro-American community." Although few Jews worked on the SNCC staff, SNCC relied on its ties to northern Jews for much of its fundraising. Carson points out that several of SNCC's more radical leaders, most notably Stokely Carmichael, were products of "a shared Afro-American-Jewish radical culture." By 1967, however, SNCC's increasingly anti-Israel stand had alienated most of its Jewish supporters.

505   ____. *In Struggle: SNCC and the Black Awakening of the 1960's*. Cambridge.: Harvard University Press, 1981. 359 pages.

Carson chronicles the brief history of the Student Nonviolent Coordinating Committee from its origins in the student sit-in movement of 1960 to its disintegration during the repression of the Black Power movement in 1969. He claims that during this brief span SNCC was arguably the most militant and uncompromising organization in the southern civil rights movement. Carson describes how SNCC members were leaders in the sit-ins; carried on the Freedom Rides; worked in rural Georgia, Alabama, and Mississippi; and helped launch the Mississippi Freedom Democratic party. He concludes that after the Freedom Summer of 1964 the organization was increasingly torn by internal conflicts, and turned in a more nationalistic direction. Other valuable works on SNCC include Zinn's *SNCC: The New Abolitionists* (1965, see entry 548) and Foreman's *The Making of Black Revolutionaries* (1972, see entry 511).

506   ____. "SNCC and the Albany Movement." *Journal of Southwest Georgia History* 2 (Fall 1984): 15–25.

See entry 278.

507   CARSON, CLAYBORNE, JR., ed. *The Student Voice, 1960–1965: Periodical of the Student Nonviolent Coordinating Committee*. Westport, CT: Meckler Corp., 1990. 252 pages.

The Student Voice was a monthly newsletter published by the Student Nonviolent Coordinating Committee. The fifty-seven issues collected in this volume were published between June 1960 and December 1965. They chronicle the evolution of SNCC during the time when it was the most militant organization in the southern civil rights movement.

508 CLARK, KENNETH B. "The Civil Rights Movement: Momentum and Organization." In *We Shall Overcome*, edited by David J. Garrow, vol. 1, 151–80. Brooklyn, NY: Carlson Publishing, 1989. Orig. pub. in *Daedalus* 95, no. 1 (1966): 239–67.

Clark reviews the history, leadership, philosophy, and strategy of each of the five major civil rights organizations: the NAACP, the National Urban League, SCLC, SNCC, and CORE. He identifies difficulties facing each organization, but argues that "these problems can be seen as symptoms of the irresistable strength of the civil rights movement."

509 CLUSTER, DICK, ed. *They Should Have Served that Cup of Coffee: Seven Radicals Remember the 60s.* Boston: South End Press, 1979. 268 pages.

The first chapter of this book consists of interviews with three movement veterans who worked with SNCC: John Lewis describes the climate of the early sit-ins and the Freedom Rides, Bernice Johnson Reagon discusses her involvement in the Albany movement, and Jean Smith talks about voter registration work in Mississippi.

510 COLES, ROBERT. "Social Struggle and Weariness." *Psychiatry* 27 (November 1964): 305–15.

Coles relates his observations of twenty-three SNCC activists and how they deal with the stresses they encounter. He finds that many show clinical signs of depression including "exhaustion, weariness, despair, frustration, and rage," which he equates with "battle fatigue." He discusses the causes and treatment of these symptoms.

511 FORMAN, JAMES. *The Making of Black Revolutionaries.* 2d ed. Washington, DC: Open Hand Publishing, 1985. 568 pages. Orig. pub. New York: MacMillan, 1972.

James Forman served as executive secretary of SNCC in the critical years of 1962 to 1966. A former Chicago school teacher, he was one of the few older SNCC leaders and one of the most radical. This book describes his personal evolution from a militant integrationist to a revolutionary nationalist. Forman provides a firsthand account of SNCC's dangerous mission in the Deep South, and gives insights to the internal tensions and external pressures that led to SNCC's eventual collapse. For other views of SNCC during this time, see Carson (1984, entry 505); King (1987, entry 518); and Sellers (1973, entry 537).

512 FRUCHTER, NORM. "Mississippi: Notes on SNCC." *Studies on the Left* (Winter 1965): 74–80.

See entry 349.

513 FRY, JOHN R. "The Voter Registration Drive in Selma, Alabama." In *We Shall Overcome*, edited by David J. Garrow, vol. 1, 249–69. Brooklyn, NY: Carlson Publishing, 1989. Orig. pub. in *Presbyterian Life*, 15 January 1964, 12–22.

See entry 192.

514   GIDDINGS, PAULA. *When and Where I Enter: The Impact of Black Women on Race and Sex in America.* New York: William Morrow & Co., 1984. 408 pages.

In this comprehensive history of black women in America, Giddings devotes two chapters to women in the civil rights movement. Chapter 15, "Dress Rehearsal for the Sixties," describes the contributions of women like Rosa Parks and Jo Ann Gibson Robinson in the Montgomery bus boycott, Daisy Bates in the Little Rock crisis, and Ella Baker in SCLC. Chapter 16, "SNCC: Coming Full Circle," chronicles the role of women within SNCC, where they were "propelled . . . into the forefront of the struggle in a way that was not possible in more hierarchical male-led organizations." Among the women whom Giddings credits with making major contributions in SNCC were Diane Nash, Ruby Doris Smith, Jean Wiley, Gloria Richardson, Lucretia Collins, Bernice Johnson Reagon, Bertha Gober, Unita Blackwell, Fanny Lou Hamer, Arnelle Ponder, and Cynthia Washington.

515   GOOD, PAUL. "Odyssey of a Man and a Movement." *New York Times Magazine,* 25 June 1967. Reprinted in *Black Protest in the Sixties,* edited by August Meier and Elliot Rudwick, 252–66. Chicago: Quadrangle Books, 1970.

Good profiles veteran civil rights activist John Lewis shortly after his ouster as chair of SNCC. He reviews Lewis's involvement in the civil rights movement from the Nashville sit-ins of 1960 and the 1961 Freedom Rides to the 1966 Meredith march. Lewis is described as a man dedicated to Christian nonviolence, but disillusioned by the violence and bitterness surrounding him.

516   HAYDEN, TOM. "SNCC in Action: Dignity for the Enslaved and for All of Us." In *The New Student Left,* edited by Mitchell Cohen and Dennis Hale, 75–86. Boston: Beacon Press, 1966. Orig. pub. as "Revolution in Mississippi," 1961.

See entry 361.

517   _____. "SNCC: The Qualities of Protest." *Studies on the Left* 5 (1965): 113–24.

SDS leader Hayden uses this review of Zinn's *SNCC: The New Abolitionists* (1964, see entry 548) as a vehicle for expressing his views on SNCC and the civil rights movement. Hayden is favorably disposed toward SNCC and praises its growing willingness to question liberal political formulas and consider more radical alternatives. He defends the actions of the MFDP at the 1964 Democratic convention and cites it as an example of grass roots organizing that needs to be replicated across the nation. Hayden sounds one note of caution, however, regarding the need for the black movement to form alliances with poor whites who also would benefit from radical social change.

518   KING, MARY. *Freedom Song: A Personal Story of the 1960's Civil Rights Movement.* New York: William Morrow & Co., 1987. 592 pages.

Mary King was a white college student who became involved in the civil rights movement in 1962 and soon went to work for the Student Non-violent Coordinating Committee as an assistant to Julian Bond, the organization's press secretary. For the next three years King was closely involved with the movement across the South as she relayed stories from local SNCC activists to the national news media. This book is the story of her personal evolution and the changes she observed within SNCC.

519   KOPKIND, ANDREW. "The Future of Black Power." *New Republic*, 7 January 1967, 16–18.

Kopkind examines events at the December 1966 staff conference of SNCC, focusing on the debate between the "black nationalists" and the "Howard group" regarding the continued presence of whites within the organization.

520   _____. "New Radicals in Dixie: Those Subversive Civil Rights Workers." *New Republic*, 10 April 1965, 13–16.

Kopkind dismisses charges that the civil rights movement has been infiltrated by communists. Although he acknowledges ties with a few "old-line leftist organizations" such as Southern Conference Education Fund (SCEF) and the Highlander Folk School, he concludes that "SNCC's radicalism is its own, not of another society's or another generation's making."

521   LADNER, JOYCE. "Return to the Source." *Essence*, June 1977.

Civil rights activist Ladner is prompted by the occasion of a 1976 SNCC reunion to recall in this essay her participation in SNCC and the changes it caused in her life, and the ways the South has changed.

522   LAWSON, JAMES M., JR. "We Are Trying to Raise the Moral Issue." In *Negro Protest Thought in the Twentieth Century*, edited by Francis L. Broderick and August Meier, 274–81. Indianapolis: Bobbs-Merrill, 1965. Address to SNCC conference, Raleigh, NC, April 1960.

Lawson was an influential advisor to the Nashville student protestors and played an important role in launching SNCC. Here he justifies the sit-ins on moral and religious grounds.

523   LESTER, JULIUS. *All Is Well*. New York: William Morrow & Co., 1976. 319 pages.

This very personal autobiography of the veteran civil rights activist and one-time Black Power spokesperson combines Lester's reflections on the movement with a description of his own spiritual quest.

524   LEWIS, JOHN. "A Trend toward Aggressive Nonviolent Action." In *Negro Protest Thought in the Twentieth Century*, edited by Francis L. Broderick and August Meier, 313–21. Indianapolis: Bobbs-Merrill, 1965. Orig. pub. in *Dialogue* 4 (Spring 1964): 7–9.

Lewis discusses changes in the civil rights movement and within SNCC, the objectives of the movement, SNCC's voter registration efforts, and plans for the Mississippi Summer Project.

525 LONG, MARGARET. "The unity of the Rifting Negro Movement." *Progressive*, February 1964, 10–14.

Long explores the rivalry and differences among the four leading civil rights organizations—the NAACP, CORE, SLCC, and SNCC. Although she finds the schisms "endlessly interesting," she maintains that ultimately they are "unimportant" because they recognize that they all are working for the same cause. Of the four organizations, Long holds that it is "the grubby and long-suffering youngsters of SNCC" who are really in the forefront of bringing change to the South.

526 MATUSOW, ALLEN J. "From Civil Rights to Black Power: The Case of SNCC, 1960–1966." In *Twentieth Century America: Recent Interpretations*, edited by Barton J. Bernstein and Allen J. Matusow, 531–36. New York: Harcourt, Brace and World, 1969.

Matusow presents a brief history of SNCC to explain the development of the Black Power ideology, which he sees as "the creation of a small group of civil rights workers who in the early 1960's manned the barricades of black protest in the Deep South." Although SNCC's disenchantment with the liberal establishment was already well developed by 1963, Matusow sees the 1964 Freedom Summer in Mississippi as being the crucial factor in its turn to a more radical position. He claims that internal sexual tensions between black and white staffers caused many within SNCC to question the feasibility of racial integration and stimulated the growth of black nationalism, which surfaced at the 1966 Meredith march. Curiously, Matusow makes no mention of SNCC's work with the Lowndes County Freedom Organization—the original Black Panther party—which contributed to the emergence of Black Power. For more on the change within SNCC see Carson, *In Struggle* (1981, entry 505) and Forman, *The Making of Black Revolutionaries* (1972, entry 511).

527 MEIER, AUGUST. "Negro Protest Movements and Organizations." In *We Shall Overcome*, edited by David J. Garrow, vol. 2, 763–76. Brooklyn, NY: Carlson Publishing, 1989. Orig. pub. in *Journal of Negro Education* 32 (Fall 1963): 437–50.

Meier describes the differing strategies employed by the NAACP, CORE, and SNCC. He discusses the rivalry and competition among them as a helpful contribution to the civil rights movement: "For in their attempt to outdo each other, each organization puts forth stronger effort than it otherwise would, and is constantly searching for new avenues along which to develop a program."

528 MOSES, BOB. "Mississippi: 1961–1962." *Liberation* 14 (January 1970): 7–17.

See entry 394.

529 NASH, DIANE. "Inside the Sit-Ins and Freedom Rides: Testimony of a Southern Student." In *We Shall Overcome*, edited by David J. Garrow, vol. 3, 955–74. Brooklyn, NY: Carlson Publishing, 1989. Orig. pub. in

The New Negro, edited by Matthew Ahmann, 43–60. Notre Dame, IN: Fides Publishers, 1961.

See entry 448.

530   NEARY, JOHN. *Julian Bond: Black Rebel.* New York: William Morrow & Co., 1971. 256 pages.

This journalistic biography primarily focuses on the period following Bond's 1966 election to the Georgia legislature. One chapter is devoted to his involvement with SNCC from 1960 to 1966.

531   NEWFIELD, JACK. *A Prophetic Minority.* New York: New American Library, 1966. 212 pages.

In this portrait of the New Left, Newfield devotes three chapters to the young activists of the civil rights movement, with special emphasis on SNCC. He looks at the student sit-in movement, SNCC's organizing efforts in Amite County, Mississippi, and changes within SNCC during 1965 and 1966. He includes admiring profiles of Robert Moses and Stokely Carmichael.

532   PAYNE, BRUCE. "SNCC: An Overview Two Years Later." In *The New Student Left*, edited by Mitchell Cohen and Dennis Hale, 86–103. Boston: Beacon Press, 1966. Orig. pub. in *The Activist*, November 1965.

Payne examines eight elements of SNCC's unofficial ideology: freedom, brotherhood, nonviolence, the power structure, middle-class values, the vote, leadership and consensus, and participatory democracy. He argues that the aims of participatory democracy and consensus politics are "largely wrong-headed and doomed to failure."

533   PAYNE, CHARLES. "Ella Baker and Models of Social Change." *Signs* 14, no. 4 (1989): 885–99.

Payne describes the career of Ella Baker and her contributions to the civil rights movement. During the 1940s she worked for the NAACP as director of branches. In 1957 she joined the fledgling SCLC as its first executive director. In 1960 she organized the conference which led to the creation of SNCC. She remained an influential advisor to SNCC and later helped organize the Mississippi Freedom Democratic party. Payne discusses Baker's philosophy, especially her ideas on group-centered leadership and the distinction between organizing and mobilizing.

534   ROBERTS, GENE. "The Story of Snick: From 'Freedom High' to 'Black Power.'" *New York Times Magazine*, 25 September 1966, 27–29. Reprinted in *Black Protest in the Sixties*, edited by August Meier and Elliot Rudwick, 139–153. Chicago: Quadrangle Books, 1970.

Roberts describes the growth of black consciousness within SNCC. He is critical of this development, and accuses SNCC of spreading violence, suggests that it may be influenced by communists, and claims that it has lost touch with southern blacks. He sees the election of Stokely Carmichael as chair as a critical turning point for SNCC that "exemplifies its moodiness, brilliance and contradictions."

535 ROMAINE, ANNE. "Interview with Fannie Lou Hamer." *Southern Exposure* (Spring 1981): 47–48.
See entry 401.

536 ROTHSCHILD, MARY AICKIN. *A Case of Black and White: Northern Volunteers and the Southern Freedom Summers, 1964–1965.* Westport, CT: Greenwood Press, 1982. 213 pages.
See entry 402.

537 SELLERS, CLEVELAND, with ROBERT TERRELL. *River of No Return: The Autobiography of a Black Militant and the Life and Death of SNCC.* New York: William Morrow & Co., 1973. 279 pages.
Sellers became involved in the sit-in movement as a high school student in Denmark, South Carolina, in 1960. When he enrolled at Howard University in 1962, he gravitated to the Nonviolent Action Group that was led by Stokely Carmichael. In 1964 he was active in the protests in Cambridge, Maryland, and then went to Mississippi where he worked as a SNCC field secretary in the Mississippi Summer Project. In November 1965 he was elected SNCC's program secretary and remained in that position for the next three years while SNCC was torn apart by factional debates over its mission. *River of No Return* is both an autobiography of Sellers and a history of SNCC, but since he was not a part of the organization during its formative years, he had to rely on secondary sources and the recollections of SNCC veterans. For the period of 1964 to 1968, Sellers provides a valuable account of the dynamics of a volatile organization and an intimate portrait of some of its most colorful personalities. Especially interesting is his account of the relationships between Martin Luther King and the young SNCC activists during the Meredith march of 1966. For a contrasting view on several points see Mary King's *Freedom Song* (1988, entry 518).

538 SESSIONS, JIM, and SUE THRASHER. "A New Day Begins: An Interview with John Lewis." *Southern Exposure* 4 (Fall 1976): 14–24.
John Lewis joined the civil rights movement in 1960 as a ministerial student in Nashville. He subsequently participated in the Freedom Rides and became a leader of SNCC and later a head of the Voter Education Project. In this interview he reflects on his youth and early involvement in the movement.

539 SINSHEIMER, JOSEPH A. "Never Turn Back: An Interview with Sam Block." *Southern Exposure* 15 (Summer 1987): 37–50.
See entry 411.

540 STOPER, EMILY. *The Student Nonviolent Coordinating Committee: The Growth of Radicalism in a Civil Rights Organization.* Brooklyn, NY: Carlson Publishing, 1989. 331 pages. Ph.D. dissertation, Harvard University, 1968.
Stoper traces the history of SNCC from 1960 to 1966. She describes its internal development and organizational philosophy, its growing disillusion-

ment with the federal government, and its relations with other civil rights organizations. Her work is based on interviews with fifty-one SNCC activists. Transcripts of interviews with ten key figures are included in this volume.

541 _____. "The Student Nonviolent Coordinating Committee: Rise and Fall of a Redemptive Organization." *Journal of Black Studies* 8 (September 1977): 13–34. Reprinted in *We Shall Overcome*, edited by David J. Garrow, vol. 3, 1041–1062. Brooklyn, NY: Carlson Publishing, 1989.

Stoper classifies SNCC as a "redemptive" organization—one which not only seeks to change society, but "also to change its members by requiring them to exemplify in their own lives the new order." She seeks to explain the apparent paradox of SNCC's rapid disintegration as an organization, which came so closely after its greatest achievement, the 1964 Mississippi Summer Project. She finds the reason for this enigma in the tension between SNCC's unique organizational ethos and its pursuit of purposive goals. Her conclusions are based on interviews with fifty-one former SNCC members. This article is a condensed version of her Harvard Ph.D. dissertation (1989, see entry 540).

542 STUDENT NONVIOLENT COORDINATING COMMITTEE. "Nonviolence is the Foundation." In *Black Protest Thought in the Twentieth Century*, edited by August Meier, Elliot Rudwick, and Francis L. Broderick, 307–8. Indianapolis: Bobbs-Merrill, 1971.

This is the statement of purpose adopted by SNCC at its first general conference on 17 April 1960.

543 WARREN, ROBERT PENN. "Two for SNCC." *Commentary* 39 (1965): 38–48.

Warren interviewed Robert Moses in February 1964 and Stokley Carmichael in early 1965. He discusses here their personal backgrounds and their movement involvement. The same material is also contained in Warren's *Who Speaks for the Negro?* (1965, see entry 162).

544 WASHINGTON, CYNTHIA. "We Started from Different Ends of the Spectrum." *Southern Exposure* 4, no. 4 (1977), 14–15. Reprinted in *Reweaving the Web of Life*, edited by Pam McAllister, 112–14. Philadelphia: New Society Publishers, 1982.

Washington, a SNCC project director in Mississippi during 1964, reflects on her experiences in the civil rights and women's movements. She states: "We did the same work as men. . . . Our skills and abilities were recognized and respected, but that seemed to place us in some category other than female."

545 WATTERS, PAT. *Encounter with the Future.* Atlanta: Southern Regional Council, 1965. 34 pages.

Watters describes the growing radicalism within SNCC following the Mississippi Summer Project of 1964.

546 _____. "The Negroes Enter Southern Politics." *Dissent* (July-August
     1966): 361–68.

Watters reviews political developments in the South between the passage of the Voting Rights Act in 1965 and the Democratic primaries in 1966. He examines SNCC's efforts to build an all-black political party in Lowndes County, Alabama, and its decision to exclude white workers on its staff. Although he doubts that black separatism will be a successful political strategy, he traces its origins to the disappointment felt by young activists following the 1964 Democratic convention.

547 _____. "Their Text is a Civil Rights Primer." *New York Times Magazine*, 20 December 1964. Reprinted in *Black Protest in the Sixties*, edited by August Meier and Elliot Rudwick, 79–88. Chicago: Quadrangle Books, 1970.
     See entry 422.

548 ZINN, HOWARD. *SNCC: The New Abolitionists*. Boston: Beacon Press, 1964. 286 pages.

Zinn captures the idealism of the young SNCC workers. He covers the period from its founding in 1960 through early 1965. Zinn served as an advisor to SNCC while teaching at Spellman College in Atlanta and writes from an insider's perspective.

SCLC

549 ABERNATHY, RALPH D. *And the Walls Came Tumbling Down*. New York: Harper & Row, 1989. 641 pages.

From the Montgomery bus boycott in 1955 to the Memphis sanitation workers' strike in 1968, Ralph Abernathy was the loyal friend and companion to Martin Luther King, Jr. and second in command of the Southern Christian Leadership Conference. The two men experienced most of the period's major civil rights campaigns together. When King was assassinated, Abernathy became head of SCLC but never experienced the success that King had enjoyed and eventually was removed from this position. This book is Abernathy's autobiography, from his origins on a humble farm in Marengo County, Alabama, and his experiences in the Jim Crow army to his flirtation with Republican politics during the Reagan years.

550 _____. "The Nonviolent Movement: The Past, the Present and the Future." In *Black Life and Culture in the United States*, edited by Rhoda L. Goldstein, 180–209. New York: Thomas Y. Crowell, 1971. Orig. pub. in *Drum Major* 1 (August 1971): 18–35.

Abernathy recalls his involvement in the early days of the civil rights movement with Martin Luther King, Jr. in Alabama, as well as the efforts of SCLC to continue King's work following his assassination in 1968.

551 AIKEN, MICHAEL, N. J. DEMERATH III, and GERALD MARWELL. "Conscience and Confrontation." *New South* 21 (Spring 1966): 19–28.

Aiken and his colleagues report the preliminary results of their study of white volunteers for SCLC's Summer Community Organization and Political Education Project (SCOPE) in the summer of 1965. They found that the volunteers were not rebels against society, but enjoyed close relations with their families, and were committed to education, religion, and democratic values. The volunteers were not more liberal on racial issues than other college students, but did show greater concern about a larger number of social problems. These data are examined in more depth in Demerath et al., *The Dynamics of Idealism* (1971, see entry 831).

552 CLARK, KENNETH B. "The Civil Rights Movement: Momentum and Organization." In *We Shall Overcome*, edited by David J. Garrow, vol. 1, 151–80. Brooklyn, NY: Carlson Publishing, 1989. Orig. pub. in *Daedalus* 95, no. 1 (1966): 239–67.

See entry 508.

553 CLARK, SEPTIMA P. "Literacy and Liberation." *Freedomways* 4, no. 1 (1964): 113–24.

Clark describes the work of her Citizenship Education program for teaching literacy, preparing voters, and developing local leadership. This program was begun under the sponsorship of the Highlander Folk School and was first implemented on Johns Island in South Carolina.

554 _____. *Ready From Within: Septima Clark and the Civil Rights Movement.* Edited by Cynthia S. Brown. Navarro, CA: Wild Trees Press, 1986. 134 pages.

Septima Clark played an important role in the civil rights movement, but never received much public recognition for her contributions. A school teacher in Charleston, South Carolina, she became active in civil rights organizations during the early 1950s. In 1956 she was fired from her teaching position because of her membership in the NAACP and went to work as director of workshops for the Highlander Folk School. In that position she developed a highly successful Citizenship Education program, which taught adult literacy as a means of helping blacks register to vote. This program was first tried on the Sea Islands of South Carolina and later spread to black communities throughout the South. In 1961 the program was taken over by SCLC, and it continued until her retirement in 1970. This slim volume is based on six days of interviews Cynthia Brown conducted with Septima Clark in 1979. See also Clark's earlier autobiography *Echo in My Soul* (1962, entry 644).

555 COTTON, DOROTHY. "A Conversation with Ralph Abernathy." *Journal of Current Social Issues* 9, no. 3 (1970): 21–30.

Abernathy discusses his youth in rural Alabama, his early involvement with Martin Luther King, Jr. in Montgomery, the mission of the Southern

Christian Leadership Conference, and the future of the civil rights movement.

556   FAIRCLOUGH, ADAM. "The Preachers and the People: The Origins and Early Years of the Southern Christian Leadership Conference, 1955–1959." *Journal of Southern History* 52 (1986): 403–40.

Based on the author's extensive research of primary and secondary sources, this article focuses on the early years of the Southern Christian Leadership Conference, especially the bus boycotts in Montgomery and Tallahassee. In addition to profiles of Martin Luther King, Jr. and the other ministers in SCLC, Fairclough provides useful information on the roles of Ella Baker, Bayard Rustin, and Stanley Levinson. For more on the history of SCLC see Fairclough's book *To Redeem the Soul of America* (1987, entry 558).

557   _____. "The Southern Christian Leadership Conference and the Second Reconstruction, 1957–1973." *South Atlantic Quarterly* 80 (Spring 1981): 177–94. Reprinted in *We Shall Overcome*, edited by David J. Garrow, vol. 1, 231–48. Brooklyn, NY: Carlson Publishing, 1989.

Fairclough traces the history of SCLC from its origins in 1957 to its decline following Martin Luther King, Jr.'s assassination in 1968. He describes its unusual organizational structure, the leadership of Martin Luther King, Jr. the contributions of key aides such as Wyatt Walker, Hosea Williams, James Bevel, and Andrew Young, and its relationships with other civil rights organizations. He recount's the organization's problems following the urban riots of 1965 and the "fiasco" of the Poor People's Campaign. Despite his criticisms, Fairclough is generally favorable in his evaluation of SCLC, which he describes as "one of the most successful . . . reform groups in recent American history." These themes are further developed in his book-length study of SCLC *To Redeem the Soul of America* (1987, see entry 558).

558   _____. *To Redeem the Soul of America: The Southern Christian Leadership Conference and Martin Luther King, Jr.* Athens: University of Georgia Press, 1987. 504 pages.

Fairclough has produced a clearly written and carefully researched history of the Southern Christian Leadership Conference from its founding in 1957 through the 1980s. He examines the organization behind Martin Luther King, Jr., exposes its shortcomings, and praises many of its tactics. Fairclough sees SCLC's greatest success in its ability to create the conditions which enabled the movement "to bypass the South's white-controlled political and judicial institutions, making a direct appeal to the centers of federal power."

559   GARROW, DAVID J. *Bearing the Cross: Martin Luther King, Jr., and the Southern Christian Leadership Conference.* New York: Random House, 1986. 800 pages.

More than a biography of Martin Luther King, Jr. this incredibly well-researched volume is also a history of the civil rights movement, and especially of those events such as the ones in Montgomery, Albany, Birmingham, and the

March on Washington and the Chicago Open Housing Campaign that directly involved King. Garrow gives considerable insight to the operation and organization of SCLC and the colorful personalities who worked with King.

560 _____. *Protest at Selma: Martin Luther King, Jr. and the Voting Rights Act of 1965.* New Haven: Yale University Press, 1978. 346 pages.
See entry 195.

561 GOOD, PAUL. "'No Man Can Fill Dr. King's Shoes' but Abernathy Tries." *New York Times Magazine*, 26 May 1968. Reprinted in *Black Protest in the Sixties*, edited by August Meier and Elliot Rudwick, 284–301. Chicago: Quadrangle Press, 1970.

Good describes the problems facing Ralph Abernathy as he attempts to organize the Poor People's Campaign following the assassination of Martin Luther King, Jr. One dilemma according to Good is "how to assert himself while keeping fresh the King legend." Another difficulty, he points out, is keeping faith in nonviolence in the face of increasingly bitter criticism from young militants.

562 LEVINE, RICHARD. "Jesse Jackson: Heir to Dr. King?" *Harper's*, March 1969, 58–70.
See entry 483.

563 LONG, MARGARET. "The Unity of the Rifting Negro Movement." *Progressive*, February 1964, 10–14.
See entry 525.

564 MCFADDEN, GRACE JORDAN. "Septima P. Clark and the Struggle for Human Rights." In *Women in the Civil Rights Movement*, edited by Vicki L. Crawford, Jacqueline Anne Rouse, and Barbara Woods, 85–97. Brooklyn, NY: Carlson Publishing, 1990.

McFadden describes the contributions of Septima P. Clark, who was affiliated with the Southern Christian Leadership Conference and with the Highlander Folk School, where she developed citizenship schools to prepare blacks in the rural South for voter registration. Some of this material is also covered in Clark's two autobiographies, *Echo in My Soul* (1962, see entry 644) and *Ready From Within* (1986, see entry 554).

565 ORANGE, JAMES. "With the People." *Southern Exposure* 9 (Spring 1981): 110–16.

James Orange first became involved in the civil rights movement in 1963 when he helped organize student demonstrations in Birmingham. As a SCLC staff organizer he worked in Selma, Chicago, Memphis, and on the Poor People's Campaign. Subsequently, he became a union organizer. In this interview he describes his involvement in the movement.

566 PAYNE, CHARLES. "Ella Baker and Models of Social Change." *Signs* 14, no. 4 (1989): 885–99.
See entry 533.

567   PEAKE, THOMAS R. *Keeping the Dream Alive: A History of the Southern Christian Leadership Conference from King to the 1980s.* New York: Peter Lang Publishing, 1987. 502 pages.
   Peake traces the history of SCLC from its founding in 1957 into the 1980s. He emphasizes the evolution of the organization's "dream"—its vision for social change in America. Peake identifies three features which distinguished SCLC's role in the civil rights movement: (1) its unique relationship with Martin Luther King, Jr. (2) its religious orientation and strong ties to local churches, and (3) its southern roots and orientation.

568   PENDERGRAST, NAN. "Twenty-five Years of Love in Action—an Interview with Joseph Lowery." *Fellowship* 1 (February 1983): 10–12.
   Pendergrast describes Lowery's twenty-five year involvement with SCLC and the civil rights movement. She discusses his views on nonviolence, international peace, and changes he has observed.

569   REAGIN, EWELL. "A Study of the Southern Christian Leadership Conference." In *We Shall Overcome*, edited by David J. Garrow, vol. 3, 975–84. Brooklyn, NY: Carlson Publishing, 1989. Orig. pub. in *Review of Religious Research* 9 (Winter 1968): 88–96.
   Reagin describes "the origins, development, and employment of ideology by SCLC in the Chicago movement" of 1966.

570   RUSTIN, BAYARD. "Even in the Face of Death." *Liberation* 2 (February 1957): 12–14.
   Rustin describes the January 1957 meeting of sixty black leaders in Atlanta, which resulted in the formation of SCLC.

571   SOUTHERN CHRISTIAN LEADERSHIP CONFERENCE. "The Ultimate Aim is the 'Beloved Community'" In *Negro Protest Thought in the Twentieth Century*, edited by Francis L. Broderick and August Meier, 269–73. Indianapolis: Bobbs-Merrill, 1965. Orig. pub. in *This Is SCLC* (1964), a leaflet prepared by the Southern Christian Leadership Conference.
   This article sets forth SCLC's objectives and philosophy, especially its advocacy of civil disobedience.

572   WALKER, WYATT T. "Albany, Failure or First Step?" *New South* 18 (June 1963): 3–8.
   See entry 303.

573   WIGGINTON, ELLIOT, and SUE THRASHER. "To Make the World We Want: An Interview with Dorothy Cotton." *Southern Exposure* 10 (September 1982): 25–31.
   Dorothy Cotton became involved in the civil rights movement as a college student in Petersburg, Virginia, where Wyatt T. Walker built a local movement to oppose segregation in the public library. When Walker joined the SCLC staff in Atlanta, Cotton followed him. Here she describes the work of the Citizenship Education Program and decision-making within SCLC.

CORE

574   BELL, INGE POWELL. "Case Study of a Southern CORE Group." In *Racial Conflict*, edited by Gary T. Marx, 406–15. Boston: Little, Brown & Co., 1971. Excerpt from *CORE and the Strategy of Nonviolence* by Inge Powell Bell. New York: Random House, 1968.

Bell describes the organization and membership of a CORE chapter in an anonymous southern city. She discusses its relationships with the white and black communities, and examines its efforts to build a consensus within the black community.

575   _____. *CORE and the Strategy of Nonviolence*. New York: Random House, 1968. 214 pages.

Bell's sociological study of CORE focuses on the period from 1961 to 1963 when the organization was in "the process of transition from a small, pacifist, predominantly white intellectual group to a more militant, more pragmatic, and less philosophical mass organization in which middle class Negroes and Negro students were replacing whites in positions of influence."

576   _____. "CORE and the Strategy of Nonviolence." In *Minority Responses*, edited by Minako Kurokawa, 249–58. New York: Random House, 1970.

A shortened version of her 1968 book by the same title (see entry 575).

577   _____. "Status Discrepancy and the Radical Rejection of Nonviolence." *Sociological Inquiry* 38 (1968): 51–63.

Bell interviewed an equal number of black CORE members from both southern and northern chapters. She found that it was "the Northern higher status Negroes who were most inclined toward a radical rejection of nonviolence." She hypothesizes that the large discrepancy between their racial status and their socioeconomic status produced a high level of relative deprivation which "almost inevitably led to ideological radicalism."

578   CLARK, KENNETH B. "The Civil Rights Movement: Momentum and Organization." In *We Shall Overcome*, edited by David J. Garrow, vol. 1, 151–80. Brooklyn, NY: Carlson Publishing, 1989. Orig. pub. in *Daedalus* 95, no. 1 (1966): 239–67.

See entry 508.

579   CONGRESS of RACIAL EQUALITY. "An Alternative to Bitterness and Mere Sentiment." In *Negro Protest Thought in the Twentieth Century*, edited by Francis L. Broderick and August Meier, 296–304. Indianapolis: Bobbs-Merrill, 1965. Orig. pub. in *All About CORE*, a pamphlet prepared by the Congress of Racial Equality, 1963.

This article sets forth CORE's philosophy of nonviolent direct action against racial discrimination.

580　EHLE, JOHN. *The Free Men.* New York: Harper & Row, 1965. 340
　　　pages.
　　See entry 433.

581　FARMER, JAMES. *Freedom—When?* New York: Random House, 1965.
　　　197 pages.
　　See entry 308.

582　_____. *Lay Bare the Heart: An Autobiography of the Civil Rights Move-
　　　ment.* New York: Arbor House, 1985. 370 pages.

James Farmer spent most of his adult life deeply involved in the civil rights
movement. As one of the founders of CORE, he pioneered the use of nonviolent direct action against segregation. Nearly twenty years after its creation, the
organization achieved national recognition when it organized the Freedom
Rides. With the rise of Black Power Farmer left CORE and, for a short time,
worked in the Nixon administration. This book traces his career in the movement and gives his personal views on events during this tumultuous era.

583　_____. "We Must Be in a Position of Power." In *Negro Protest Thought
　　　in the Twentieth Century*, edited by Francis L. Broderick and August
　　　Meier, 421–28. Indianapolis: Bobbs-Merrill, 1971. Address to the
　　　CORE national convention, Durham, NC, 1 July 1965.

Farmer advocates a strategy for CORE consisting of community organizing and independent political action.

584　GAITHER, TOM. "Jailed-In." In *Nonviolence in America*, edited by
　　　Staughton Lynd, 399–415. Indianapolis: Bobbs-Merrill, 1966. Orig.
　　　pub. by League for Industrial Democracy, New York, 1961.
　　See entry 478.

585　JONES, MACK H., and ALEX WILLINGHAM. "The White Custodians of the
　　　Black Experience: A Reply to Meier and Rudwick." *Social Science
　　　Quarterly* 51 (June 1970): 31–36.

A critical response to Rudwick and Meier's "Organizational Structure
and Goal Succession: A Comparative Analysis of the NAACP and CORE,
1964–1968" (1970, see entry 605). The authors accuse Rudwick and Meier of
a consistent anti-nationalist bias.

586　KOTZ, NICK, and MARY LYNN KOTZ. *A Passion for Equality: George
　　　Wiley and the Movement.* New York: W. W. Norton & Co., 1977. 372
　　　pages.

George Wiley is best known as the founder and chief organizer of the
National Welfare Rights Organization. Before his involvement with the
NWRO, however, he was a local and national leader of CORE. The authors
describe Wiley's evolution from a Syracuse University chemistry professor,
to an activist for school desegregation, to a full-time civil rights organizer.

587　LOMAX, LOUIS E. "The Freedom Rides." In *The Civil Rights Reader:
　　　Basic Documents of the Civil Rights Movement*, edited by Leon Freid-

man, 51–60. New York: Walker, 1968. Orig. pub. in *The Negro Revolt*, by Louis E. Lomax. New York: Harper & Row, 1962.

Lomax presents a detailed chronology of the Freedom Rides, which he describes as a major victory for James Farmer and CORE.

588 LOUIS, DEBBIE. *And We Are Not Saved: A History of the Movement as People.* Garden City, NY: Doubleday, 1970. 462 pages.

Louis's study of the civil rights movement between 1959 and 1965 focuses on the young people who joined the movement and the diverse "psychological and cultural factors which brought about" their participation. She maintains that by understanding the "varying depth of their commitment and the varying ends that commitment was made to achieve," one can better understand both the success and the ultimate decline of the movement.

589 MABEE, CARLETON. "Two Decades of Sit-Ins: Evolution of Non-Violence. *The Nation*, 12 August, 1961, 78–81.

Mabee traces the development of nonviolent direct action tactics against segregation by CORE during the 1940s. He describes the evolution of the organization from its founding in 1942 through its use of sit-ins against a variety of forms of segregation, mainly in the North.

590 MAHONEY, WILLIAM. "In Pursuit of Freedom." In *Nonviolence in America*, edited by Staughton Lynd, 415–28. Indianapolis: Bobbs-Merrill, 1966. Orig. pub. in *Liberation* 6 (September 1961): 7–11.

Mahoney describes his experiences in the 1961 Freedom Rides and his subsequent imprisonment in Mississippi's Parchman Penitentiary.

591 MEIER, AUGUST. "Negro Protest Movements and Organizations." In *We Shall Overcome*, edited by David J. Garrow, vol. 2, 763–76. Brooklyn, NY: Carlson Publishing, 1989. Orig. pub. in *Journal of Negro Education* 32 (Fall 1963): 437–450.

See entry 527.

592 MEIER, AUGUST, and ELLIOT RUDWICK. *CORE: A Study in the Civil Rights Movement, 1942–1968.* New York: Oxford University Press, 1973. 563 pages.

Drawing upon extensive interviews with key figures, as well as manuscript sources and other published accounts, Meier and Rudwick offer here the definitive historical and sociological analysis of the rise and decline of this dynamic civil rights organization.

593 ———. "The First Freedom Ride." *Phylon* 30 (1969): 213–22.

Meier and Rudwick describe CORE's 1947 Journey of Reconciliation, which was the model for the 1961 Freedom Rides.

594 ———. "How CORE Began." *Social Science Quarterly* 49 (March 1969): 789–99.

Meier and Rudwick trace the founding of CORE by a small group of Christian pacifists in Chicago in 1942. They describe its objectives, philosophy, tactics, and some of its early efforts. For a more comprehensive portrait of the organization see Meier and Rudwick's *CORE: A Study in the Civil Rights Movement* (1973, entry 592).

595 MOODY, ANNE. *Coming of Age in Mississippi.* New York: Dell Publishing Co., 1968. 348 pages.
See entry 390.

596 MOORE, RONNIE M. "We Are Catching Hell Down Here." In *Black Protest Thought in the Twentieth Century*, edited by August Meier, Elliot Rudwick, and Francis L. Broderick, 340–46. Indianapolis: Bobbs-Merrill, 1971. Memorandum to Richard Haley, Marvin Rich, and Jim McCain, 6 September 1963.
See entry 312.

597 PECK, JAMES. *Freedom Ride.* New York: Simon and Schuster, 1962. 160 pages.
While James Peck was one of the organizers of CORE's Freedom Ride in 1961, only one of his book's ten chapters discusses the Freedom Ride. The rest are accounts of other nonviolent protests against segregation. Peck provides a valuable eyewitness description of the Freedom Ride, but, since he was knocked unconscious and hospitalized when the Freedom Riders actually arrived in Birmingham on May 14, readers will have to look elsewhere for a complete account of this dramatic protest.

598 ———. "Freedom Rides—1947 and 1961." In *Nonviolent Direct Action, American Cases: Social Psychological Analyses*, edited by A. P. Hare and Herbert H. Blumberg, 49–75. Washington, DC: Corpus Books, 1968.
Peck describes his participation in two Freedom Rides organized by CORE. The first took place in 1947 and ended with the arrest of the Freedom Riders in North Carolina. The second, and better-known, Freedom Ride began on 4 May 1961 in Washington, D.C., and ended for Peck on May 14 when the riders were attacked upon their arrival in Birmingham, Alabama.

599 PINARD, MAURICE, JEROME KIRK, and DONALD VON ESCHEN. "Processes of Recruitment in the Sit-In Movement." *Public Opinion Quarterly* 33 (Fall 1969): 355–69.
Pinard and his associates distributed questionnaires to participants in 1961 sit-ins at restaurants along Route 40 between Baltimore and Wilmington. In this report, they analyze 386 completed questionnaires and find that the participants were predominantly white and upper-middle class. Lower status participants, however, were found to be more active in the movement as a whole than those from more privileged backgrounds.

600 RICH, MARVIN. "The Congress of Racial Equality and its Strategy." *Annals of the American Academy of Political and Social Science* 357 (1965): 113–18.
Rich reviews CORE's history, its organizational structure, its changing goals, and its commitment to nonviolent direct action.

601 ROBBINS, JHAN, and JUNE ROBBINS. "'Why Didn't They Hit Back?'" In *Nonviolent Direct Action*, edited by A. Paul Hare and Herbert H. Blumberg, 107–27. Washington, DC: Corpus Books, 1968. Orig. pub. in *Redbook* 52 (July 1963): 110–15.
See entry 493.

602 ROGERS, KIM LACY. "Organizational Experience and Personal Narrative: Stories of New Orleans' Civil Rights Leadership." *Oral History Review* 13 (1985): 23–54.
See entry 314.

603 RUDWICK, ELLIOT, and AUGUST MEIER. "Integration vs. Separatism: The NAACP and CORE Face Challenge from Within." In *Along the Color Line*, edited by August Meier and Elliot Rudwick, 238–64. Urbana: University of Illinois Press, 1976.
Rudwick and Meier examine the response of the NAACP and CORE to the Black Power thrust of the mid-1960s. They find that the NAACP stuck with its traditional ideology of racial integration in part because of its bureaucratic, centralized organizational structure, and also because its leaders and membership remained committed to this goal. CORE, on the other hand, had a looser, decentralized structure, with a rapidly changing membership that pushed it to adopt the Black Power ideology.

604 _____. "NAACP and CORE: Some Additional Theoretical Considerations." *Social Science Quarterly* 51 (June 1970): 37–41.
Rudwick and Meier continue their discussion of the responses of the NAACP and CORE to the accomplishments of the civil rights movement. They argue that differences in the composition of their memberships led the NAACP to view the passage of civil rights legislation as significant progress while the same laws were viewed as token concessions by CORE.

605 _____. "Organizational Structure and Goal Succession: A Comparative Analysis of the NAACP and CORE." *Social Science Quarterly* 51 (June 1970): 9–24.
Rudwick and Meier compare CORE and the NAACP during the 1960s. They point out that while both organizations began the decade dedicated to the goal of racial integration, by the end of the 1960s CORE had become a leading proponent of racial separatism. The key to explaining this difference, they maintain, is a rapid change in CORE's decision-making elite, while the NAACP's leadership remained stable.

606 VAN MATRE, JAMES. "The Congress of Racial Equality and the Re-Emergence of the Civil Rights Movement." In *The Civil Rights Movement in Florida and the United States*, edited by Charles U. Smith, 135–75. Tallahassee, FL: Father & Son Press, 1989.
Van Matre describes CORE's origins in the 1940s, and the community organizing techniques used by CORE field workers in Louisiana and Florida during the 1960s.

607 YANCEY, WILLIAM L. "Organizational Structures and Environments: A Second Look at the NAACP and CORE." *Social Science Quarterly* 51 (June 1970): 25–30.

Yancey follows Rudwick and Meier's analysis of organizational change in the NAACP and CORE to point out that the "traditional model of organizational crystallization does not apply" to either organization.

NAACP

608 ARNOLD, MARTIN. "There Is No Rest for Roy Wilkins." *New York Times Magazine*, 28 September 1969. Reprinted in *Black Protest in the Sixties*, edited by August Meier and Elliot Rudwick, 315–28. Chicago: Quadrangle Books, 1970.

Arnold offers a portrait of NAACP leader Wilkins at a time when he was under criticism from young militants within and outside that organization. Wilkins is described as a "successful politician" who is well connected to "the white power structure." Wilkins laments that "we offer the young people nothing spectacular."

609 BLAND, RENDALL W. *Private Pressure and Public Law: The Legal Career of Justice Thurgood Marshall.* Port Washington, NY: Kennikat Press, 1973. 206 pages.

Bland examines Marshall's legal career, especially the thirty-two cases he argued on behalf of the NAACP before the U.S. Supreme Court, and his impact on the civil rights movement. He concludes that Marshall's life proves that it is possible "for a minority group to accomplish most reasonable objectives or to redress legitimate grievances within the framework of American constitutional law."

610 CLARK, KENNETH B. "The Civil Rights Movement: Momentum and Organization." In *We Shall Overcome*, edited by David J. Garrow, vol. 1, 151–80. Brooklyn, NY: Carlson Publishing, 1989. Orig. pub. in *Daedalus* 95, no. 1 (1966): 239–67.

See entry 508.

611 COHEN, ROBERT CARL. *Black Crusader: A Biography of Robert Franklin Williams.* Secaucus, NJ: Lyle Stuart, 1972. 361 pages.

Williams gained a reputation as a radical civil rights leader for his advocacy of armed self-defense as head of the Monroe, North Carolina, NAACP chapter. He was subsequently expelled from the NAACP and fled to Cuba when accused of kidnapping in a 1962 confrontation. Williams published and broadcast calls for black revolution from Cuba and later from China. Cohen is generally sympathetic to Williams's position.

612 GRAVES, CARL R. "The Right to be Served: Oklahoma City's Lunch Counter Sit-Ins, 1958–1964." In *We Shall Overcome*, edited by David

J. Garrow, vol. 1, 283–97. Brooklyn, NY: Carlson Publishing, 1989. Orig. pub. in *Chronicles of Oklahoma* 59 (Summer 1981): 361–73.
See entry 480.

613   JONES, MACK H., and ALEX WILLINGHAM. "The White Custodians of the Black Experience: A reply to Meier and Rudwick." *Social Science Quarterly* 51 (June 1970): 31–36.
See entry 585.

614   KLUGER, RICHARD. *Simple Justice: The History of Brown v. Board of Education and Black America's Struggle for Equality.* New York: Alfred A. Knopf, 1976. 823 pages.
Kluger provides a comprehensive account of the five school desegregation suits filed by the NAACP, which culminated in the *Brown v. Board of Education* decision in 1954. He describes the origins of each suit, the legal strategies employed by the NAACP, and the judicial decision process that resulted in the Supreme Court's unanimous decision.

615   LOMAX, LOUIS E. "The Negro Revolt against 'the Negro Leaders.'" In *We Shall Overcome*, edited by David J. Garrow, vol. 2, 603–10. Brooklyn, NY: Carlson Publishing, 1989. Orig. pub. in *Harper's* (June 1960): 41–48.
Lomax views the emergence of the southern sit-in movement as a rejection of the traditional "Negro leadership class," especially the NAACP. He claims that these demonstrations have "shifted the main issue to one of individual dignity, not civil rights."

616   LONG, MARGARET. "The Unity of the Rifting Negro Movement." *Progressive*, February 1964, 10–14.
See entry 525.

617   MCNEIL, GENNA RAE. *Groundwork: Charles Hamilton Houston and the Struggle for Civil Rights.* Philadelphia: University of Pennsylvania Press, 1983. 308 pages.
McNeil describes Houston's work as an educator at Howard University Law School and as an attorney for the NAACP that helped prepare the way for the *Brown* decision in 1954. His death in 1950 denied him the satisfaction of seeing the culmination of his efforts.

618   MARGER, MARTIN N. "Social Movement Organization and Response to Environmental Change: The NAACP, 1960–1973." *Social Problems* 32, no. 1 (1984): 16–32.
Marger examines the NAACP as it "struggled to maintain its relevance to the black protest movement in the face of competition from organizations espousing more radical goals and strategies." He finds that while its membership remained constant, "its revenue increased as it became professionalized and drew substantially greater funding from external sources."

619   MEIER, AUGUST. "Negro Protest Movements and Organizations." In *We Shall Overcome*, edited by David J. Garrow, vol. 2, 763–76. Brooklyn,

NY: Carlson Publishing, 1989. Orig. pub. in *Journal of Negro Education* 32 (Fall 1963): 437–50.
See entry 527.

620	_____. "The Revolution against the NAACP." In *We Shall Overcome*, edited by David J. Garrow, vol. 2, 729–36. Brooklyn, NY: Carlson Publishing, 1989. Orig. pub. in *Journal of Negro Education* 32 (Spring 1963): 146–52.
This review of Louis Lomax's *The Negro Revolt* (1962, see entry 63) is largely a defense of the NAACP against the book's "serious distortions." Meier maintains that Lomax is overly critical of the NAACP leadership and fails to report the extent of the organization's involvement in direct action against segregation. Meier also claims that the competition between civil rights organizations has infused "new life" into the activities of the NAACP.

621	MORSELL, JOHN A. "The National Association for the Advancement of Colored People and Its Strategy." *Annals of the American Academy of Political and Social Science* 357 (1965): 97–101.
Morsell describes the civil rights program of the NAACP, which he views as the major source of leadership for the movement.

622	PAYNE, CHARLES. "Ella Baker and Models of Social Change." *Signs* 14, no. 4 (1989): 885–99.
See entry 533.

623	RENDER, SYLVIA LYONS. "Roy Wilkins, 1901–1981: A Tribute." *Quarterly Journal of the Library of Congress* 39, no. 2 (1982): 116–25.
Render provides a pictoral essay on Wilkin's life and his career in civil rights as an executive of the NAACP.

624	ROGERS, KIM LACY. "Organizational Experience and Personal Narrative: Stories of New Orleans' Civil Rights Leadership." *Oral History Review* 13 (1985): 23–54.
See entry 314.

625	RUDWICK, ELLIOT, and AUGUST MEIER. "Integration vs. Separatism: The NAACP and CORE Face Challenge from Within." In *Along the Color Line*, edited by August Meier and Elliot Rudwick, 238–64. Urbana: University of Illinois Press, 1976.
See entry 603.

626	_____. "NAACP and CORE: Some Additional Theoretical Considerations." *Social Science Quarterly* 51 (June 1970): 37–41.
See entry 604.

627	_____. "Organizational Structure and Goal Succession: A Comparative Analysis of the NAACP and CORE." *Social Science Quarterly* 51 (June 1970): 9–24.
See entry 605.

628 SALTER, JOHN R., JR. *Jackson, Mississippi: An American Chronicle of Struggle and Schism.* 1979. Reprint. Malabar, FL: R. E. Krieger Publishing Co., 1987. 248 pages.
See entry 407.

629 TUSHNET, MARK V. *The NAACP's Legal Strategy against Segregated Education. 1925–1950.* Chapel Hill: University of North Carolina Press, 1987. 222 pages.
Tushnet describes the NAACP's legal strategy against segregation in education in the era prior to the direct attack on "separate but equal," which culminated in the *Brown* decision.

630 WATSON, DENTON L. *Lion in the Lobby: Clarence Mitchell, Jr.'s Struggle for the Passage of the Civil Rights Laws.* New York: William Morrow & Co., 1990. 846 pages.
As director of the NAACP's Washington office from 1950 to 1978, Clarence Mitchell, Jr., was the leading lobbyist on behalf of civil rights legislation during the peak years of the civil rights movement. In this hefty book, Watson provides a detailed account of the lobbying process and how Mitchell helped secure the passage of the landmark civil rights bills of 1957, 1960, 1963, and 1964.

631 WILKINS, ROY. "For 'Shock Troops' and 'Solid Legal Moves.'" In *Negro Protest Thought in the Twentieth Century,* edited by Francis L. Broderick and August Meier, 281–87. Indianapolis: Bobbs-Merrill, 1965. Address to mass meeting of Jackson, Mississippi, branch of NAACP, 7 June 1961.
The NAACP leader describes that organization's involvement in direct action against segregation, and defends the usefulness of its traditional legal and political strategy.

632 _____. *Standing Fast: The Autobiography of Roy Wilkins.* New York: Viking, 1982. 361 pages.
From the death of Walter White in 1955 to his own retirement in 1977, Roy Wilkins was the main leader of the NAACP. The last five chapters of this autobiography cover the period of the civil rights movement. Wilkins points out that the instigators of the Montgomery bus boycott were former NAACP officers, the sit-in technique was pioneered in 1958 by an NAACP youth council in Oklahoma, and NAACP lobbyists played a critical role in securing the passage of the 1964 Civil Rights Act. He defends the programs and policies of the organization he headed.

633 _____. "We Must Use Every Tool." In *Negro Protest Thought in the Twentieth Century,* edited by Francis L. Broderick and August Meier, 397–400. Indianapolis: Bobbs-Merrill, 1965. Orig. pub. as "Freedom tactics for 18,000,000." *New South* 18, no. 1 (1964), 3–7.
Wilkins defends the NAACP's position against criticism from more militant organizations by arguing that a variety of tactics is needed to realize the

movement's goals. He is critical of those who attempt "to solve all problems everywhere by a single method."

634   WILLIAMS, ROBERT F. "The Swimming Pool Showdown." *Southern Exposure* 8 (Summer 1980): 22–24.
      See entry 438.

635   WOODS, BARBARA A. "Modjeska Simkins and the South Carolina Conference of the NAACP, 1939–1957." In *Women in the Civil Rights Movement,* edited by Vicki L. Crawford, Jacqueline Anne Rouse, and Barbara Woods, 99–120. Brooklyn, NY: Carlson Publishing, 1990.
      See entry 497.

636   YANCEY, WILLIAM L. "Organizational Structures and Environments: A Second Look at the NAACP and CORE." *Social Science Quarterly* 51 (June 1970): 25–30.
      See entry 607.

National Urban League

637   CLARK, KENNETH B. "The Civil Rights Movement: Momentum and Organization." In *We Shall Overcome,* edited by David J. Garrow, vol. 1, 151–80. Brooklyn, NY: Carlson Publishing, 1989. Orig. pub. in *Daedalus* 95, no. 1 (1966): 239–67.
      See entry 508.

638   WEISS, NANCY J. *Whitney M. Young, Jr., and the Struggle for Civil Rights.* Princeton, NJ: Princeton University Press, 1989. 286 pages.
      Weiss's biography of Young focuses on his role as leader of the National Urban League. She credits Young with bringing the National Urban League into the civil rights movement: "In so doing, he kept the league from becoming peripheral to the black struggle, and he positioned it to take advantage of a political and social climate conducive to black employment and social welfare." She feels that the two areas in which he was most successful in capitalizing on this new climate were the corporate establishment and the federal government, especially the Kennedy and Johnson administrations.

639   _____. "Whitney M. Young, Jr.: Committing the Power Structure to the Cause of Civil Rights." In *Black Leaders of the Twentieth Century,* edited by John Hope Franklin and August Meier, 331–58. Urbana: University of Illinois Press, 1982.
      Weiss examines Young's roles as head of the National Urban League and as a civil rights leader in general. She concludes that Young was successful in communicating "the needs and aspirations of black Americans to the white establishment." According to Weiss, he was effective because "he excelled as a mediator," "understood the power structure," and "knew the

processes of social change." The same themes are developed at greater length in Weiss's *Whitney M. Young, Jr., and the Struggle for Civil Rights* (1989, see entry 638).

640   YOUNG, WHITNEY M., JR. "For Protest Plus 'Corrective Measures.'" In *Negro Protest Thought in the Twentieth Century*, edited by Francis L. Broderick and August and Meier, 287–96. Indianapolis: Bobbs-Merrill, 1965. Address to national conference of the National Urban League, 1963.

Young defends the National Urban League's traditional social service programs, saying there is a need both for protest and for programs that help blacks take advantage of new opportunities.

641   _____. "The Urban League and Its Strategy." *Annals of the American Academy of Political and Social Science* 357 (1965): 102–7.

Young outlines the objectives and programs of the National Urban League. He stresses the goals of eliminating discrimination and promoting self-help efforts. He emphasizes the league's belief that "interracial cooperation is an indispensable prerequisite to the achievement of significant and lasting gains for Negro citizens."

Highlander Folk School

642   ADAMS, FRANK, and MYLES HORTON. *Unearthing Seeds of Fire: The Idea of Highlander.* Winston-Salem, NC: John F. Blair, 1975. 255 pages.

Adams describes the work of the Highlander Folk School in Monteagle, Tennessee which played a vital role in the civil rights movement by providing training for civil rights organizers and for developing the Citizenship Education program. Chapter 7 describes the Citizenship Schools established on the Sea Islands of South Carolina during the 1950s by Esau Jenkins, Bernice Robinson, and Septima Clark. Chapters 8 and 9 deal with Highlander's conferences on southern race relations and the resulting effort by the state of Tennessee to close the school. Chapters 10 and 11 chronicle Highlander's continued association with the civil rights movement. Adams is no dispassionate observer—he obviously identifies with Highlander and its objectives. For more on the significance of Highlander see Aldon Morris, *The Origins of the Civil Rights Movement* (1984, entry 1016).

643   BLEDSOE, THOMAS. *Or We'll All Hang Separately: The Highlander Idea.* Boston: Beacon Press, 1969. 266 pages.

Bledsoe presents here descriptions of the Highlander Folk School, including a profile of its founder Myles Horton, and a narrative of the attempts to destroy the school. One chapter is devoted to that Tennessee school's role in the civil rights movement.

644   CLARK, SEPTIMA P. *Echo in My Soul.* New York: E.P. Dutton, 1962. 243
      pages.

Clark was an influential civil rights organizer who created the Citizenship Education Program while working for the Highlander Folk School. This
autobiography focuses on her early years in South Carolina. For more on her
later years, see her autobiography *Ready From Within* (1986, entry 554).

645   _____. "Literacy and Liberation." *Freedomways* 4, no. 1 (1964): 113–24.
      See entry 553.

646   _____. *Ready From Within: Septima Clark and the Civil Rights Move-
      ment.* Edited by Cynthia S. Brown. Navarro, CA: Wild Trees Press,
      1986. 134 pages.
      See entry 554.

647   EGERTON, JOHN. "The Trial of the Highlander Folk School." *Southern
      Exposure* 6, no. 1 (1978): 82–89.

Egerton describes the legal attack on the Highlander Folk School by the
state of Tennessee. He relates how in 1959 the state legislature authorized
an investigation of "subversive activities" at the school. Egerton claims that
the main charge against the school was that it supported racial integration,
which was equated with communism. He tells how the committee urged the
district attorney to bring suit against Highlander; relates the subsequent raid
by state agents; and describes the ensuing trial at which the school was
convicted of selling beer without a license. After two unsuccessful appeals,
the school's property was sold at an auction in 1961.

648   GLEN, JOHN M. *Highlander: No Ordinary School.* Lexington: Univer-
      sity Press of Kentucky, 1988. 309 pages.

Glen traces the history of the Highlander Folk School from 1932 to
1962. The last third of the book focuses on Highlander's role in the civil
rights movement. Glen claims that "until 1961 the Tennessee school was in
the forefront of the drive to end racial segregation in the South." He describes its conferences and training programs for civil rights workers, its
program of citizenship schools for poor blacks, and the successful attempt by the state of Tennessee to close Highlander for its integrationist
acitivities.

649   HORTON, AIMEE ISGRIG. *The Highlander Folk School: A History of its
      Major Programs, 1932–1961.* Brooklyn, NY: Carlson Publishing,
      1989. 334 pages. Ph.D. thesis, University of Chicago, 1971.

This comprehensive history of the Highlander Folk School devotes sixty
pages to a discussion of its civil rights activities between 1953 and 1965. For
more on Highlander and its role in the civil rights movement see Morris (1984,
entry 1016), Myles Horton (1990, entry 650) and Clark (1982, entry 664).

650   HORTON, MYLES, with JUDITH and HERBERT KOHL. *The Long Haul: An
      Autobiography.* New York: Doubleday, 1990. 231 pages.

During the 1940s and 1950s the Highlander Folk School in Monteagle,

Tennessee was the only place in the South where blacks and whites could meet together to discuss their common problems. Highlander played an important, though little noted, part in the development of the civil rights movement. Myles Horton was the founder and, for fifty years, the guiding spirit behind Highlander. This autobiography is based on interviews conducted by Judith and Herbert Kohl. It includes Horton's reflections on the school's mission as well as his own philosophy of adult education.

651   HUGHES, ALVIN. "A New Agenda for the South: The Role and Influence of the Highlander Folk School, 1953–1961." *Phylon* 46, no. 3 (1985): 242–50.

Hughes examines the role of the Highlander Folk School in "defining the new southern agenda for social justice in the 1950s and early 1960s." He shows that the Tennessee school for adult education contributed to the civil rights movement by holding workshops on school desegregation for community leaders from 1953 to 1957 and by sponsoring training sessions on civil rights for black and white college students. He concludes that Highlander "paved the way for liberal white Southerners to participate in the movement, and for better racial understanding through involvement in the fight for democracy in the South."

652   LANGSTON, DONNA. "The Women of Highlander." In *Women in the Civil Rights Movement*, edited by Vicki L. Crawford, Jacqueline Anne Rouse, and Barbara Woods, 145–67. Brooklyn, NY: Carlson Publishing, 1990.

The Highlander Folk School of Monteagle, Tennessee, played a vital role in the civil rights movement by providing a "halfway house" where movement activists could come together for conferences and training. It also developed a system of "Citizenship Schools," which educated illiterate blacks and prepared them for voter registration. Langston describes the work of the Highlander School, especially the efforts of Septima Clark, Esau Jenkins, and Bernice Robinson who organized the Citizenship Schools.

653   McFADDEN, GRACE JORDAN. "Septima P. Clark and the Struggle for Human Rights." In *Women in the Civil Rights Movement*, edited by Vicki L. Crawford, Jacqueline Anne Rouse, and Barbara Woods, 85–97. Brooklyn, NY: Carlson Publishing, 1990.
See entry 564.

654   OLDENDORF, SANDRA B. "The South Carolina Sea Islands Citizenship Schools, 1957–1961." In *Women in the Civil Rights Movement*, edited by Vicki L. Crawford, Jacqueline Anne Rouse, and Barbara Woods, 169–82. Brooklyn, NY: Carlson Publishing, 1990.
See entry 491.

6

The Federal Government

Executive

655 ANDERSON, J. W. *Eisenhower, Brownell, and the Congress: The Tangled Origins of the Civil Rights Bill of 1956–1957.* Tuscaloosa: University of Alabama Press, 1964. 139 pages.

Anderson argues that the passage of the 1957 Civil Rights Act can be understood only in the context of the failure of the 1956 bill. He claims that the 1956 bill was never endorsed by President Eisenhower, but was introduced into Congress by Attorney General Herbert Brownell "in direct violation of the explicit instructions of the White House." Only during the presidential campaign of 1956 was Eisenhower persuaded to speak in favor of the bill's provisions.

656 BALL, HOWARD, DALE KRANE, and THOMAS P. LAUTH. *Compromised Compliance: Implementation of the 1965 Voting Rights Act.* Westport, CT: Greenwood Press, 1982. 300 pages.

The authors examine the implementation and enforcement of the 1965 Voting Rights Act by the Civil Rights Division of the U.S. Justice Department. They argue that the decisions on how the act was to be implemented were based on careful assessment of political pressures. They describe how from 1965 to 1971 efforts were concentrated on gaining compliance with section 4 of the act, which dealt with voter registration. After 1971 they claim that demands by civil rights organizations forced the Civil Rights Division to shift its attention to section 5, which required Justice Department approval of changes in voting arrangements. The authors also claim that the implementation strategy that the Civil Rights Division lawyers finally agreed on was a compromise designed to gain the compliance of white powerholders in the South while also satisfying the demands of civil rights organizations.

657   BELKNAP, MICHAEL R. *Federal Law and Southern Order: Racial Violence and Constitutional Conflict in the Post-Brown South.* Athens: University of Georgia Press, 1987. 387 pages.

Belknap studies the role of the federal government in controlling anti-civil rights violence in the South. Although he feels that the "blatant abdication of responsibility by southern officials forced the Kennedy administration to take dramatic and forceful action" in a few cases, most notably the Freedom Rides and the integration of the University of Mississippi, Belknap claims that these gestures were "temporary departures from a general policy of leaving the problem of racist terrorism to the states." Not until the murders of civil rights workers in 1964 did the federal government begin to attack and prosecute those responsible for anti-civil rights killings. Belknap examines these efforts and concludes that the decline in southern violence after 1965 was not primarily due to federal prosecutions or greater black political strength, but to changing attitudes of white southerners who became more committed to "preserving law and order and to protecting people and ideas they did not like."

658   BERMAN, WILLIAM C. *The Politics of Civil Rights in the Truman Administration.* Columbus: Ohio State University Press, 1970. 261 pages.

Berman examines the treatment of civil rights issues by the Truman administration, both those inherited from Roosevelt (e.g., Fair Employment Practices Committee [FEPC]) and those that Truman himself originated (e.g., military desegregation). He describes Truman as a shrewd politician who used the issue of civil rights "to obtain maximum political benefit for him and his party." He observes that Truman's rhetorical support for civil rights was not always matched by his legislative efforts. He does, however, credit Truman with helping "to move the issue of civil rights into the forefront of American life."

659   BERNSTEIN, BARTON. "The Ambiguous Legacy: The Truman Administration and Civil Rights." In *Politics and Policies of the Truman Administration,* edited by Barton Bernstein, 269–314. Chicago: Quadrangle Books, 1970.

Bernstein assesses Truman's record on civil rights. He concludes that his "efforts fell far short of the promise of American democracy . . . [b]ut his contributions were still significant." He describes Truman on the subject of civil rights as "a reluctant liberal, troubled by terror and eager to establish limited equality."

660   BICKEL, ALEXANDER M. "Civil Rights: The Kennedy Record." *New Republic,* 15 December 1962, 11–16.

Bickel examines the civil rights record of the Kennedy administration's first two years with a focus on desegregation of transportation, voting rights, education, federal grants-in-aid, and appointment of federal judges. He finds that the administration's efforts have consisted almost entirely of executive actions, especially litigation. He gives Kennedy a mixed review, with high marks for his effective desegregation of interstate bus lines and terminals, and lower marks for his handling of school integration and some of his appointments to the federal bench in the South.

661 BRAUER, CARL M. *John F. Kennedy and the Second Reconstruction.* New York: Columbia University Press, 1977. 396 pages.

Brauer traces the civil rights policies, enforcement of civil rights laws, and symbolic gestures of the Kennedy administration. While Brauer acknowledges Kennedy's initial caution concerning civil rights and some errors, such as the appointment of racist judges in the South, he gives Kennedy generally high marks on civil rights. He summarizes Kennedy's record: "He used his executive powers broadly, promoting an end to racial discrimination in voting, schools, the federal government, jobs, public facilities, and housing. He committed the moral authority of the President to racial justice in the most clear cut terms ever. And he proposed and made significant progress toward securing the most important piece of civil rights legislation in a century." Not everyone will agree, however, with Brauer's assessment that "Kennedy's exercise of leadership probably helped instill in many potential civil rights activists a confidence and daring that they would not otherwise have had."

662 BULLOCK, CHARLES S., III, and CHARLES M. LAMB, eds. *Implementation of Civil Rights Policy.* Monterey, CA: Brooks/Cole Publishing Co., 1984. 223 pages.

This book consists of essays by political scientists evaluating the implementation of federal policy in five specific areas: the Voting Rights Act, equal educational opportunity, fair employment laws, racial desegregation in higher education, and equal housing opportunity. In his concluding essay Bullock identifies six variables that help explain the relative success of implementation efforts.

663 BURK, ROBERT F. *The Eisenhower Administration and Black Civil Rights.* Knoxville: University of Tennessee Press, 1984. 287 pages.

Burk discusses the response of the Eisenhower administration to the early stirrings of the civil rights movement, including the *Brown* decision, the Little Rock crisis, and the Civil Rights Acts of 1957 and 1960.

664 DULLES, FOSTER RHEA. *The Civil Rights Commission: 1957–1965.* Ann Arbor: University of Michigan Press, 1968. 274 pages.

The U.S. Civil Rights Commission was created by the Civil Rights Act of 1957 in response to the first stirrings of the civil rights movement. Dulles examines the commission's first seven years and credits it with keeping up a "steady, insistent pressure . . . which gave a substantial basis for transforming the emotional reaction to the (civil rights) demonstrations and protests into remedial measures." It did this, according to Dulles, by gathering facts on the extent of racial discrimination, stimulating action by Congress and the White House, and "serving as the conscience of the nation." Although President Eisenhower and commission members initially viewed its mission as helping to contain the movement, Dulles maintains that it "progressively became a more outspoken champion of civil rights."

665   DURAM, JAMES C. *A Moderate Among Extremists: Dwight D. Eisen-hower and the School Desegregation Crisis.* Chicago: Nelson-Hall Publishers, 1981. 306 pages.

Duram's account of events resulting from the 1954 *Brown* decision is sympathetic toward Eisenhower's handling of the crisis. He argues that Eisenhower tried to negotiate a moderate course between the demands of the extreme segregationists and the extreme integrationists. Eisenhower feared that rapid desegregation would result in widespread confrontation between state and federal authorities. He also was reluctant to take forceful action because of his limited conception of the scope of executive powers. Duram concludes: "We are left with increased respect for the wisdom of Eisenhower's view that the school desegregation issue was a tremendously complex issue, one that raised basic questions about the nature of American society and defied rapid solution."

666   FLEMING, HAROLD C. "The Federal Executive and Civil Rights, 1961–1965." In *The Negro American,* edited by Talcott Parsons and Kenneth B. Clark, 371–400. Boston: Beacon Press, 1965. Orig. pub. in *Daedalus* 94, no. 4 (1965): 921–48.

Fleming offers a detailed analysis of the civil rights policies of the Kennedy administration. He reviews the administrative organization of civil rights responsibilities within the White House, in addition to executive orders on housing and employment, enforcement of civil rights laws, and school desegregation. He maintains that by the time of his assassination Kennedy "had moved from a position of cautious and sparing use of his personal influence for civil rights to a posture of leadership that was bold and unreserved." He credits the civil rights movement with porviding the pressure that caused Kennedy's shift. Fleming concludes: "The federal executive tends to innovate forcefully and effectively only in response to an evident sense of national urgency . . . .The quality of federal civil rights performance, then, depends directly on the ability of Negro Americans to dramatize their cause in such a way that it enlists the support of other influential segments of the society."

667   GOLDEN, HARRY. *Mr. Kennedy and the Negroes.* Cleveland, OH: World Publishing, 1964. 319 pages.

In this laudatory volume Golden compares John Kennedy with Abraham Lincoln as an "emancipator" of blacks. When Kennedy did not move quickly to secure civil rights legislation, Golden invokes the excuse of "political considerations" to justify his caution. He praises Kennedy for setting a "moral tone" favorable to black rights and argues that the main beneficiaries of the civil rights revolution will be white southerners. For a more critical view of Kennedy's civil rights record see Navasky (1971, entry 695).

668   GRAHAM, HUGH DAVIS. *The Civil Rights Era: Origins and Development of National Policy.* New York: Oxford University Press, 1990. 578 pages.

In this massively detailed study of federal civil rights policy during the

Kennedy, Johnson, and Nixon administrations, Graham examines its formulation by the Executive office and its enactment by Congress, but his special focus is on the implementation of policy by federal agencies as shaped by the courts. He distinguishes between Phase I of the civil rights movement with its emphasis on anti-discrimination legislation and Phase II, following 1965, "when the problems and politics of implementation produced a shift of administrative and judicial enforcement from a goal of equal treatment to one of equal results." He sees this change as part of a larger expansion of government regulatory power away from the adjudicatory model employed by older agencies to a "notice-and-comment rule-making" approach used by new regulatory agencies such as EEOC and OFCC.

669　GUTHMAN, EDWIN O. *We Band of Brothers.* New York: Harper & Row, 1971. 399 pages.

Guthman was Robert Kennedy's special assistant in the Justice Department from 1961 to 1965. This volume of personal reminiscences of his years with Kennedy includes two chapters on the civil rights movement. He covers the Freedom Rides, the desegregation of the Universities of Mississippi and Alabama, and the 1963 Birmingham demonstrations.

670　GUTHMAN, EDWIN O., and JEFFREY SHULMAN, eds. 1988. *Robert Kennedy in His Own Words: The Unpublished Recollections of the Kennedy Years.* New York: Bantam Books, 1988. 493 pages.

This book consists of transcripts of interviews with Robert Kennedy on various aspects of the administration of his brother, President John F. Kennedy. Of special interest are three interviews conducted by Anthony Lewis of *The New York Times* during December of 1964. These interviews cover such critical topics as the Freedom Rides, judicial appointments, the FBI and J. Edgar Hoover, desegregation of the Universities of Mississippi and Alabama, the demonstrations in Birmingham, and the 1963 Civil Rights Bill. These interviews provide invaluable insight into the thinking of the Kennedy administration on civil rights.

671　HART, JOHN. "Kennedy, Congress and Civil Rights." *Journal of American Studies* 13, no. 2 (1979): 165–78.

Hart challenges the "revisionist" interpretation of Kennedy's civil rights record. He credits Kennedy with exercising considerable political skill and leadership in overcoming "a complex pattern of opposition" to civil rights in Congress and championing a moderate and pragmatic program that was moving toward passage at the time of his assassination.

672　HARVEY, JAMES C. *Black Civil Rights During the Johnson Administration.* Jackson: College & University Press of Mississippi, 1973. 245 pages.

Harvey reviews federal policy from 1963 to 1969. He includes chapters on the Civil Rights Act of 1964, the Voting Rights Act of 1965, housing, employment, voting, and education. Although he maintains that "more gains were made in desegregating some of America's major institutions during the

Johnson administration than in any previous ones," Harvey faults Johnson for not addressing the needs of the black masses and for his 1965 decision to dismantle the centralized coordination of federal civil rights activities under the vice president.

673   _____. *Civil Rights During the Kennedy Administration.* Hattiesburg: University and College Press of Mississippi, 1971. 87 pages.

In this brief study Harvey evaluates the Kennedy record on civil rights and compares it to the Roosevelt, Truman, and Eisenhower administrations. He cites progress in specific areas such as the appointment of blacks to important posts, ending discrimination in the armed forces, public housing, school desegregation, voting, employment, and government contracts. He finds that Kennedy relied primarily on executive powers such as litigation and negotiation during 1961 and 1962. Harvey sees 1963 as a "turning point," when Kennedy adopted a more aggressive stance on civil rights, due largely to the Birmingham demonstrations. He states in summary: "President Kennedy changed the image of the presidency from a position of seeming neutrality on civil rights as under Eisenhower to one of positive actions on behalf of the frustrated blacks."

674   HENDERSON, THELTON. "The Law and Civil Rights: The Justice Department in the South." In *We Shall Overcome*, edited by David J. Garrow, vol. 2, 407–16. Brooklyn, NY: Carlson Publishing, 1989. Orig. pub. in *New University Thought* 3 (1963): 36–45.

In this interview Henderson, a former attorney for the Justice Department, describes the department's procedures for challenging voter discrimination in the South as well as his observations on SNCC's voter registration efforts in Selma, Alabama.

675   HERBERS, JOHN. *The Lost Priority: What Happened to the Civil Rights Movement in America?* New York: Funk & Wagnalls, 1970. 236 pages.

Herbers covered the civil rights movement for *The New York Times*. He examines events in Washington during the spring and summer of 1965 that, in his opinion, resulted in the loss of faith in the federal government and the rejection of nonviolence by militant blacks. He argues that the escalation of the Vietnam War, the handling of the Moynihan report, the White House conference on civil rights, and the lack of civil rights enforcement "encouraged the trend away from nonviolence." Herbers concludes that as blacks in increasing numbers adopted the tactic of violence, white reaction further widened the gap between the races.

676   HUMPHREY, HUBERT H. *Beyond Civil Rights: A New Day of Equality.* New York: Random House, 1968. 193 pages.

Humphrey describes his own record on civil rights and the accomplishments of the Johnson administration.

677   JOHNSON, LYNDON. "To Fulfill These Rights." In *The Great Society Reader*, edited by Marvin E. Gettleman and David Mermelstein,

251–60. New York: Random House, 1967. Commencement speech delivered at Howard University, 4 June 1965.

This address to Howard University's graduating class of 1965, written by Richard Goodwin and shaped by the ideas of Daniel Patrick Moynihan, calls for the government to "move beyond opportunity to achievement." In it Johnson identifies remaining barriers to racial equality and pledges that his administration will work for their removal.

678   KATZ, MILTON S. "E. Frederick Morrow and Civil Rights in the Eisenhower Administration." *Phylon* 42, no. 2 (1981): 133–44.

Morrow was the only black appointee in the Eisenhower White House. Katz reviews Morrow's six years working for the Eisenhower administration and finds little evidence that he helped advance the cause of civil rights. He concludes that Morrow's positive contribution was that "his presence helped to keep the civil rights issue from being even more ignored than it was."

679   LAWSON, STEVEN F. "Civil Rights." In *Exploring the Johnson Years*, edited by Robert A. Divine, 93–125. Austin: University of Texas Press, 1981.

Lawson reviews Lyndon Johnson's record on civil rights and assesses the civil rights materials contained in the Lyndon B. Johnson Library. He finds the archival holdings impressive, but cautions future researchers not to rely on them exclusively when studying Johnson's civil rights program.

680   _____. "'I Got It from the *New York Times*': Lyndon Johnson and the Kennedy Civil Rights Program." *Journal of Negro History* 67 (Summer 1982): 159–72.

This article includes the transcript of a 1963 phone conversation between Lyndon Johnson and Theodore Sorenson. Johnson gives his candid assessment of the administration's pending civil rights bill and offers his advice on gaining its passage.

681   _____. "Preserving the Second Reconstruction: Enforcement of the Voting Rights Act, 1965–1975." *Southern Studies* 22, no. 1 (1983): 55–75.

Lawson compares the decade of 1965 to 1975 to the Reconstruction era one hundred years earlier. He finds that although black political power in the South has not reached the levels it did during the first Reconstruction, "it is based on a more solid basis of acceptance." Compared to other areas of racial equality, he finds that "black enfranchisement has generated much less bitter conflict." Despite the gains in black political strength, Lawson cautions against "a premature withdrawal of federal supervision."

682   LAWSON, STEVEN F., and MARK I. GELFAND. "Consensus and Civil Rights: Lyndon B. Johnson and the Black Franchise." *Prologue* 8 (Summer 1976): 65–76.

Lawson and Gelfand review Johnson's civil rights record as senator, vice president, and president, but concentrate on the period 1964 to 1965.

While praising Johnson's accomplishments in extending the franchise to southern blacks, they acknowledge that he "did not always respond quickly or adequately" when they "demanded a share in running Democratic party affairs." These two sides of Johnson—"the politician as reformer and the politician as realist"—can be seen in his handling of the MFDP challenge at the 1964 Democratic convention. Although civil rights activists were not satisfied with the proposed compromise, it "strengthened his long-range legislative plans" by gaining the cooperation of powerful southern committee chairs in Congress.

683   LEUCHTENBERG, WILLIAM E. "The White House and Black America: From Eisenhower to Carter." In *Have We Overcome?: Race Relations Since Brown*, edited by Michael V. Namorato, 121–45. Jackson: University Press of Mississippi, 1979.

Leuchtenburg reviews the civil rights records of six presidents. The Eisenhower administration is described as a "misfortune" for blacks. Kennedy is faulted for too much caution in his first two years, but his actions in 1963 are cited as evidence of a deeper commitment to the cause of civil rights. Johnson gets high marks for his civil rights record, especially in his first two years. Nixon is described as having done "little to advance the cause of civil rights, and quite a bit to set it back." Ford and Carter receive scant mention.

684   LICHTMAN, ALLAN. "The Federal Assault against Voting Discrimination in the Deep South, 1957–1967." *Journal of Negro History* 54 (October 1969): 346–67.

Lichtman traces the efforts of the Civil Rights Division of the U.S. Department of Justice from 1957 to 1967 to "eliminate unconstitutional denials of the right to vote." He divides the decade into four periods to correspond to the tenure of the four assistant attorneys general who each supervised the division at the time. He finds that the activities of the Civil Rights Division differed significantly in each period, ranging from very limited involvement from 1957 to 1959, to vigorous enforcement from 1961 to 1964. He also points out that the passage of the Voting Rights Act of 1965 altered the scope of federal activities as the division shifted from litigation to administrative procedures.

685   McCOY, DONALD, and RICHARD T. RUETTEN. *Quest and Response: Minority Rights in the Truman Administration.* Lawrence: University of Kansas Press, 1973. 427 pages.

McCoy and Ruetten review the record of the Truman administration regarding minority rights. They conclude that "by the end of the Truman administration substantial progress" advancing the political and economic status of minorities had been made. The authors state that favorable economic conditions, the application of minority pressure, and greater tolerance of some whites helped make these gains possible. They also claim that the advances of the Truman years laid the foundation for the emergence of the civil rights movement during the Eisenhower and Kennedy administrations.

686 McKNIGHT, GERALD D. "A Harvest of Hate: The FBI's War against Black Youth—Domestic Intelligence in Memphis, Tennessee." In *We Shall Overcome*, edited by David J. Garrow, vol. 2, 657–78. Brooklyn, NY: Carlson Publishing, 1989. Orig. pub. in *South Atlantic Quarterly* 86 (Winter 1987): 1–21.
See entry 445.

687 ———. "The 1968 Memphis Sanitation Strike and the FBI: A Case Study in Urban Surveillance." In *We Shall Overcome*, edited by David J. Garrow, vol. 2, 637–56. Brooklyn, NY: Carlson Publishing, 1989. Orig. pub. in *South Atlantic Quarterly* 83 (Spring 1984): 138–56.
See entry 446.

688 McMILLEN, NEIL R. "Black Enfranchisement in Mississippi: Federal Enforcement and Black Protest in the 1960's." *Journal of Southern History* 43, no. 3 (1977): 351–72. Reprinted in *We Shall Overcome*, edited by David J. Garrow, vol. 2, 679–700. Brooklyn, NY: Carlson Publishing, 1989.
See entry 385.

689 MARSHALL, BURKE. "Federal Protection of Negro Voting Rights." *Law and Contemporary Problems* 27 (Summer 1962): 455–67.
Marshall, assistant attorney general in the Kennedy administration, lists some of the problems encountered by southern blacks attempting to register and vote. He also describes the efforts of Justice Department attorneys to legally challenge these practices using the Civil Rights Acts of 1957 and 1960. Marshall argues that the difficulty in obtaining and enforcing a court order in these cases underscores the limited effectiveness of these acts.

690 ———. *Federalism and Civil Rights*. New York: Columbia University Press, 1964. 85 pages.
This book consists of two lectures delivered by Marshall at Columbia University in 1964, in which he addresses the question of federal involvement in civil rights enforcement. The first lecture deals with voting rights and the second covers the administration of justice. He defends the Justice Department's lack of involvement in cases of blatant abuses by southern law enforcement personnel by falling back on the doctrine of federalism. Since law enforcement is a state responsibility, he argues, the federal government may not intervene unless federal laws or court orders have been violated.

691 MATUSOW, ALLEN J. *The Unraveling of America: A History of Liberalism in the 1960s*. New York: Harper & Row, 1984. 542 pages.
Matusow's history of liberal politics in the 1960s includes two chapters on civil rights. He describes the 1964 Civil Rights Act as "the great liberal achievement of the decade" because it brought the southern segregation system to an end. He finds that by the end of the decade, however, liberal politicians were retreating from the goal of racial justice.

692   MIROFF, BRUCE. "Presidential Leverage over Social Movements: The Johnson White House and Civil Rights." *Journal of Politics* 43 (February 1981): 2–23.

Miroff examines efforts by the Johnson administration to control the course of the civil rights movement. He identifies three objectives: (1) moderating the actions of the movement, (2) managing the appearance of black politics, and (3) shifting the channels of black action toward party politics. He argues that behind-the-scenes moves by the Johnson White House were successful in moderating movement actions, especially during the 1964 presidential election campaign.

693   MORGAN, RUTH P. *The President and Civil Rights: Policy-Making by Executive Order.* New York: St. Martin's Press, 1970. 107 pages.

Morgan examines the use of presidential executive orders for civil rights from 1941 to 1965. She focuses on three areas—the armed forces, fair employment, and fair housing. She concludes that the executive order can be a valuable "safety valve" for dealing with controversial issues "when a policy void exists because of congressional inaction."

694   MORROW, E. FREDERICK. *Black Man in the White House: A Diary of the Eisenhower Years by the Administrative Officer for Special Projects, 1955–1961.* New York: Coward-McCann, 1963. 308 pages.

Morrow recounts his experiences as the top-ranking black in the Eisenhower White House. Included are his observations on Martin Luther King, the Little Rock crisis, and the 1957 Civil Rights Act.

695   NAVASKY, VICTOR. *Kennedy Justice.* New York: Atheneum, 1971. 482 pages.

Navasky offers a critical account of the operation of the Justice Department. Chapter 3 deals with John and Robert Kennedy's handling of the desegregation crisis at Ole Miss. Particularly valuable is a lengthy transcript of telephone conversations between the Kennedys and Governor Ross Barnett of Mississippi at the time of the crisis.

696   O'REILLY, KENNETH. "The FBI and the Civil Rights Movement during the Kennedy Years—from the Freedom Rides to Albany." *Journal of Southern History* 54, no. 2 (1988): 201–32.

O'Reilly provides a detailed description of the FBI's involvement with the civil rights movement from 1961 to 1963. He focuses on the Freedom Rides, especially the mob violence in Birmingham, the murder of Medgar Evers, the bombing of Birmingham's Sixteenth Street Baptist Church, and the federal prosecution of civil rights activists in Albany, Georgia. In each of these cases O'Reilly faults the FBI for failing to protect civil rights workers and for providing assistance to segregationists on local police forces. He also blames the Kennedy administration for its failure to curb the FBI's abuses. O'Reilly expands this research in his *Racial Matters* (1989, see entry 697).

697 ———. *"Racial Matters": The FBI's Secret File on Black America, 1960–1972.* New York: Free Press, 1989. 400 pages.

O'Reilly traces the actions of the FBI toward the civil rights movement and the subsequent black liberation movement. He documents J. Edgar Hoover's personal opposition to racial equality, the bureau's close ties to racist southern lawmen, and its unwillingness to protect civil rights workers. As the decade progressed, the bureau's stance changed from passive inaction to active opposition. He recounts the bureau's campaign of harassing Martin Luther King, Jr. and its infamous COINTELPRO program that resulted in the destruction of the Black Panther party. O'Reilly claims that Hoover decided "to destroy the civil rights movement" following the March on Washington, but he does not blame Hoover alone. He also criticizes presidents Kennedy, Johnson, and Nixon who allowed Hoover to operate without restraint.

698 ORFIELD, GARY. *The Reconstruction of Southern Education: The Schools and the 1964 Civil Rights Act.* New York: John Wiley & Sons, 1969. 376 pages.

Orfield examines the implementation of the school desegregation provisions contained in the 1964 Civil Rights Act. He covers not only the federal bureaucracy charged with carrying out this policy, but also includes two case studies—Chicago and Virginia. He maintains that the desegregation of southern schools "has demanded a historic restructuring of national-state relations and has constituted a fundamental element of an unprecedented peacetime social revolution."

699 PANETTA, LEON. *Bring Us Together: The Nixon Team and the Civil Rights Retreat.* Philadelphia: Lippincott, 1971. 380 pages.

Panetta was director of the Office for Civil Rights in the Department of Health, Education and Welfare during 1969 and 1970. He is highly critical of the Nixon administration's "lack of principle" regarding civil rights in general and school desegregation in particular.

700 PARMENT, HERBERT. *Eisenhower and the American Crusades.* New York: Macmillan Publishing Co., 1972. 660 pages.

Parment's standard biography of Eisenhower contains descriptions of presidential reaction to major civil rights issues during his administration, including the Emmett Till lynching, the Montgomery bus boycott, the *Brown* decision, the 1957 and 1960 Civil Rights Acts, and the Little Rock school desegregation crisis. Parment concludes that Eisenhower's cautious approach to civil rights "only convinced the black leaders that real gains required meeting stiff conservative opposition with bolder means."

701 RUSTIN, BAYARD, and TOM KAHN. "Johnson So Far: Civil Rights." *Commentary* 39 (June 1965): 43–46.

Rustin and Kahn praise Johnson for his speech to Congress calling for voting rights legislation because in it he declared that "the government is an ally of the Negro struggle, even when that struggle assumes unconventional or extra-legal forms." Johnson is credited with presiding over "important shifts in the distribution of political power." To fully deal with the social and economic needs of blacks, however, will require a comprehensive attack on the underlying problem of poverty. They suggest that "rougher political terrain is ahead."

702   SAUNDERS, DORIS E., ed. *The Kennedy Years and the Negro: A Photographic Record.* Chicago: Johnson Publishing, 1964. 143 pages.

Photos of John Kennedy and prominent blacks are included with the texts of presidential statements on civil rights.

703   SMITH, BAXTER. "New Evidence of FBI 'Disruption' Program." *Black Scholar* 6 (July 1975): 43–48.

Smith describes efforts of the FBI to harrass and discredit civil rights organizations and leaders including Robert Williams, Martin Luther King, and Malcolm X.

704   STERN, MARK. "The Democratic Presidency and Voting Rights in the Second Reconstruction." In *Blacks in Southern Politics,* edited by Laurence W. Moreland, Robert P. Steed, and Tod A. Baker, 49–73. New York: Praeger Publishers, 1987.

Stern examines the political concerns and strategic considerations of John F. Kennedy and Lyndon Johnson regarding black civil rights in the context of Democratic party coalition politics. He argues that Kennedy's initial reluctance to take vigorous action on civil rights stemmed from his narrow electoral margin and his dependence on southern congressional leaders. This changed following the Birmingham demonstrations when, according to Stern, "the costs of avoiding the black rights issue became higher than the costs of supporting the issue." No longer able to preserve the New Deal coalition between northern liberals and southern conservatives, first Kennedy and then Johnson decided to enfranchise southern blacks as a replacement for the white southerners who had abandoned the Democratic party.

705   SUNDQUIST, JAMES L. *Politics and Policy: The Eisenhower, Kennedy, and Johnson Years.* Washington, DC: Brookings Institution, 1968. 560 pages.

Equal rights is one of six major political issues covered in this study of the federal government's response to national needs between 1953 and 1966.

706   WALTON, HANES, JR. *When the Marching Stopped: The Politics of Civil Rights Regulatory Agencies.* Albany: State University of New York Press, 1988. 263 pages.

Walton examines the workings of civil rights regulatory agencies established in the wake of the civil rights movement.

707   WHITEHEAD, DON. *Attack on Terror: The FBI against the Ku Klux Klan in Mississippi.* New York: Funk & Wagnalls, 1970. 321 pages.
See entry 423.

708 WOFFORD, HARRIS. *Of Kennedys and Kings: Making Sense of the Sixties.* New York: Farrar, Straus, & Giroux, 1980. 503 pages.

Wofford was a special assistant to John F. Kennedy for civil rights in the 1960 presidential campaign and during the first years of the Kennedy administration. This book contains the definitive account of John Kennedy's fateful phone call to Corretta King during the 1960 presidential campaign and Robert Kennedy's subsequent call to a Georgia judge, which led to Martin Luther King being released from prison. Many political observers say this event was crucial in winning black support for Kennedy and may have decided the election in his favor.

709 WOLK, ALLAN. *The Presidency and Black Civil Rights: Eisenhower to Nixon.* East Rutherford, NJ: Fairleigh Dickinson University Press, 1971. 276 pages.

Wolk examines the civil rights compliance efforts of the federal government from the Eisenhower to Nixon administrations, but most of his attention is directed to the Kennedy and Johnson years. The three agencies that are most closely studied are the Civil Rights Division of the Justice Department; the Department of Health, Education and Welfare; and the Community Relations Service. He finds that the civil rights implementation efforts of each administration varied with the outlook of the president and the conditions that existed during his incumbency. Eisenhower is seen as limited by "his own strict interpretation of his Constitutional duties and by his personal beliefs." Kennedy is portrayed as "stifled by his inability to cope with a recalcitrant Congress." Johnson is seen as more successful because he held an expansive view of presidential powers, enjoyed a broad popular mandate to act, had a more liberal Congress to work with, and was an experienced and skillful politician.

Legislative

710 ANDERSON, J. W. *Eisenhower, Brownell, and the Congress: The Tangled Origins of the Civil Rights Bill of 1956–1957.* Tusculoosa: University of Alabama Press, 1964. 139 pages.
See entry 655.

711 BERMAN, DANIEL M. *A Bill Becomes a Law: Congress Enacts Civil Rights Legislation.* 2d ed. New York: Macmillan Publishing Co., 1966. 146 pages.

Berman relates the legislative histories of the Civil Rights Acts of 1960 and 1964. These acts are then used to illustrate the law-making process in Congress.

712 BURSTEIN, PAUL. *Discrimination, Jobs, and Politics: The Struggle for Equal Employment Opportunity in the United States since the New Deal.* Chicago: University of Chicago Press, 1985. 247 pages.
Burstein traces the evolution of equal employment laws from

Roosevelt's Executive Order 8802 in 1941 to the passage of Equal Employment Opportunity (EEO) legislation in the 1960s. He is especially concerned with the relationship between the actions of civil rights advocates, changes in public opinion, and congressional action. He argues that public opinion supportive of EEO was the "fundamental determinant" of its success, but that the civil rights movement forced members of Congress to pay closer attention to public opinion on this issue. Burstein also claims that by provoking a violent response from southern bigots the movement also increased the public salience of this issue.

713 _____. "Public Opinion, Demonstrations, and the Passage of Anti-Discrimination Legislation." *Public Opinion Quarterly* 43 (Summer 1979): 157–73.

Burstein examines the effect of civil rights demonstrations and changes in public opinion on the passage of civil rights legislation. He concludes that "Congress passes legislation when the proportion of the public supporting a right in principle is well over half—usually two-thirds—and increasing." He feels that the rise in public concern about civil rights followed demonstrations that "helped transform continuing changes in public opinion into support for specific legislation."

714 CATER, DOUGLAS. "How the Senate Passed the Civil Rights Bill." *The Reporter*, 5 September 1957, 9–13.

Cater describes the political infighting that led to the passage of the 1957 Civil Rights Act. He argues that a major reason for the failure to pass a stronger bill was "the animosity that continued to divide those who should have been working together."

715 COFFIN, TRIS. "How Lyndon Johnson Engineered Compromise on Civil Rights Bill." *New Leader*, 5 August 1957, 3–4.

Coffin describes how Lyndon Johnson secured the votes needed to pass the 1957 Civil Rights Bill in the Senate. Among the reasons Johnson worked for a compromise on this bill, according to Coffin, are his "aversion to controversy and conflict" and his belief that the country is "not eager for reforms."

716 COLBY, DAVID C. "The Voting Rights Act and Black Registration in Mississippi." *Publius* 16 (Fall 1986): 123–37.
See entry 331.

717 CONGRESSIONAL QUARTERLY. *Revolution in Civil Rights, 1945–1968.* 4th ed. Washington, DC: Congressional Quarterly, Inc., 1968. 119 pages.
See entry 27.

718 FINDLAY, JAMES F. "Religion and Politics in the Sixties: The Churches and the Civil Rights Act of 1964." *Journal of American History* 77 (June 1990): 69–70.

Findlay describes the organized efforts of the National Council of

Churches to build support for the passage of the 1964 Civil Rights Act. He concentrates on the Council's Commission on Religion and Race and its "Midwest strategy," which was aimed at persuading conservative Republican representatives and senators to vote for the bill and then for cloture. He concludes that their efforts were highly successful, but that this was only a temporary commitment to social activism and within a few years the churches "fell back into traditional ways."

719   FOSTER, LORN S. "The Voting Rights Act: Black Voting and the New Southern Politics." *Western Journal of Black Studies* 7, no. 3 (1983): 120–29.

Foster reviews the enforcement of the Voting Rights Act, especially Section 5, by the Voting Section in the Civil Rights Division of the Department of Justice. He presents data on the number of changes submitted for review, organized by state, year, and type of change. He also presents data on black and white voter registration for eleven southern states from 1960 to 1980. He concludes that Section 5 has "been very effective in expanding Black electoral participation and the number of Black elected officials."

720   HARRIS, ROBERT V. *The Quest for Equality: The Constitution, Congress and the Supreme Court.* Baton Rouge: Louisiana State University Press, 1960. 172 pages.

Harris examines the history of the "equal protection" clause of the Fourteenth Amendment from its origin in the 39th Congress to the *Brown* decision.

721   HART, JOHN. "Kennedy, Congress and Civil Rights." *Journal of American Studies* 13, no. 2 (1979): 165–78.

See entry 671.

722   LAWSON, STEVEN F. *Black Ballots: Voting Rights in the South, 1944–1969.* New York: Columbia University Press, 1976. 474 pages.

Lawson chronicles the struggle for black voting rights, beginning with the NAACP's successful challenge of the white primary and the attempt to repeal the poll tax. He then describes the passage and implementation of voting rights sections in the Civil Rights Acts of 1957, 1960, and 1964 and the Voting Rights Act of 1965. The main emphasis is on Congress, the White House, the Justice Department, and national politics.

723   LOEVY, ROBERT D. *To End All Segregation: The Politics of the Passage of the Civil Rights Act of 1964.* Lanham, MD: University Press of America, 1990. 373 pages.

Loevy chronicles the passage of the 1964 Civil Rights Act, especially the senatorial cloture vote that ended the eighty-three day southern filibuster against the bill. In his opinion, "Everett Dirkson was the key to the cloture vote and final passage of the civil rights bill." He was so powerful, according to Loevy, that backers of the bill had no choice but to give Dirkson "whatever he demanded in return for his support."

724   LYTLE, CLIFFORD M. "The History of the Civil Rights Bill of 1964." *Journal of Negro History* 51 (October, 1966): 275–96.

Lytle examines "some of the major factors which led to the passage of the 1964 Civil Rights Bill." He focuses on two primary features of this struggle: the "dynamic political agitation" of the civil rights movement, which shaped public opinion on the problem of discrimination, and the organizational and procedural tactics used by supporters of civil rights legislation in the House and the Senate.

725   SITKOFF, HARVARD. "The Second Reconstruction." *Wilson Quarterly* 8 (1984): 49–59.

Sitkoff briefly reviews the development of the civil rights movement from the New Deal to Black Power. He views the passage of civil rights legislation as the result of "disciplined, organized pressure . . . by blacks who had grown tired of waiting."

726   STUDENT NONVIOLENT COORDINATING COMMITTEE. "Enforcement of the Educational Provisions of the Civil Rights Act of 1964." In *The Great Society Reader*, edited by Marvin E. Gettleman and David Mermelstein, 294–305. New York: Random House, 1967.

This research report was prepared in 1965 by SNCC staff members Betty Garman and Marion Barry, Jr. It documents the slow pace of compliance with school desegregation provisions of the 1964 Civil Rights Act and criticizes the "freedom of choice" plans submitted by many southern school districts. The strongest criticism, however, is reserved for Commissioner of Education Francis Keppel, for not insisting on stronger enforcement procedures.

727   THERNSTROM, ABIGAIL. "The Odd Evolution of the Voting Rights Act." *Public Interest* 55 (Spring 1979): 49–76.

Thernstrom claims that since its passage in 1965 the Voting Rights Act has been reinterpreted as a guarantee of maximum political effectiveness for black voters, not merely as a means of providing equal electoral opportunity. This, she argues, was not the intent of Congress when the bill was originally passed. She traces a series of court decisions and Justice Department policies that have expanded the act's original scope. She expounds these views in more detail in *Whose Votes Count?* (1987, see entry 728). For an opposing point of view see Frank Parker's *Black Votes Count* (1990, entry 398).

728   _____. *Whose Votes Count? Affirmative Action and Minority Voting Rights*. Cambridge: Harvard University Press, 1987. 316 pages.

Thernstrom advances the critique of the implementation of the 1965 Voting Rights Act that she began in her 1979 *Public Interest* article. She incorporates extensive research on judicial opinions, congressional debate, and Justice Department actions. Support for these policies has continued under Republican administrations, she argues, because Republican candidates often benefit from the consolidation of black voting strength into predominately black districts. As a result, liberal white Democrats are victimized when they loose crucial black support.

729 THOMPSON, KENNETH H. *The Voting Rights Act and Black Electoral Participation.* Washington, DC: Joint Center for Political Studies, 1982. 45 pages.

Thompson addresses two questions: (1) the impact of the Voting Rights Act on black electoral participation and (2) the likely impact of the act during the 1980s.

730 WATSON, DENTON L. *Lion in the Lobby: Clarence Mitchell, Jr.'s Struggle for the Passage of the Civil Rights Laws.* New York: William Morrow & Co., 1990. 846 pages.

See entry 630.

731 WHALEN, CHARLES, and BARBARA WHALEN. *The Longest Debate: A Legislative History of the 1964 Civil Rights Act.* Cabin John, MD: Seven Locks Press, 1985. 289 pages.

The authors follow the Civil Rights Act of 1964 from its introduction into the House to its eventual passage by the Senate. They identify five forces that accounted for its adoption: (1) blacks decided it was time for effective civil rights legislation, (2) protest was becoming widespread, (3) the excesses of opponents helped the cause of the protestors, (4) civil rights leaders exploited these excesses to attract support to their cause, and (5) the Leadership Conference on Civil Rights framed the debate in moral terms and activated religious leaders to support the bill. The authors also describe the strategies of the principal actors in this drama, including Lyndon Johnson, who limited his personal involvement; Richard Russell, who was unable to muster the necessary nonsouthern votes to defeat cloture; and Everett Dirksen, whose support was critical to the bill's passage.

732 WOODWARD, C. VANN. "The Great Civil Rights Debate." *Commentary* (October 1957): 285–95.

Woodward sees the imaginary ghost of Thaddeus Stevens in the Senate chamber during the debate on the 1957 Civil Rights Act. He points out in this article many parallels between the issues being debated in 1957and those that surfaced during Reconstruction.

Legal/Judicial

733 AMAKER, NORMAN C. "De Facto Leadership and the Civil Rights Movement: Perspective on the Problems and Role of Activists and Lawyers in Legal and Social Change." In *We Shall Overcome*, edited by David J. Garrow, vol. 1, 1–54. Brooklyn, NY: Carlson Publishing, 1989. Orig. pub. in *Southern University Law Review* 6 (Spring 1980): 225–78.

Based on his experience representing Martin Luther King, Jr. and other leaders of the Birmingham and Selma movements, Amaker examines the relationship between leaders of social movements and their lawyers. He provides examples of ways in which the law was used both to thwart the civil rights movement and to help it attain its goals. He also discusses the ways in which demonstrations helped shape civil rights legislation.

734 BARDOLPH, RICHARD A., ed. *The Civil Rights Record: Black Americans and the Law, 1840–1970.* New York: Thomas Y. Crowell, 1970. 558 pages.
See entry 117.

735 BARKAN, STEVEN. "Legal Control of the Southern Civil Rights Movement." *American Sociological Review* 49 (August 1984): 552–65.
Barkan examines the white response to civil rights protests in five southern communities. He finds that a violent response by local authorities generated widespread sympathy and federal intervention that enabled civil rights forces to succeed. Where white resistance was "legalistic," that is, "eschewing violence in favor of frequent questionable arrests, high bail, court proceedings lacking due process, and injunctions without legal foundation," the local movements were often defeated.

736 _____. *Protestors on Trial: Criminal Justice in the Southern Civil Rights and Vietnam Antiwar Movements.* New Brunswick, NJ: Rutgers University Press. 1985. 198 pages.
Barkan compares the legal treatment of arrested civil rights protestors with opponents of the Vietnam War. He examines the legal controls used against the civil rights movement in Albany, Birmingham, Danville, Selma, and the Mississippi Summer Project. He argues that local authorities were able to use the law to impose major and, in some cases, insurmountable barriers to the movement's success. Only when law enforcement personnel engaged in excessive brutality were the civil rights forces able to overcome the obstacles imposed by white legalism. In comparing the two movements, Barkan concludes that the antiwar movement was better able to use the law to advance its cause than was the civil rights movement.

737 BARROW, DEBORAH J., and THOMAS G. WALKER. *A Court Divided: The Fifth Circuit Court of Appeals and the Politics of Judicial Reform.* New Haven: Yale University Press, 1988. 274 pages.
This case study relates the effort to divide the Fifth Circuit into two smaller jurisdictions. The second chapter describes the increase in civil rights cases coming before the court from 1961 to 1963 and the internal conflicts between liberals who favored integration and those opposed to federal involvement in racial matters. For a more comprehensive study of the Fifth Circuit's record on civil rights see Read and McGough, *Let Them Be Judged* (1978, entry 790).

738 BASS, JACK. *Unlikely Heroes.* New York: Simon & Schuster, 1981. 352 pages.
Bass subtitles his book "The dramatic story of the Southern judges of

the Fifth Circuit who translated the Supreme Court's *Brown* decision into a revolution for social equality." His heroes are Judges Elbert Tuttle, John Minor Wisdom, John Brown, and Richard Rives, who consistently ruled in favor of black civil rights in cases brought before them on the Fifth Circuit Court of Appeals. The villains in the book include Judges Ben Cameron and W. Harold Cox, who tried to use the court to preserve segregation.

739 BELKNAP, MICHAEL R. "The Legal Legacy of Lemuel Penn." *Howard Law Journal* 25 (1982): 457–524.

Belknap credits the 1964 murder of Lemuel Penn by Georgia Klansmen with helping to secure federal protection for civil rights workers. He argues that the Supreme Court's *Guest* decision, which resulted from the federal prosecution of the Klansmen responsible for Penn's death, signaled a willingness "to greatly expand the scope of congressional power in this area." Congress subsequently included Section 245 in the Civil Rights Act of 1968, which imposed penalties on anyone using violence or threats of violence against people seeking to exercise their civil rights.

740 _____. "The Vindication of Burke Marshall: The Southern Legal System and the Anti-Civil Rights Violence of the 1960s." *Emory Law Journal* 33 (Winter 1984): 93–131.

Assistant Attorney General Burke Marshall insisted that the federal government could not take over local law enforcement responsibilities to stop violent attacks on civil rights workers. Belknap examines here the apparent failure of this policy in the early 1960s and its eventual vindication in the mid-1960s. He argues that southern law enforcement agencies began to crack down on anti-civil rights violence and southern juries began to convict those responsible for racial terrorism. This came about, he claims, not due to pressure from the federal government, but because of growing "white concern about the deterioration of law and order."

741 BERGER, MORROE. *Equality By Statute: The Revolution in Civil Rights.* rev. ed. New York: Doubleday, 1967. 253 pages.

Berger's sociological study examines changes in judicial interpretation of civil rights from the 1860s to the 1960s.

742 BERMAN, DANIEL M. *It Is So Ordered: The Supreme Court Rules on School Segregation.* New York: W. W. Norton & Co., 1966. 161 pages.

A brief history of the 1954 *Brown* decision. See Kluger (1975, entry 614) for a more extensive treatment of the same subject.

743 BERRY, MARY F. *Black Resistance, White Law: A History of Constitutional Racism in America.* New York: Appleton-Century Crofts, 1971. 268 pages.

In this history of "constitutionally sanctioned violence against blacks and violent suppression of black resistance," Berry devotes one chapter to the civil rights movement. She uses the cases of the integration of the University of Mississippi and the 1963 Birmingham demonstrations to illustrate how "the Kennedy administration seriously intervened in cases of racial violence."

744   BINION, GAYLE. "The Implementation of Section 5 of the 1965 Voting Rights Act: A Retrospective on the Role of the Courts." *Western Political Quarterly* 32 (June 1979): 154–73.

Binion reviews Supreme Court decisions regarding Section 5 of the 1965 Voting Rights Act, which requires local governments to secure Justice Department approval before changing their electoral systems. She concludes that "it was decisions of the Supreme Court . . . that have made Section 5 an enormously important section of the Voting Rights Act." She notes two exceptions to this generalization: decisions immunizing court-ordered reapportionment plans from review and limiting the attorney general's authority to object to plans submitted by local authorities.

745   BLAND, RENDALL W. *Private Pressure and Public Law: The Legal Career of Justice Thurgood Marshall.* Port Washington, NY: Kennikat Press, 1973. 206 pages.
        See entry 609.

746   BLAUSTEIN, ALBERT P., and CLARENCE CLYDE FERGUSON, JR. *Desegregation and the Law: The Meaning and Effect of the School Segregation Cases.* 2d ed. New York: Vintage Books, 1962. 359 pages.

Blaustein and Ferguson explain the meaning of the school segregation cases, the constitutional questions involved in the *Brown* decision, and the workings of the judicial process.

747   BRAITERMAN, MARVIN. "Harold and the Highwaymen." In *Southern Justice,* edited by Leon Friedman, 88–102. New York: Pantheon Books, 1965.
        See entry 322.

748   BRENNER, JESSE H. "The Case of the Disappearing Docket." In *Southern Justice,* edited by Leon Friedman, 103–6. New York: Pantheon Books, 1965.
        See entry 324.

749   BURNS, HEYWOOD. "The Federal Government and Civil Rights." In *Southern Justice,* edited by Leon Friedman, 228–54. New York: Pantheon Books, 1965.

Burns reviews the involvement of the federal government, especially the Department of Justice, in the civil rights movement and finds its efforts inadequate. Although sympathetic to the limitations of their position, he concludes that the president must use the power of his office to initiate "bold affirmative action necessary to complete the unfinished business of democracy."

750   CHEVIGNY, PAUL G. "A Busy Spring in the Magnolia State." In *Southern Justice,* edited by Leon Friedman, 13–34. New York: Pantheon Books, 1965.
        See entry 329.

751 COLLINS, ROBERT F., NILS R. DOUGLAS, and LOLIS E. ELIE. "Clinton, Louisiana." In *Southern Justice*, edited by Leon Friedman, 112–26. New York: Pantheion Books, 1965.

See entry 307.

752 DURR, CLIFFORD. "Sociology and the Law: A Field Trip to Montgomery, Alabama." In *Southern Justice*, edited by Leon Friedman, 43–56. New York: Pantheon Books, 1965.

See entry 184.

753 ELY, JAMES W. "Negro Demonstrations and the Law: Danville as a Test Case." *Vanderbilt Law Review* 27 (October 1974): 927–68. Reprinted in *We Shall Overcome*, edited by David J. Garrow, vol. 1, 189–230. Brooklyn, NY: Carlson Publishing, 1989.

See entry 455.

754 FINGERHOOD, SHIRLEY. "The Fifth Circuit Court of Appeals." In *Southern Justice*, edited by Leon Friedman, 214–27. New York: Pantheon Books, 1965.

Fingerhood examines the civil rights record of the federal judges on the Fifth Circuit Court of Appeals, which receives cases from Alabama, Mississippi, Louisiana, Texas, Georgia, and Florida. She finds four of the judges to be consistently pro-civil rights, two to be consistently opposed, and three with mixed records. If judges hostile to civil rights came to outnumber "the Four," she fears that "the entire complexion of the civil rights movement may change."

755 FREUND, PAUL A. "The Civil Rights Movement and the Frontiers of Law." In *The Negro American*, edited by Talcott Parsons and Kenneth B. Clark, 363–70. Boston: Beacon Press, 1966.

Freund points out that the civil rights movement has expanded the frontiers of the law "in many sectors that are far broader than the interests of the movement itself." Among the examples he cites are the questions of the meaning of equality and the basis of the duty of obedience to law.

756 FREYER, TONY. *The Little Rock Crisis: A Constitutional Interpretation.* Westport, CT: Greenwood Press, 1984. 186 pages.

See entry 250.

757 FRIEDMAN, LEON. "Federal Courts of the South: Judge Bryan Simpson and his Reluctant Brethren." In *Southern Justice*, edited by Leon Friedman, 187–213. New York: Pantheon Books, 1965.

See entry 262.

758 FRIEDMAN, LEON, ed. *Southern Justice.* New York: Pantheon Books, 1965. 306 pages.

See entry 129.

759 GALPHIN, BRUCE M. "Judge Pye and the Hundred Sit-Ins." *New Republic* 30 May 1964, 8–9.

See entry 283.

760   GRAGLIA, LINO S. *Disaster by Decree: The Supreme Court Decisions on Race and the Schools*. Ithaca, NY: Cornell University Press, 1976. 351 pages.

Graglia examines the effects of the Supreme Court's rulings on school desegregation. While he agrees that the *Brown* decision "could be understood and justified," he disagrees with subsequent decisions which require "compulsory integration." He argues that these rulings were the result of a greatly expanded conception of the court's power and brought no benefit to anyone involved. He is especially adamant in his opposition to busing as a means of achieving racial integration; he describes it as "enormously costly, conferring no known benefit, and inconsistent with the most basic desires of parents to protect and provide for the welfare of their children."

761   GUTMAN, JEREMIAH S. "Oktibbeha County, Mississippi." In *Southern Justice*, edited by Leon Friedman, 80–87. New York: Pantheon Books, 1965.

See entry 353.

762   HAMILTON, CHARLES V. *The Bench and the Ballot: Southern Federal Judges and Black Voting Rights*. New York: Oxford University Press, 1973. 258 pages.

Hamilton examines the enforcement of voting rights legislation in federal courts between 1957 and 1965. He give examples of judicial aggressiveness in three Alabama counties—Macon, Bullock, and Montgomery. He also presents three cases of judicial resistance in Mississippi counties—Forrest, Bolivar, and Jefferson Davis. He concludes: "The federal courts virtually nullified all legal means to deter black voting."

763   _____. "Federal Law and the Courts in the Civil Rights Movement." In *The Civil Rights Movement in America*, edited by Charles W. Eagles, 97–120. Jackson: University Press of Mississippi, 1986.

Hamilton argues that the federal courts played a critical role in attaining the movement's primary goal of eliminating de jure segregation. He states that, because congressional support for civil rights was limited, the movement was forced to turn to the courts, where the Supreme Court and many (but not all) district and circuit judges showed a willingness to interpret the Constitution in their favor. Hamilton claims that the possibility of judicial relief helped sustain the movement and preserved the integrity of the national political system until Congress was willing to take action on its own.

764   _____. "Southern Judges and Negro Voting: The Judicial Approach to the Solution of Controversial Social Problems." *Wisconsin Law Review* 65 (Winter 1965): 71–102.

Hamilton analyzes the performance of southern federal judges in voter registration cases. He uses Judge Johnson of Alabama to illustrate "judicial activism;" Judges Cox, Cameron, and Clayton of Mississippi as examples of "judicial reaction;" and Judge Dawkins of Louisiana to portray "judical gradualism." He concludes that community pressure on federal judges "has not proven to be an insurmountable obstacle." This topic is covered more fully in Hamilton's *The Bench and the Ballot* (1973, see entry 762).

765   HAMMER, RICHARD. "Yankee Lawyers in Mississippi Courts." *Harper's*, November 1966, 79–88.
See entry 359.

766   HARRIS, ROBERT V. *The Quest for Equality: The Constitution, Congress and the Supreme Court.* Baton Rouge: Louisiana State University Press, 1960. 172 pages.
See entry 720.

767   HECK, EDWARD V., and JOSEPH STEWART, JR. "Ensuring Access to Justice: The Role of Interest Group Lawyers in the 60s Campaign for Civil Rights." *Judicature* 66, no. 2 (1982): 84–94.
See entry 362.

768   HENDERSON, THELTON. "The Law and Civil Rights: The Justice Department in the South." In *We Shall Overcome*, edited by David J. Garrow, vol. 2, 407–16. Brooklyn, NY: Carlson Publishing, 1989. Orig. pub. in *New University Thought* 3 (1963): 36–45.
See entry 674.

769   HONNOLD, JOHN. "The Bourgeois Bar and the Mississippi Movement." *American Bar Association Journal* 52 (March 1966): 228–32.
See entry 366.

770   HORWITZ, MORTON J. "The Jurisprudence of *Brown* and the Dilemmas of Liberalism." In *Have We Overcome? Race Relations Since Brown*, edited by Michael V. Namorato, 173–87. Jackson: University Press of Mississippi, 1979.
Horwitz examines the legal philosophy behind the *Brown v. Board of Education* decision.

771   KING, DONALD B., and CHARLES W. QUICK, eds. 1965. *Legal Aspects of the Civil Rights Movement.* Detroit: Wayne State University Press, 1965. 447 pages.
See entry 141.

772   KLUGER, RICHARD. *Simple Justice: The History of Brown v. Board of Education and Black America's Struggle for Equality.* New York: Alfred A. Knopf, 1976. 823 pages.
See entry 614.

773   KUNSTLER, WILLIAM M. *Deep in My Heart.* New York: William Morrow & Co., 1966. 387 pages.
Movement lawyer Kunstler describes his defense of civil rights workers in many of the major campaigns in the Deep South beginning with the Freedom Rides of 1961 and including the protests in Albany, Georgia; Bir-

mingham, Alabama; Danville, Virginia; St. Augustine, Florida; and the Mississippi Summer Project of 1964.

774   LOMAX, LOUIS E. "What Mass Protests Can't Do." *Saturday Review,* 6 July 1963, 11–12.

Lomax emphasizes that despite the shift within the civil rights movement from legal cases to mass demonstrations, "there is a continuing and increasing need for legalism in civil rights actions."

775   LUSKY, LOUIS. "Justice with a Southern Accent: Do Our Federal Courts Need Emancipating?" *Harper's,* March 1964, 69–77.

Through a review of the handling of civil rights cases, Lusky finds the lower federal courts ineffective in protecting civil rights activists. He uses the 1961 arrest of 315 Freedom Riders in Jackson, Mississippi, to illustrate how local officials have been able to use the courts to thwart the legal rights of civil rights protestors. He concludes that the "courts are not doing the job for which they were established" and recommends that the president, Congress, and the Supreme Court "provide them with the support they so desperately need."

776   McCORD, JOHN H., ed. *With All Deliberate Speed: Civil Rights Theory and Reality.* Urbana: University of Illinois Press, 1969. 205 pages.
See entry 144.

777   McNEIL, GENNA RAE. *Groundwork: Charles Hamilton Houston and the Struggle for Civil Rights.* Philadelphia: University of Pennsylvania Press, 1983. 308 pages.
See entry 617.

778   MARSHALL, BURKE. *Federalism and Civil Rights.* New York: Columbia University Press, 1964. 85 pages.
See entry 690.

779   ———. "The Pattern of Southern Disfranchisement of Negroes." In *Freedom Now! The Civil Rights Struggle in America,* edited by Alan F. Westin, 95–103. New York: Basic Books, 1964. Orig. pub. in *Law and Contemporary Problems* 27 (Summer 1963): 455–76.

Marshall, head of the Justice Department's Civil Rights Division, describes here a variety of techinques used in southern states to prevent blacks from registering and voting.

780   ———. "The Protest Movement and the Law." In *We Shall Overcome,* edited by David J. Garrow, vol. 2, 701–19. Brooklyn, NY: Carlson Publishing, 1989. Orig. pub. in *Virginia Law Review* 51 (June 1965): 785–803.

Marshall discusses the problems of law enforcement created by the use of civil disobedience in the civil rights movement. He questions how society can support or tolerate a movement "which relies on genuine disobedience to law for its source of energy, and on the threat of violence alone to induce social change."

781 MELTSNER, MICHAEL. "Southern Appelate Courts: A Dead End." In *Southern Justice*, edited by Leon Friedman, 136–54. New York: Pantheon Books, 1965.

Meltsner reviews the disposition of civil rights cases in southern state courts. He concludes: "Negro rights will continue to remain abstract and unrealized until federal courts develop workable techniques for prompt and effective control of southern state courts."

782 MILLER, LOREN. *The Petitioners: The Story of the Supreme Court of the United States and the Negro.* New York: Pantheon Books, 1966. 461 pages.

The last 100 pages of this comprehensive review of Supreme Court cases relating to black civil rights covers the period from the *Brown* decision to the passage of the 1964 Civil Rights Act. Miller deals with legal challenges to segregation in transportation and public accommodations, as well as with the legality of sit-in demonstrations and the attempts to outlaw the NAACP. This book is well written and free of legal jargon.

783 MORGAN, CHARLES, JR. *One Man, One Voice.* New York: Holt, Rinehart and Winston, 1979. 348 pages.
See entry 217.

784 _____. "Segregated Justice." In *Southern Justice*, edited by Leon Friedman, 155–64. New York: Pantheon Books, 1965.

Morgan explains how jury selection practices that exclude blacks from serving on juries helps to perpetuate racial inequality in the legal system.

785 MURRAY, PAULI. "Protest against the Legal Status of the Negro." *Annals of the American Academy of Political and Social Science* 357 (1965): 55–64.

Murray sees the civil rights movement as the culmination of a long tradition of protest. She attributes the rise of the movement to a changing self-image of African Americans and a redefinition of their constitutional rights by the Supreme Court. According to Murray, the growth of militant protests can be attributed to the "failure of legal process in parts of the South to facilitate these changes."

786 OPPENHEIM, JACK. "The Abdication of the Southern Bar." In *Southern Justice*, edited by Leon Friedman, 127–35. New York: Pantheon Books, 1965.
See entry 397.

787 PARKER, FRANK R. *Black Votes Count: Political Empowerment in Mississippi After 1965.* Chapel Hill: University of North Carolina Press, 1990. 254 pages.
See entry 398.

788 PELTASON, JACK W. *Fifty-Eight Lonely Men: Southern Federal Judges and School Desegregation.* New York: Harcourt, Brace and World, 1961. 270 pages.

Peltason examines the role of federal district judges in the struggle for school desegregation in the South. He finds that "many southern federal district judges had permitted the evasion" of enforcing the Supreme Court's *Brown* decision. He concludes that these judges need "rigid mandates that compel them to act." He blames the Supreme Court for delegating too much discretion to the district judges, who are vulnerable to local political pressure.

789 POLLITT, DANIEL H. "Dime Store Demonstrations : Events and Legal Problems of First Sixty Days." *Duke Law Journal* 10 (Summer 1960): 315–65.

Pollitt reviews the first two months of sit-in activity in ten southern states. He considers the legality of four measures used against the civil rights demonstrators: (1) charges of violating anti-trust laws, (2) charges of creating a breach of peace, (3) expulsions from school, and (4) charges of trespassing. In each case he finds that the application of sanctions against the sit-in demonstrators "wrongfully deprives them of fundamental rights of citizenship protected by federal statute and constitutional amendment."

790 READ, FRANK T., and LUCY S. McGOUGH. *Let Them Be Judged: The Judicial Integration of the Deep South.* Metuchen, NJ: Scarecrow Press, 1978. 658 pages.

Read and McGough examine the Fifth Circuit Court of Appeals and its rulings on civil rights between 1954 and 1971. Because the court heard appeals from the six Deep South states, its rulings on jury selection, on voting rights, and, most importantly, on school desegregation, had a major impact on the advance of black rights in the South. Perhaps no other federal court experienced such violent differences of opinion among its members than the Fifth Circuit, which included dedicated integrationists like John Minor Wisdom and Richard T. Rives, and die-hard segregationists such as William Harold Cox and Benjamin F. Cameron.

791 RODGERS, HARRELL R., JR., and CHARLES S. BULLOCK III. *Law and Social Change: Civil Rights Laws and Their Consequences.* New York: McGraw-Hill, 1972. 230 pages.

Rodgers and Bullock investigate the implementation of civil rights laws in five areas: voting, public accommodations, school desegregation, employment, and housing. They conclude that change has been "basically inadequate . . . very difficult to produce and very slow in coming." According to the authors, the main reason for this inadequate response is because Congress and the executive branch "take no action they do not have to take and respond only incrementally when they do act."

792 SCHULMAN, ROBERT P. "Clarksdale Customs." In *Southern Justice*, edited by Leon Friedman, 107–11. New York: Pantheon Books, 1965.
See entry 408.

793 SILVERMAN, CORINNE. *The Little Rock Story.* Inter-University Case Program. Tuscaloosa: University of Alabama Press, 1959. 38 pages.

This case study of the Little Rock school desegregation crisis of 1957 to 1959 focuses primarily on the legal and constitutional question of federalism.

794 STERN, GERALD M. "Judge William Harold Cox and the Right to Vote in Clarke County, Mississippi." In *Southern Justice,* edited by Leon Friedman, 165–86. New York: Pantheon Books, 1965.
See entry 413.

795 STEWART, Joseph, JR., and JAMES F. SHEFFIELD, JR. "Does Interest Group Litigation Matter? The Case of Black Political Mobilization in Mississippi." *Journal of Politics* 49 (August 1987): 780–98.
See entry 414.

796 STRONG, DONALD S. *Negroes, Ballots, and Judges.* Tuscaloosa: University of Alabama Press, 1968. 100 pages.

Strong examines voting rights litigation in federal courts in Louisiana, Mississippi, and Alabama from 1957 to 1965. Because of the difficulty of legally defining what constitutes discrimination against black voters and the problems of enforcement, Strong concludes that the "effort to enforce the Fifteenth Amendment by means of the judiciary was not a success story, at least not when compared with the results produced by the Voting Rights Act of 1965."

797 TEACHOUT, PETER R. "Louisiana under Law." In *Southern Justice,* edited by Leon Friedman, 57–79. New York: Pantheon Books, 1965.
See entry 315.

798 TUSHNET, MARK V. *The NAACP's Legal Strategy against Segregated Education. 1925–1950.* Chapel Hill: University of North Carolina Press, 1987. 222 pages.
See entry 629.

799 WILKINSON, J. HARVIE. *From Brown to Bakke: The Supreme Court and School Integration, 1954–1978.* New York: Oxford University Press, 1979. 368 pages.

Wilkinson reviews major Supreme Court decisions relating to school desegregation, beginning with the 1954 *Brown* case and covering the *Brown* II decision, the school busing controversy, desegregation in northern cities, and the *Bakke* decision.

800 WILSON, JAMES B. "Municipal Ordinances, Mississippi Style." In *Southern Justice,* edited by Leon Friedman, 35–42. New York: Pantheon Books, 1965.
See entry 424.

801 YARBROUGH, TINSLEY E. *Judge Frank Johnson and Human Rights in Alabama.* Tuscaloosa: University of Alabama Press, 1981. 270 pages.

Frank M. Johnson was appointed to the U.S. District Court for the Middle District of Alabama by President Eisenhower in 1955. He had been on the bench less than a year when he ruled that Montgomery's bus segregation ordinance was unconstitutional. For the next two decades Johnson remained in the public spotlight as he helped dismantle Alabama's system of racial discrimination. For his efforts, "he and his family were subjected to ostracism, threats, violence, and vitriolic editorial and verbal abuse." Yarbrough traces Johnson's career through 1978, paying special attention to his running battle with George Wallace, his law school classmate and former friend.

802   _____. *A Passion for Justice: J. Waties Waring and Civil Rights.* New
         York: Oxford University Press, 1987. 282 pages.
      See entry 499.

7

Participants in the Movement

Participants

803 BELL, INGE POWELL. "Status Discrepancy and the Radical Rejection of Nonviolence." *Sociological Inquiry* 38 (1968): 51–63.
See entry 577.

804 COLES, ROBERT. "Serpents and Doves: Non-violent Youth in the South." In *Youth: Change and Challenge*, edited by Erik H. Erikson, 188–216. New York: Basic Books, 1963.
Coles describes the psychological adjustment of civil rights workers who must cope with constant danger in the Deep South. He offers in-depth portraits of several black and white volunteers.

805 _____. "Social Struggle and Weariness." *Psychiatry* 27 (November 1964): 305 15.
See entry 510.

806 COLES, ROBERT, and JOSEPH BRENNER. "American Youth in a Social Struggle: The Mississippi Summer Project. *American Journal of Orthopsychiatry* 35 (October 1965): 907–26.
See entry 333.

807 FENDRICH, JAMES M. "Activists Ten Years Later: A Test of Generational Unit Continuity." *Journal of Social Issues* 30 (1974): 95–118.
Fendrich compares the political attitudes and behaviors of former civil rights activists, student government leaders, and nonpolitical students. He finds that the activists are concentrated more in knowledge and human services occupations, belong in higher numbers to change-oriented voluntary organizations, and participate to a greater degree in institutional and noninstitutional politics.

808   _____. "Black and White Activists Ten Years Later: Political Socialization and Adult Left-Wing Politics." *Youth & Society* 8, no. 1 (1976):
81–104.

Fendrich reports the results of his ten-year follow-up on black and
white student civil rights activists. He finds that participation in "confrontation politics was a radicalizing experience for whites," but not for the former
black student protestors.

809   _____. "Keeping the Faith or Pursuing the Good Life: A Study of the
Consequences of Participation in the Civil Rights Movement." *American Sociological Review* 42, no. 1 (1977): 144–57.

Fendrich measures the political attitudes of black and white former
civil rights activists and finds the whites to be more radical in their views.
He argues that the white activists were motivated more by ideological
values while the black activists were motivated by personal and collective gain.

810   FENDRICH, JAMES M., and ELLIS S. KRAUSS. "Student Activism and Adult
Left-Wing Politics: A Causal Model of Political Socialization for Black,
White, and Japanese Students of the 1960's Generation." In *Research
in Social Movements, Conflict and Change,* edited by Lewis
Kriesberg, vol. 1, 231–55. Greenwich, CT: JAI Press, 1978.

Fendrich and Krauss analyze the long-term consequences of participation in student protest using three sample groups: black and white college
students active in the civil rights movement, and Japanese student activists.
They report that the white and Japanese former activists remain more committed to "radical left-wing principles," while the politically active blacks
are more likely to folow a "liberal reformist ideology."

811   FENDRICH, JAMES M., and KENNETH M. LOVOY. "Back to the Future:
Adult Political Behavior of Former Student Activists." *American Sociological Review* 52 (December 1988): 780–84.

Fendrich and Lovoy compare former civil rights activists with former
student government leaders and uninvolved students twenty-five years after
they left college. They report that the former civil rights activists remain very
much involved in a variety of political behaviors with a strong liberal-radical
orientation.

812   FENDRICH, JAMES M., and CHARLES U. SMITH. "Florida A & M Civil Rights
Activists: A Partial Legacy." In *The Civil Rights Movement in Florida
and the United States,* edited by Charles U. Smith, 292–310.
Tallahassee, FL: Father & Son Press, 1989.

Fendrich and Smith examine the adult political attitudes and protest
behavior of former Florida A & M students. Former student activists are
found to have higher social statuses, more graduate education, and also
found to be more involved in protest activities.

813 FENDRICH, JAMES M, and ALLISON T. TARLEAU. "Marching to a Different Drummer: Occupational and Political Correlates of Former Student Activists." *Social Forces* 53 (December 1973): 245–52.

Fendrich and Tarleau compare the occupational statuses and political attitudes of a sample of former student civil rights activists from Florida State University, with a control group of former student government leaders. The former civil rights activists are seen as much more likely to be employed in public sector jobs and as leaning further to the left in their political orientation.

814 FERNANDEZ, ROBERTO M., and DOUG MCADAM. 1987. "Multi-Organizational Fields and Recruitment to Social Movements." In *Organizing for Social Change: Social Movement Organizations Across Cultures*, edited by Bert Klandermas, 315–43. Greenwich, CT: JAI Press, 1987. See entry 345.

815 FISHMAN, JACOB R., and FREDERIC SOLOMON. "Youth and Social Action: Perspectives on the Student Sit-In Movement." *American Journal of Orthopsychiatry* 33 (1963): 872–82.

Fishman and Solomon describe the psychological processes they observed in interviews with twenty young people involved in the sit-in movement. They view the sit-ins as a means to "channel aggression into a positive identification with the traditional ego-ideal of the white majority." At the same time, they see the sit-ins as a way to act out "early childhood frustrations and parental conflicts and wishes." They term this behavior "prosocial acting out."

816 GESCHWENDER, BARBARA, and JAMES A. GESCHWENDER. "Relative Deprivation and Participation in the Civil Rights Movement." *Social Science Quarterly* 54 (1973): 403–11.

The Geschwenders distinguish three types of relative deprivation: aspirational deprivation, progressive deprivation, and reference group deprivation. Using data on participation in the civil rights movement gathered from black college students, they report here that the participants "derived their discontent from the perception of black aspirational deprivation" and "derived their hope from the experience of relative success in their own lives."

817 MEIER, AUGUST. "Who Are the 'True Believers'?—A Tentative Typology of the Motivations of Civil Rights Activists." In *Protest, Reform, and Revolt*, edited by Joseph R. Gusfield, 473–82. New York: John Wiley & Sons, 1970.

Meier offers his observations on the social characteristics of black and white activists in the civil rights movement. He maintains that the movement "draws different social types among Negroes and whites." Meier reports that the blacks are more likely to be upwardly-mobile people of working class origins. The whites, he believes, are more likely to be intellectuals from leading colleges and upper middle class backgrounds. Meier contends that this social class difference may help explain the racial tensions within the movement that surfaced in 1965.

818   ORBELL, JOHN M. "Protest Participation among Southern Negro College Students." In *The Black Revolt*, edited by James A. Geschwender, 158–71. Englewood Cliffs, NJ: Prentice Hall Press, 1971. Orig. pub. in *American Political Science Review* 61 (June 1967): 446–56.

Orbell presents his analysis of data gathered from 264 southern black college students interviewed in 1962. He reports that protest activity is greater among students attending high quality colleges located in urban counties. He also states that protest is more frequent among students from higher income families and among those who perceive group rather than individual deprivation.

819   ORUM, ANTHONY M. *Black Students in Protest: A Study of the Origins of the Black Student Movement.* Washington, DC: American Sociological Association, 1972. 89 pages.

Orum studied the characteristics of southern black college students involved in the sit-in protests. He reports here that the protestors did not differ from other students with respect to social class variables, although the activists were more involved "in campus life and committed to bringing about innovation." He also states that in the communities in which the sit-ins first occurred, blacks were "a fairly small and relatively prosperous proportion of the population."

820   ORUM, ANTHONY M., and AMY W. ORUM. "The Class and Status Bases of Negro Student Protest." *Social Science Quarterly* 49, no. 3 (1968): 521–33.

The Orums examine three hypotheses advanced to explain "the participation of Negro college students in the Negro protest movement." They find that neither the "vulgar Marxist," nor the "rising expectations," nor the "relative deprivation" hypothesis offers a satisfactory explanation of the growth of the civil rights movement.

821   PINARD, MAURICE, JEROME KIRK, and DONALD VON ESCHEN. "Processes of Recruitment in the Sit-In Movement." *Public Opinion Quarterly* 33 (Fall 1969): 355–69.
See entry 599.

822   SEARLES, RUTH, and J. ALLEN WILLIAMS, JR. "Negro College Students: Participation in Sit-Ins." *Social Forces* 40 (March 1962): 215–20.

Searles and Williams report their analysis of questionnaires completed by 827 students at three black colleges in North Carolina. They find that those who are active in the sit-in movement are not alienated or disaffected from American society. The authors conclude that students involved in the protests are more optimistic about the extent of public support for their objectives, and express less anti-white sentiment than those not active in the movement.

823 SMITH, CHARLES U. "The Sit-Ins and the New Negro Student." *Journal of Intergroup Relations* 2 (1961): 223–29. Reprinted in *American Race Relations Today*, edited by Earl Raab, 69–75. Garden City, NY: Anchor Books, 1962.
See entry 273.

824 SOLOMON, FREDERIC, and JACOB R. FISHMAN. "The Psychosocial Meaning of Nonviolence in the Student Civil Rights Activities." *Psychiatry* 27, no. 2 (1964): 91–99.
Solomon and Fishman "delineate the psychosocial dimensions of five leading features of nonviolence" based on their interviews with nineteen experienced black civil rights workers. The five dimensions they identify are: (1) prohibition of violence, (2) overt display of fearlessness and dignity, (3) show of friendliness toward opponents, (4) awareness of the potential for national and international publicity, and (5) the sense of inevitability about the progress of desegregation.

825 _____. "Youth and Social Action: II. Action Identity Formation in the First Student Sit-In Demonstration." *Journal of Social Issues* 29, no. 2 (1964): 36–47.
Solomon and Fishman present a psychological case history of one student involved in the original sit-in in Greensboro, North Carolina. They describe his behavior as a "pro-social acting out"—risk-taking behavior that has its origin in "shame, anger and self-deprecating depression," but that results in a socially constructive outcome.

826 SURACE, SAMUEL J., and MELVIN SEEMAN. "Some Correlates of Civil Rights Activism." *Social Forces* 46 (1967): 197–207.
Surace and Seeman report here the results of a study of students in evening extension courses and of civil service personnel. They find that the variables of previous interracial contact, absence of powerlessness, and lack of conformity help explain support of civil rights for white respondents but not for blacks. It should be noted that very few of the 300 respondents reported any participation in civil rights activities.

Whites in the Movement

827 AIKEN, MICHAEL, N. J. DEMERATH III, and GERALD MARWELL. "Conscience and Confrontation." *New South* 21 (Spring 1966): 19–28.
See entry 551.

828 BLUMBERG, RHODA L. "Careers of Women Civil Rights Activists." *Journal of Sociology and Social Welfare* 7 (1980): 708–29.
See entry 471.

829 _____. "White Mothers in the American Civil Rights Movement." In *Research in the Interweave of Social Roles: Women and Men*, edited by Helena A. Lopata, vol. 1, 33–50. Greenwich, CT: JAI Press, 1980.
See entry 472.

830 DEMERATH, N. J., III, GERALD MARWELL, and MICHAEL T. AIKEN. "Criteria and Contingencies of Success in a Radical Political Movement." *Journal of Social Issues* 27, no. 1 (1971): 63–80.
This study examines 166 white summer volunteers who worked for SCLC in various southern communities during the summer of 1965. It examines the subjects' personal sense of satisfaction with their efforts and finds that it is related to the project's ability to build community organizations, the degree of project cohesiveness, and the extent of personal fulfillment. The authors also discuss the differences between the "sympathetic" activism of outside volunteers and the "self-interested" activism of local residents. The full report of this study is contained in *The Dynamics of Idealism*, by the same authors (1971, see entry 831).

831 _____. *Dynamics of Idealism: White Activists in a Black Movement*. San Francisco: Jossey-Bass, 1971. 228 pages.
Demerath et al. studied 300 volunteers who spent two and a half months working on voter registration projects for SCLC in six southern states in the summer of 1965. Participants completed questionnaires at the beginning and conclusion of the project and a small sample was interviewed four years later. They report here that the summer's experience resulted in relatively little "radicalization in a revolutionary direction" among the volunteers. More significant, the authors feel, was their "diffusion of concern"—an increase in the perceived importance of social problems other than civil rights, i.e., the war in Vietnam, nuclear disarmament, and poverty.

832 LEVY, CHARLES J. *Voluntary Servitude: Whites in the Negro Movement*. New York: Appleton-Century Crofts, 1968. 125 pages.
This is an impressionistic account of "what happens when members of a dominant group seek membership in a dominated group." It is based on Levy's four years of "unstructured participant observation" at a southern black college and in a civil rights organization. He describes four stages through which whites pass when trying to gain acceptance by blacks. Levy concludes that the pervasive mistrust between the races makes it impossible for whites to ever be fully accepted by blacks.

833 MCADAM, DOUG. *Freedom Summer*. New York: Oxford University Press, 1988. 322 pages.
See entry 382.

834 _____. "Recruitment to High Risk Activism: The Case of Freedom Summer." *American Journal of Sociology* 92, no. 1 (1986): 64–90.
See entry 383.

835 MCADAM, DOUG, and ROBERTO M. FERNANDEZ. "Microstructural Bases of Recruitment to Social Movements." In *Research in Social Movements, Conflicts and Change,* edited by Louis Kriesberg, vol. 12, 1–33. Greenwich, CT: JAI Press, 1990.

McAdam and Fernandez studied the recruitment of student volunteers for the 1964 Mississippi Summer Project at the University of California in Berkeley and at the University of Wisconsin in Madison. They concentrated on the relationships among volunteers to determine whether or not an "I'll go if you go" pattern prevailed. They report here that the dynamics of recruitment differed at the two schools due to, they speculate, the absence of a tradition of strong civil rights activism at the University of Wisconsin.

836 MARWELL, GERALD, MICHAEL T. AIKEN, and N. J. DEMERATH III. "The Persistence of Political Attitudes among 1960's Civil Rights Activists." *Public Opinion Quarterly* 51 (1987): 359–75.

Marwell et al. present a follow-up on the white civil rights activists first studied twenty years earlier in *The Dynamics of Idealism* (1971, see entry 831). They report that the activists hold liberal positions on a wide variety of political topics and that "their overall pattern of response . . . is basically stable."

837 MARX, GARY T., and MICHAEL USEEM. "Majority Involvement in Minority Movements: Civil Rights, Abolition, Untouchability." *Journal of Social Issues* 27, no. 1 (1971): 81–104.

Marx and Useem compare the role of majority group participants in three movements that sought to improve the status of minority group members. They identify three common sources of tension between minority and majority group participants in these movements: (1) minority group acitivists viewed themselves as more radical and committed to the cause than majority activists, (2) majority group members tended to assume a disproportionate number of decision-making positions, and (3) some movement members carried prejudices and hostilities toward members of other groups. They also point out that outsiders frequently played essential roles in the early phases of these movements, but as the movements continued, pressures developed to reduce the involvement of majority group members.

838 PINKNEY, ALPHONSO. *The Committed: White Activists in the Civil Rights Movement.* New Haven: College and University Press, 1968. 239 pages.

Pinkney analyzed questionnaires from 176 whites active in the civil rights movement during 1963 and 1964, and conducted thirty-three in-depth interviews. He examined sociological background characteristics, personality characteristics, extent of civil rights involvement, social supports for actions, motivations for participation, hardships encountered, and general attitudes about civil rights. He reports here that the white activists shared "a sense of estrangement from the values of the larger society" and a determination to bring social practices "in line with principles."

839   POUSSAINT, ALVIN F. "Problems of White Civil Rights Workers in the
        South." *Psychiatric Opinion* 3 (December 1966): 18–24.

Poussaint analyzes the stresses encountered by white civil rights workers in the South. He notes that complete rejection by southern whites was
anticipated, "but few white workers were prepared for the little-suspected
difficulties they would encounter as white people living in the black community." He goes on to describe some of the sources of black-white conflict
including the "White African Queen Complex" and the "Tarzan Complex."

840   _____. "The Stresses of the White Female Worker in the Civil Rights
        Movement in the South." *American Journal of Psychiatry* 123, no. 4
        (1966): 401–7.

Poussaint focuses on white female volunteers in the movement and
examines the psychological pressures they face while living and working in
the black community. White women, he points out, frequently become the
focus for black anger. He claims that many white females contribute to their
own difficulties due to the "White African Queen Complex"—"a tabooed
and repressed fantasy of the intelligent, brave, and beautiful white woman
leading the poor, downtrodden, and oppressed black man to freedom and
salvation."

841   ROTHSCHILD, MARY AICKIN. *A Case of Black and White: Northern Vol-
        unteers and the Southern Freedom Summers, 1964–1965.* Westport,
        CT: Greenwood Press, 1982. 213 pages.
        See entry 402.

842   _____. "White Women Volunteers in the Freedom Summers: Their Life
        and Work in a Movement for Social Change." *Feminist Studies* 5, no.
        3 (1979): 466–95.

Rothschild examines the backgrounds and experiences of 650 white
women who volunteered to work with SNCC and SCLC in the summers of
1964 and l965. She focuses on the institutional sexism the women encountered and finds that "job assignments and responsibilities were clearly sex-
role stereotyped." In addition, she points out that white women were sexu-
ally "tested" by black males. She finds it ironic that while they were working
for racial equality, most Freedom Summer participants "never questioned
the unequal status of men and women."

Women in the Movement

843   BAKER, ELLA. "Developing Community Leadership." In *Black Women
        in White America: A Documentary History*, edited by Gerda Lerner,
        345–52. New York: Vintage Books, 1973.

In this 1970 interview Baker covers her career in the civil rights movement working for the NAACP in the 1940s and 1950s; organizing for SCLC
beginning in 1957; and helping to found SNCC in 1960 and the MFDP in

1964. The interview also contains her comments on the role of women in the movement.

844 BATES, DAISY. *The Long Shadow of Little Rock.* New York: David McKay Co., 1962. 234 pages.
See entry 244.

845 BLUMBERG, RHODA L. "Careers of Women Civil Rights Activists." *Journal of Sociology and Social Welfare* 7 (1980): 708–29.
See entry 471.

846 _____. "Rediscovering Women Leaders of the Civil Rights Movement." In *Dream and Reality: The Modern Black Struggle for Freedom and Equality,* edited by Jeannine Swift, 19–28. Westport, CT: Greenwood Press, 1991.
Blumberg uses recently published biographies of civil rights activists and her own research to reassess the role of women in the civil rights movement. She claims that the movement created unusual opportunities for women to lead, but gender-related barriers limited "their recognition and mobility in leadership roles." Rather than protesting their unequal treatment, Blumberg states, black and white women "welcomed and encouraged black male leadership as it became available."

847 _____. "White Mothers in the American Civil Rights Movement. In *Research in the Interweave of Social Roles: Women and Men,* edited by Helena A. Lopata, vol. 1, 33–50. Greenwich, CT: JAI Press, 1980.
See entry 472.

848 _____. "Women in the Civil Rights Movement: Reform or Revolution." *Dialectical Anthropology* 15 (1990): 133–39.
Blumberg claims that "revolutionary conditions propelled women into leadership and mass action in the early stages of the civil rights movement." She notes that as the movement grew, men began to monopolize formal leadership roles. According to Blumberg, for a variety of reasons "women gave up their prominence in the movement and allowed their contributions to be obscured."

849 BROCK, ANNETTE K. "Gloria Richardson and the Cambridge Movement." In *Women in the Civil Rights Movement,* edited by Vicki L. Crawford, Jacqueline Anne Rouse, and Barbara Woods, 121–44. Brooklyn, NY: Carlson Publishing, 1990.
See entry 473.

850 BURKS, MARY FAIR. "Trailblazers: Women in the Montgomery Bus Boycott." In *Women in the Civil Rights Movement,* edited by Vicki L. Crawford, Jacqueline Anne Rouse, and Barbara Woods, 71–83. Brooklyn, NY: Carlson Publishing, 1990.
See entry 174.

851   CANTAROW, ELLEN. "Mother to a Movement. *In These Times*, 4–10 February 1987, 24.
Cantarow offers a brief biography of Ella Baker, "one of the Civil Rights movement's great, behind-the-scenes leaders."

852   CANTAROW, ELLEN, and SUSAN G. O'MALLEY. "Ella Baker: Organizing for Civil Rights." In *Moving the Mountain: Women Working for Social Change*, edited by Ellen Cantarow, 52–93. Old Westbury, NY: Feminist Press, 1980.
Ella Baker was an influential organizer who worked behind the scenes for several civil rights organizations. During the 1940s she was the national director of branches for the NAACP. In 1958 she became executive secretary of SCLC. In 1960 she organized the conference that led to the formation of the SNCC. She remained a key advisor to SNCC leaders and in 1964 helped organize the MFDP. Cantarow and O'Malley relied on personal interviews to compile this portrait of Baker's life and work.

853   CARSON, JOSEPHINE. *Silent Voices: The Southern Negro Woman Today.* New York: Delacorte Press, 1969. 273 pages.
Carson reports her conversations with a variety of black women in the South in the late 1960s. Although this book's primary focus is on the condition of black women, many of its subjects were involved in the civil rights movement and offer their observations on the role of women in the movement.

854   CLARK, SEPTIMA P. *Echo in My Soul.* New York: E. P. Dutton, 1962. 243 pages.
See entry 644.

855   _____. *Ready From Within: Septima Clark and the Civil Rights Movement.* Edited by Cynthia S. Brown. Navarro, CA: Wild Trees Press, 1986. 134 pages.
See entry 554.

856   CRAWFORD, VICKI L. "Beyond the Human Self: Grassroots Activists in the Mississippi Civil Rights Movement." In *Women in the Civil Rights Movement*, edited by Vicki L. Crawford, Jacqueline Anne Rouse, and Barbara Woods, 13–26. Brooklyn, NY: Carlson Publishing, 1990.
See entry 335.

857   CRAWFORD, VICKI L., JACQUELINE ANNE ROUSE, and BARBARA WOODS, eds. *Women in the Civil Rights Movement: Trailblazers and Torchbearers, 1941–1965.* Vol. 16, *Black Women in United States History*, edited by Darlene Clark Hine. Brooklyn, NY: Carlson Publishing, 1990. 290 pages.
See entry 123.

858   DURR, VIRGINIA FOSTER. *Outside the Magic Circle: The Autobiography of Virginia Foster Durr.* Edited by Hollinger F. Barnard. Tuscaloosa: University of Alabama Press, 1985. 360 pages.
See entry 185.

859 EVANS, SARA. *Personal Politics: The Roots of Women's Liberation in the Civil Rights Movement and the New Left.* New York: Alfred A. Knopf, 1979. 274 pages.

Evans's thesis is that the young female participants in the civil rights movement and members of the New Left were the catalyst that launched the modern women's movement. While involved in the South, civil rights volunteers "found the strength and self-respect to explore the meaning of equality and an ideology that beckoned them to do so." She describes the experiences of white southern women such as Sandra Cason, Dorothy Dawson, Jane Stembridge, and Mary King in SNCC as well as the northern volunteers who came south in the summer of 1964. She traces the development of feminist consciousness within SNCC that resulted in the 1964 position paper "Women in the Movement" and the 1965 memo "Sex and Caste" by Hayden and King (see entry 864).

860 _____. "Women's Consciousness and the Southern Black Movement." *Southern Exposure* 4, no. 4 (1977): 10–18. Reprinted in *Reweaving the Web of Life,* edited by Pam McAllister, 115–26. Philadelphia: New Society Publishers, 1982.

Evans advances the thesis that the experiences of white middle-class women working in the civil rights movement led to the development of women's consciousness, which eventually resulted in the women's liberation movement. She credits the SNCC for providing opportunities for women to develop new strengths and a sense of self-worth. At the same time, she believes that their subordinate status as women within the organization gave rise to a new feminism. This culminated in 1965 when Casey Hayden and Mary King circulated a memo (see entry 864) that argued that women in the movement were relegated to a low position in a caste-like system. This thesis is developed in greater depth in Evans's *Personal Politics* (1979, see entry 859).

861 GIDDINGS, PAULA. *When and Where I Enter: The Impact of Black Women on Race and Sex in America.* New York: William Morrow & Co., 1984. 408 pages.
See entry 514.

862 GRANT, JACQUELYN. "Civil Rights Women: A Source for Doing Womanist Theology." In *Women in the Civil Rights Movement,* edited by Vicki Crawford, Jacqueline Anne Rouse, and Barbara Woods, 39–50. Brooklyn, NY: Carlson Publishing, 1990.

Grant uses the life of Mississippi civil rights activist Fannie Lou Hamer as an example of liberation theology. She examines the interrelationship between religion and the civil rights movement.

863 HAMER, FANNIE LOU. "Sick and Tired of Being Sick and Tired." *Katallagete,* Fall 1968, 19–26.
See entry 358.

864   HAYDEN, CASEY, and MARY KING. "Sex and Caste: A Kind of a Memo."
     Liberation, April 1966, 35–36.
    In this memo, first circulated in 1965, SNCC workers Hayden and King
compare the position of women in the civil rights movement to the position
of Negroes in American society. They claim that women are largely excluded from positions of power within the movement and are not treated as
equals in their personal relations with men in the movement. Evans (1977,
see entry 860 and 1979, see entry 859) credits this memo with launching the
modern feminist movement.

865   HEDGEMAN, ANNA ARNOLD. *The Trumpet Sounds: A Memoir of Negro
    Leadership.* New York: Holt, Rinehart and Winston, 1964. 202 pages.
    See entry 463.

866   KING, MARY. *Freedom Song: A Personal Story of the 1960's Civil Rights
    Movement.* New York: William Morrow & Co., 1987. 592 pages.
    See entry 518.

867   KLING, SUSAN. "Fannie Lou Hamer: Baptism by Fire." In *Reweaving
    the Web of Life*, edited by Pam McAllister, 106–11. Philadelphia: New
    Society Publishers, 1982.
    See entry 375.

868   LANGSTON, DONNA. "The Women of Highlander." In *Women in the
    Civil Rights Movement*, edited by Vicki L. Crawford, Jacqueline Anne
    Rouse, and Barbara Woods, 145–67. Brooklyn, NY: Carlson Publish-
    ing, 1990.
    See entry 652.

869   LOCKE, MAMIE E. "Is This America? Fannie Lou Hamer and the Missis-
    sippi Freedom Democratic Party." In *Women in the Civil Rights Move-
    ment*, edited by Vicki L. Crawford, Jacqueline Anne Rouse, and Bar-
    bara Woods, 27–37. Brooklyn, NY: Carlson Publishing, 1990.
    See entry 379.

870   MCFADDEN, GRACE JORDAN. "Septima P. Clark and the Struggle for
    Human Rights." In *Women in the Civil Rights Movement*, edited by
    Vicki L. Crawford, Jacqueline Anne Rouse, and Barbara Woods,
    85–97. Brooklyn, NY: Carlson Publishing, 1990.
    See entry 564.

871   MOODY, ANNE. *Coming of Age in Mississippi.* New York: Dell Publish-
    ing Co., 1968. 348 pages.
    See entry 390.

872   MUELLER, CAROL. "Ella Baker and the Origins of 'Participatory Democ-
    racy.'" In *Women in the Civil Rights Movement*, edited by Vicki L.
    Crawford, Jacqueline Anne Rouse, and Barbara Woods, 51–70.
    Brooklyn, NY: Carlson Publishing, 1990.
    Mueller traces Ella Baker's contributions to the idea of "participatory

democracy." She describes Baker's work with the NAACP and SCLC, but does not cover her life after 1960.

873 MYRICK-HARRIS, CLARISSA. "Behind the Scenes: Doris Derby, Denise Nicholas and the Free Southern Theatre." In *Women in the Civil Rights Movement*, edited by Vicki L. Crawford, Jacqueline Anne Rouse, and Barbara Woods, 219–32. Brooklyn, NY: Carlson Publishing, 1990.

The Free Southern Theatre (FST) was organized in the winter of 1963 as a vehicle for educating southern blacks about their history and about the civil rights movement. Myrick-Harris describes the work of Derby and Nicholas within the FST.

874 NASH, DIANE. "Inside the Sit-Ins and Freedom Rides: Testimony of a Southern Student." In *We Shall Overcome*, edited by David J. Garrow, vol. 3, 955–74. Brooklyn, NY: Carlson Publishing, 1989. Orig. pub. in *The New Negro*, edited by Matthew Ahmann, 43–60. Notre Dame, IN: Fides Publishers, 1961.
See entry 448.

875 NORTON, ELEANOR HOLMES. "The Woman Who Changed the South: A Memory of Fannie Lou Hamer." *MS*, July 1977, 51.
See entry 395.

876 O'DELL, JACK H. "Life in Mississippi: An Interview with Fannie Lou Hamer." *Freedomways* 5, no. 2 (1965): 231–42.
See entry 396.

877 OLDENDORF, SANDRA B. "The South Carolina Sea Islands Citizenship Schools, 1957–1961." In *Women in the Civil Rights Movement*, edited by Vicki L. Crawford, Jacqueline Anne Rouse, and Barbara Woods, 169–82. Brooklyn, NY: Carlson Publishing, 1990.
See entry 491.

878 PAYNE, CHARLES. "Ella Baker and Models of Social Change. *Signs* 14, no. 4 (1989): 885–99.
See entry 533.

879 _____. "Men Led, but Women Organized: Movement Participation of Women in the Mississippi Delta." In *Women in the Civil Rights Movement*, edited by Vicki L. Crawford, Jacqueline Anne Rouse, and Barbara Woods, 1–11. Brooklyn, NY: Carlson Publishing, 1990.
See entry 400.

880 POUSSAINT, ALVIN F. "The Stresses of the White Female Worker in the Civil Rights Movement in the South." *American Journal of Psychiatry* 123, no. 4 (1966): 401–7.
See entry 840.

881 REAGON, BERNICE JOHNSON. "Women as Culture Carriers in the Civil Rights Movement: Fannie Lou Hamer." In *Women in the Civil Rights*

Movement, edited by Vicki L. Crawford, Jacqueline Anne Rouse, and Barbara Woods, 203–17. Brooklyn, NY: Carlson Publishing, 1990.

Reagon describes Fannie Lou Hamer's influence in her life, as well as Hamer's contributions to the civil rights and women's liberation movements.

882   ROBINSON, JO ANN GIBSON. *The Montgomery Bus Boycott and the Women Who Started It: The Memoir of Jo Ann Gibson Robinson.* Edited by David J. Garrow. Knoxville: University of Tennessee Press, 1987. 190 pages.
See entry 227.

883   ROMAINE, ANNE. "Interview with Fannie Lou Hamer." *Southern Exposure* (Spring 1981): 47–48.
See entry 401.

884   ROTHSCHILD, MARY AICKIN. "White Women Volunteers in the Freedom Summers: Their Life and Work in a Movement for Social Change." *Feminist Studies* 5, no. 3 (1979): 466–95.
See entry 842.

885   STANDLEY, ANNE. "The Role of Black Women in the Civil Rights Movement." In *Women in the Civil Rights Movement,* edited by Vicki L. Crawford, Jacqueline Anne Rouse, and Barbara Woods, 183–202. Brooklyn, NY: Carlson Publishing, 1990.

Although men occupied most of the principal leadership positions within the civil rights movement, women exerted an enormous influence both as informal leaders and dedicated participants. Standley reviews the contributions of Ella Baker, Bernice Johnson Reagon, Anne Moody, Daisy Bates, Jo Ann Gibson Robinson, Diane Nash, Joyce Ladner, Septima P. Clark, and Cynthia Washington.

886   WASHINGTON, CYNTHIA. "We Started from Different Ends of the Spectrum." *Southern Exposure* 4, no. 4 (1977): 14–15. Reprinted in *Reweaving the Web of Life,* edited by Pam McAllister, 112–14. Philadelphia: New Society Publishers, 1982.
See entry 544.

887   WOODS, BARBARA A. "Modjeska Simkins and the South Carolina Conference of the NAACP, 1939–1957." In *Women in the Civil Rights Movement,* edited by Vicki L. Crawford, Jacqueline Anne Rouse, and Barbara Woods, 99–120. Brooklyn, NY: Carlson Publishing, 1990.
See entry 497.

Biographies and Autobiographies

888   ABERNATHY, RALPH DAVID. *And the Walls Came Tumbling Down.* New York: Harper & Row, 1989. 641 pages.
See entry 549.

889 _____. "The Nonviolent Movement: The Past, the Present and the Future." In *Black Life and Culture in the United States*, edited by Rhoda L. Goldstein, 180–209. New York: Thomas Y. Crowell, 1971. Orig. pub. in *Drum Major* 1 (1971): 18–35.
See entry 550.

890 ALLEN, ARCHIE E. "John Lewis: Keeper of the Dream." *New South* 26, no. 2 (1971): 15–25.
See entry 500.

891 ALVIS, JOEL L. "Racial Turmoil and Religious Reaction: The Rt. Rev. John M. Allin." *Historical Magazine of the Protestant Episcopal Church* 50 (March 1981): 83–96.
See entry 318.

892 ANDERSON, JERVIS. *A. Phillip Randolph: A Biographical Portrait.* New York: Harcourt Brace Jovanovich, 1972. 398 pages.
Anderson relates the career of A. Phillip Randolph, founder and president of the Brotherhood of Sleeping Car Porters and the top-ranking black in organized labor. Randolph also was an important civil rights leader, especially during the 1940s when he organized the March on Washington Movement.

893 ARNOLD, MARTIN. "There Is No Rest for Roy Wilkins." *New York Times Magazine*, 28 September 1969. Reprinted in *Black Protest in the Sixties*, edited by August Meier and Elliot Rudwick, 315–28. Chicago: Quadrangle Books, 1970.
See entry 608.

894 BAKER, ELLA. "Developing Community Leadership." In *Black Women in White America: A Documentary History*, edited by Gerda Lerner, 345–52. New York: Vintage Books, 1973.
See entry 843.

895 BEARDSLEE, WILLIAM R. *The Way Out Must Lead In: Life Histories in the Civil Rights Movement.* 2d ed. Westport, CT: Lawrence Hill Books, 1983. 193 pages.
Beardslee is a psychiatrist who interviewed veteran civil rights activists in 1974. All were living in the South and had been involved in the movement for ten years or longer. Among the questions he asked were their reasons for involvement in the movement, what sustained them over time, and how they dealt with personal difficulties. Eleven representative interviews, all but three anonymous, are presented here.

896 BELFRAGE, SALLY. *Freedom Summer.* New York: Viking, 1965. 246 pages.
See entry 319.

897 BERRY, JASON. *Amazing Grace: With Charles Evers in Mississippi.* New York: Saturday Review Press, 1973. 370 pages.
See entry 320.

898   "Black Voices of the South." *Ebony,* August 1971, 50–54.
    This article consists of short statements by twelve prominent southern black leaders including Julian Bond, Charles Evers, John Lewis, Ralph Abernathy, and Fannie Lou Hamer, who discuss relations between blacks and whites in the South.

899   BLAND, RENDALL W. *Private Pressure and Public Law: The Legal Career of Justice Thurgood Marshall.* Port Washington, NY: Kennikat Press, 1973. 206 pages.
    See entry 609.

900   BOND, JULIAN. "The Movement Then and Now." *Southern Exposure* 3 (1976): 5–16.
    See entry 502.

901   BOYNTON, AMELIA P. *Bridge Across Jordan.* New York: Carlton Press, 1979. 190 pages.
    See entry 172.

902   BRADEN, ANNE. "Birmingham, 1956–1979: The History that We Made." *Southern Exposure* 8 (Summer 1979): 48–54.
    See entry 173.

903   BROCK, ANNETTE K. "Gloria Richardson and the Cambridge Movement." In *Women in the Civil Rights Movement,* edited by Vicki L. Crawford, Jacqueline Anne Rouse, and Barbara Woods, 121–44. Brooklyn, NY: Carlson Publishing, 1990.
    See entry 471.

904   BROOKS, THOMAS R. "A strategist without a Movement." *New York Times Magazine,* 16 February 1969. Reprinted in *Black Protest in the Sixties,* edited by August Meier and Elliot Rudwick, 329–43. Chicago: Quadrangle Books, 1970.
    Brooks profiles civil rights organizer Bayard Rustin, describing him as a "contact man, go-between, and interpreter of the Negro movement," and as "the most articulate strategist of the drive for Negro equality." Brooks recalls Rustin's role in organizing the Montgomery bus boycott and the March on Washington as well as the radical criticisms of his position in the late 1960s.

905   BROWN, CYNTHIA S. "Rosa Parks." *Southern Exposure* 9 (Spring 1981): 16–17.
    Brown interviewed Rosa Parks and describes here Park's family, her involvement with the Highlander Folk school, and how both influenced her decision to protest for civil rights.

906   BROWN, H. RAP. *Die Nigger Die!* New York: Dial Press, 1969. 145 pages.
    See entry 503.

907 CAGIN, SETH, and PHILIP DRAY. *We Are Not Afraid.* New York: Macmillan Publishing Co., 1988. 613 pages.
See entry 325.

908 CANTAROW, ELLEN. "Mother to a Movement." *In These Times,* 4–10 February 1987, 24.
See entry 851.

909 CANTAROW, ELLEN, and SUSAN G. O'MALLEY. "Ella Baker: Organizing for Civil Rights." In *Moving the Mountain: Women Working for Social Change,* edited by Ellen Cantarow, 52–93. Old Westbury, NY: Feminist Press, 1980.
See entry 852.

910 CHESTNUT, J. L., JR., and JULIA CASS. *Black in Selma: The Uncommon Life of J. L. Chestnut, Jr.* New York: Farrar, Straus & Giroux, 1990. 432 pages.
See entry 177.

911 CLARK, KENNETH B., ed. *The Negro Protest.* Boston: Beacon Press, 1963. 56 pages.
Constitutes a transcript of Clark's interviews with James Baldwin, Malcolm X, and Martin Luther King, Jr. in the spring of 1963.

912 CLARK, SEPTIMA P. *Echo in My Soul.* New York: E. P. Dutton, 1962. 243 pages.
See entry 644.

913 _____. *Ready From Within: Septima Clark and the Civil Rights Movement.* Edited by Cynthia S. Brown. Navarro, CA: Wild Trees Press, 1986. 134 pages.
See entry 554.

914 CLUSTER, DICK. "The Borning Struggle: An Interview with Bernice Johnson Reagon." *Radical America* 12 (November/December 1978): 8–25.
See entry 280.

915 CLUSTER, DICK, ed. *They Should Have Served that Cup of Coffee: Seven Radicals Remember the 60s.* Boston: South End Press, 1979. 268 pages.
See entry 509.

916 COHEN, ROBERT CARL. *Black Crusader: A Biography of Robert Franklin Williams.* Secaucus, NJ: Lyle Stuart, 1972. 361 pages.
See entry 611.

917 COTTON, DOROTHY. "A Conversation with Ralph Abernathy." *Journal of Current Social Issues* 9, no. 3 (1970): 21–30.
See entry 555.

918 CUMMINGS, RICHARD. *The Pied Piper: Allard K. Lowenstein and the Liberal Dream*. New York: Grove Press, 1985. 569 pages.
See entry 336.

919 DeMUTH, JERRY. "Tired of Being Sick and Tired." *The Nation*, 1 June 1964, 548–51.
See entry 338.

920 DENT, RICHARD BLAKE. "The Father His Children Forgot." *American History Illustrated* 20 (1985): 10–17.
A brief biography of E. D. Nixon, the Montgomery NAACP leader who played a critical role in the formation of the Montgomery Improvement Association. Dent credits Nixon with being the "architect" of the boycott and the person responsible for selecting Martin Luther King, Jr., to lead it.

921 DENT, TOM. "Interviews with Civil Rights Activists." *Freedomways* 18, no. 3 (1978): 164–69.
Dent reviews *My Soul is Rested* (1977, see entry 154), a collection of interviews with civil rights workers by Howell Raines. Although Dent questions the ability of white reporters to accurately interpret the experiences of African Americans, he points to several valuable interviews in Raines's book. He is critical, however, of the omission of interviews with key SNCC and CORE activists and of Raines's tendency to overemphasize the magnitude of racial change in the South.

922 DURR, VIRGINIA FOSTER. *Outside the Magic Circle: The Autobiography of Virginia Foster Durr*. Edited by Hollinger F. Barnard. Tuscaloosa: University of Alabama Press, 1985. 360 pages.
See entry 185.

923 EVERS, CHARLES. *Evers*. Edited by Grace Halsell. New York: World Publishing, 1971. 196 pages.
See entry 343.

924 EVERS, MYRLIE B., and WILLIAM PETERS. *For Us, the Living*. Garden City, NY: Doubleday, 1967. 378 pages.
See entry 344.

925 FARMER, JAMES. *Lay Bare the Heart: An Autobiography of the Civil Rights Movement*. New York: Arbor House, 1985. 370 pages.
See entry 582.

926 FORMAN, JAMES. *The Making of Black Revolutionaries*. Washington, DC: Open Hand Publishing, 1985. 568 pages. Orig. pub. New York: Macmillan Co., 1972.
See entry 511.

927 _____. *Sammy Younge, Jr.: The First Black College Student to Die in the Black Liberation movement*. New York: Grove Press, 1968. 282 pages.
See entry 190.

928 FORT, VINCENT D. "The Atlanta Sit-In Movement 1960–61: An Oral Study." In *Atlanta*, edited by David J. Garrow. Brooklyn, NY: Carlson Publishing, 1989. M.A. thesis, Atlanta University, 1980.
See entry 282.

929 FRADY, MARSHALL. *Wallace.* Cleveland: World Publishing, 1970. 246 pages.
Frady provides an in-depth portrait of Alabama Governor George C. Wallace, one of the leading opponents of racial integration and the civil rights movement. Frady also describes Wallace's campaign for the presidency in 1968.

930 GARDNER, TOM. "The Montgomery Bus Boycott: Interviews with Rosa Parks, E. D. Nixon, Johnny Carr, and Virginia Durr." *Southern Exposure* 9, no. 1 (1981): 13–21.
See entry 193.

931 GARROW, DAVID J. *Bearing the Cross: Martin Luther King, Jr., and the Southern Christian Leadership Conference.* New York: Random House, 1986. 800 pages.
See entry 559.

932 GOOD, PAUL. "'No Man Can Fill Dr. King's Shoes' but Abernathy Tries." *New York Times Magazine*, 26 May 1968. Reprinted in *Black Protest in the Sixties*, edited by August Meier and Elliot Rudwick, 284–301. Chicago: Quadrangle Books, 1970.
See entry 561.

933 _____. "Odyssey of a Man and a Movement." *New York Times Magazine*, 25 June 1967. Reprinted in *Black Protest in the Sixties*, edited by August Meier and Elliot Rudwick, 252–66. Chicago: Quadrangle Books, 1970.
See entry 515.

934 _____. *The Trouble I've Seen: White Journalist/Black movement.* Washington, DC: Howard University Press, 1975. 272 pages.
See entry 39.

935 GRANT, JACQUELYN. "Civil Rights Women: A Source for Doing Womanist Theology." In *Women in the Civil Rights Movement*, edited by Vicki Crawford, Jacqueline Anne Rouse, and Barbara Woods, 39–50. Brooklyn, NY: Carlson Publishing, 1990.
See entry 862.

936 GUTHMAN, EDWIN O., and JEFFREY SHULMAN, eds. *Robert Kennedy in His Own Words: The Unpublished Recollections of the Kennedy Years.* New York: Bantam Books, 1988. 493 pages.
See entry 670.

937 HAMER, FANNIE LOU. "It's in Your Hands." In *Black Women in White America: A Documentary History*, edited by Gerda Lerner, 609–14.

New York: Pantheon Books, 1972. Speech given at NAACP Legal Defense Fund Institute, 7 May 1971.
See entry 357.

938 _____. "Sick and Tired of Being Sick and Tired." *Katallagete*, Fall 1968, 19–26.
See entry 358.

939 HAMPTON, HENRY, STEVE FAGER, and SARAH FLYNN. *Voices of Freedom: An Oral History of the Civil Rights Movement from the 1950's Through the 1980's.* New York: Bantam Books, 1990. 692 pages.
See entry 138.

940 HARRIS, DAVID. *Dreams Die Hard: Three Men's Journey Through the Sixties.* New York: St. Martin's Press, 1982. 341 pages.

On 14 March 1980 Allard Lowenstein, former member of Congress and activist for liberal causes, was shot dead by Dennis Sweeney, a mentally disturbed former student activist who was Lowenstein's protégé. Both men had been deeply involved in the civil rights movement in Mississippi. Lowenstein had helped recruit northern students to help with the Council of Federated Organization's (COFO) 1963 Freedom Vote and often claimed credit for originating the idea of the 1964 Mississippi Summer Project. Sweeney first came to Mississippi in 1963 for the Freedom Vote and returned in the summer of 1964 to work in McComb, one of the most dangerous assignments in the state. By the end of the summer the two men were on opposite sides, as militants within SNCC accused Lowenstein of "selling out" the Freedom Democratic party at the Democratic National Convention in Atlantic City. The first one-third of *Dreams Die Hard* traces their relationship from 1963 to 1965 within the context of the movement.

941 HEDGEMAN, ANNA ARNOLD. *The Trumpet Sounds: A Memoir of Negro Leadership.* New York: Holt, Rinehart and Winston, 1964. 202 pages.
See entry 463.

942 HORTON, MYLES. *The Long Haul: An Autobiography.* New York: Doubleday, 1990. 231 pages.
See entry 650.

943 HUEY, GARY. *Rebel with a Cause: P. D. East, Southern Liberalism, and the Civil Rights Movement, 1953–1971.* Wilmington, DE: Scholarly Resources, 1985. 232 pages.
See entry 368.

944 JONES, LEWIS W. "Fred L. Shuttlesworth, Indigenous Leader." In *Birmingham*, edited by David J. Garrow, 115–50. Brooklyn, NY: Carlson Publishing, 1989.
See entry 210.

945 KING, MARY. *Freedom Song: A Personal Story of the 1960's Civil Rights Movement.* New York: William Morrow & Co., 1987. 592 pages.
See entry 518.

946   KLING, SUSAN. "Fannie Lou Hamer: Baptism by Fire." In *Reweaving the Web of Life*, edited by Pam McAllister, 106–11. Philadelphia: New Society Publishers, 1982.
See entry 375.

947   _____. *Fannie Lou Hamer: A Biography*. Chicago: Women for Racial and Economic Equality, 1979. 56 pages.
See entry 376.

948   KOTZ, NICK, and MARY LYNN KOTZ. *A Passion for Equality: George Wiley and the Movement*. New York: W. W. Norton & Co., 1977. 372 pages.
See entry 586.

949   KRYN, RANDALL L. "James L. Bevel: The Strategist of the 1960s Civil Rights Movement." In *We Shall Overcome*, edited by David J. Garrow, vol. 2, 517–36. Brooklyn, NY: Carlson Publishing, 1989.
Kryn profiles Bevel's contributions to the civil rights movement. He claims that the movement would not have happened without the team of Martin Luther King, Jr. and James Bevel. King, he argues, "needed Bevel to be the strategist and organizer of the movement."

950   KUNSTLER, WILLIAM M. *Deep in My Heart*. New York: William Morrow & Co., 1966. 387 pages.
See entry 773.

951   LADNER, JOYCE. "Return to the Source." *Essence*, June 1977.
See entry 521.

952   LESTER, JULIUS. *All Is Well*. New York: William Morrow & Co., 1976. 319 pages.
See entry 523.

953   LEVINE, RICHARD. "Jesse Jackson: Heir to Dr. King?" *Harper's*, March 1969, 58–70.
See entry 483.

954   LEWIS, JOHN. "A Trend Toward Aggressive Nonviolent Action." In *Negro Protest Thought in the Twentieth Century*, edited by Francis L. Broderick and August Meier, 313–21. Indianapolis: Bobbs-Merrill, 1965. Orig. pub. in *Dialogue*, 4 (Spring 1964): 7–9.
See entry 524.

955   LIPSITZ, GEORGE. *A Life In the Struggle: Ivory Perry and the Culture of Opposition*. Philadelphia: Temple University Press, 1988. 292 pages.
See entry 311.

956   LOCKE, MAMIE E. "Is This America? Fannie Lou Hamer and the Mississippi Freedom Democratic Party." In *Women in the Civil Rights Movement*, edited by Vicki L. Crawford, Jacqueline Anne Rouse, and Barbara Woods, 27–37. Brooklyn, NY: Carlson Publishing, 1990.
See entry 379.

957 LONGENECKER, STEPHEN L. *Selma's Peacemaker: Ralph Smeltzer and Civil Rights Mediation.* Philadelphia: Temple University Press, 1987. 273 pages.
See entry 214.

958 LOUIS, DEBBIE. *And We Are Not Saved: A History of the Movement as People.* Garden City, NY: Doubleday, 1970. 462 pages.
See entry 588.

959 McFADDEN, GRACE JORDAN. "Septima P. Clark and the Struggle for Human Rights." In *Women in the Civil Rights Movement,* edited by Vicki L. Crawford, Jacqueline Anne Rouse, and Barbara Woods, 85–97. Brooklyn, NY: Carlson Publishing, 1990.
See entry 564.

960 MARS, FLORENCE. *Witness in Philadelphia.* Baton Rouge: Louisiana State University Press, 1977. 296 pages.
See entry 387.

961 MEREDITH, JAMES. *Three Years in Mississippi.* Bloomington: University of Indiana Press, 1966. 328 pages.
See entry 388.

962 MOODY, ANNE. *Coming of Age in Mississippi.* New York: Dell Publishing Co., 1968. 348 pages.
See entry 390.

963 MORRISON, JOAN, and ROBERT K. MORRISON. *From Camelot to Kent State: The Sixties Experience in the Words of Those Who Lived It.* New York: Times Books, 1987. 355 pages.
This collection of interviews with activists from the 1960s contains the recollections of five civil rights activists, including former SNCC workers John Lewis and Bob Zellner.

964 MOSES, BOB. "Mississippi: 1961–1962." *Liberation* 14 (January 1970): 7–17.
See entry 394.

965 MUELLER, CAROL. "Ella Baker and the Origins of 'Participatory Democracy.'" In *Women in the Civil Rights Movement,* edited by Vicki L. Crawford, Jacqueline Anne Rouse, and Barbara Woods, 51–70. Brooklyn, NY: Carlson Publishing, 1990.
See entry 872.

966 NEARY, JOHN. *Julian Bond: Black Rebel.* New York: William Morrow & Co., 1971. 256 pages.
See entry 530.

967 NORTON, ELEANOR HOLMES. "The Woman Who Changed the South: A Memory of Fannie Lou Hamer." *MS,* July 1977, 51.
See entry 395.

968   O'DELL, JACK H. "Life in Mississippi: An Interview with Fannie Lou Hamer." *Freedomways* 5, no. 2 (1965): 231–42.
See entry 396.

969   ORANGE, JAMES. "With the People." *Southern Exposure* 9 (Spring 1981): 110–16.
See entry 565.

970   PAYNE, CHARLES. "Ella Baker and Models of Social Change." *Signs* 14, no. 4 (1989): 885–99.
See entry 533.

971   PECK, JAMES. *Freedom Ride.* New York: Simon & Schuster, 1962. 160 pages.
See entry 597.

972   PENDERGRAST, NAN. "Twenty-five Years of Love in Action—an Interview with Joseph Lowery." *Fellowship* 1 (February 1983): 10–12.
See entry 568.

973   PFEFFER, PAULA F. *A. Philip Randolph, Pioneer of the Civil Rights Movement.* Baton Rouge: Lousiana State University Press, 1990. 336 pages.
Pfeffer chronicles the life of pioneer labor leader and civil rights activist A. Philip Randolph. This book focuses primarily on Randolph's efforts to secure improved opportunities for African Americans during the World War II era, but also describes his involvement in various marches in the 1950s that culminated in the 1963 March on Washington.

974   PFISTER, JOE. "Twenty Years and Still Marching." *Southern Exposure* 10 (January 1982): 20–27.
See entry 295.

975   RAINES, HOWELL. *My Soul Is Rested: Movement Days in the Deep South Remembered.* New York: G. P. Putnam's Sons, 1977. 472 pages.
See entry 154.

976   REAGON, BERNICE JOHNSON. "Women as Culture Carriers in the Civil Rights Movement: Fannie Lou Hamer." In *Women in the Civil Rights Movement,* edited by Vicki L. Crawford, Jacqueline Anne Rouse, and Barbara Woods, 203–17. Brooklyn, NY: Carlson Publishing, 1990.
See entry 881.

977   RENDER, SYLVIA LYONS. "Roy Wilkins, 1901–1981: A Tribute." *The Quarterly Journal of the Library of Congress* 39, no. 2 (1982): 116–25.
See entry 623.

978   ROBINSON, JO ANN GIBSON. *The Montgomery Bus Boycott and the Women Who Started It: The Memoir of Jo Ann Gibson Robinson.* Edited by David J. Garrow. Knoxville: University of Tennessee Press, 1987. 190 pages.
See entry 227.

979 ROGERS, KIM LACY. "Organizational Experience and Personal Narra-
     tive: Stories of New Orleans' Civil Rights Leadership." *Oral History
     Review* 13 (1985): 23–54.
     See entry 314.

980 ROMAINE, ANNE. "Interview with Fannie Lou Hamer." *Southern Expo-
     sure* (Spring 1981): 47–48.
     See entry 401.

981 RUGABER, WALTER. "'We Can't Cuss White People Any More. It's in
     Our Hands Now.'" *New York Times Magazine*, 4 August 1968. Re-
     printed in *Black Protest in the Sixties*, edited by August Meier and
     Elliot Rudwick, 302–14. Chicago: Quadrangle Books, 1970.
     See entry 403.

982 SELBY, EARL, and MIRIAN SELBY. *Odyssey: Journey Through Black
     America.* New York: G. P. Putnam's Sons, 1971. 381 pages.
     The authors interviewed black Americans from all walks of life in all
parts of the United States. Included among their subjects are civil rights
leaders such as Charles Evers, E. D. Nixon, Rosa Parks, John Lewis, Andrew
Young, Fannie Lou Hamer, Bayard Rustin, Al Raby, and C. T. Vivian. Their
book is based on impressions gained from their interviews as well as on
their personal observations of life in Black America.

983 SELLERS, CLEVELAND, and ROBERT TERRELL. *River of No Return: The Au-
     tobiography of a Black Militant and the Life and Death of SNCC.*
     New York: William Morrow & Co., 1973. 279 pages.
     See entry 537.

984 SESSIONS, JIM, and SUE THRASHER. "A New Day Begins: An Interview
     with John Lewis." *Southern Exposure* 4 (Fall 1976): 14–24.
     See entry 538.

985 SINSHEIMER, JOSEPH A. "Never Turn Back: An Interview with Sam
     Block." *Southern Exposure* 15 (Summer 1987): 37–50.
     See entry 411.

986 VIORST, MILTON. *Fire in the Streets: America in the 1960's.* New York:
     Simon & Schuster, 1979. 591 pages.
     See entry 94.

987 WARREN, ROBERT PENN. "Two for SNCC." *Commentary* 39 (1965):
     38–48.
     See entry 543.

988 WATSON, DENTON L. *Lion in the Lobby: Clarence Mitchell, Jr.'s Strug-
     gle for the Passage of the Civil Rights Laws.* New York: William Mor-
     row & Co., 1990. 846 pages.
     See entry 630.

989 WEBB, SHEYANN, and RACHEL WEST NELSON. *Selma, Lord, Selma: Girl-hood Memories of the Civil Rights Days.* Tuscaloosa: University of Alabama Press, 1980. 146 pages.
See entry 240.

990 WEISS, NANCY J. *Whitney M. Young, Jr., and the Struggle for Civil Rights.* Princeton: Princeton University Press, 1989. 286 pages.
See entry 638.

991 WEISS, NANCY J. "Whitney M. Young, Jr.: Committing the Power Struc-ture to the Cause of Civil Rights." In *Black Leaders of the Twentieth Century,* edited by John Hope Franklin and August Meier, 331–58. Urbana: University of Illinois Press, 1982.
See entry 639.

992 WIGGINTON, ELLIOT, and SUE THRASHER. "To Make the World We Want: An Interview with Dorothy Cotton." *Southern Exposure* 10 (September 1982): 25–31.
See entry 573.

993 WILKINS, ROY. *Standing Fast: The Autobiography of Roy Wilkins.* New York: Viking, 1982. 361 pages.
See entry 632.

994 WOODS, BARBARA A. "Modjeska Simkins and the South Carolina Con-ference of the NAACP, 1939–1957." In *Women in the Civil Rights Movement,* edited by Vicki L. Crawford, Jacqueline Anne Rouse, and Barbara Woods, 99–120. Brooklyn, NY: Carlson Publishing, 1990.
See entry 485.

995 YARBROUGH, TINSLEY E. *Judge Frank Johnson and Human Rights in Alabama.* Tuscaloosa: University of Alabama Press, 1981. 270 pages.
See entry 801.

996 _____. *A Passion for Justice: J. Waties Waring and Civil Rights.* New York: Oxford University Press, 1987. 282 pages.
See entry 499.

997 YOUTH of the RURAL ORGANIZING and CULTURAL CENTER. *Minds Stayed on Freedom: The Civil Rights Struggle in the Rural South.* Edited by Jay MacLeod. Boulder: Westview Press, 1991. 189 pages.
See entry 426.

8

Phases of the Movement

Origins of the Movement

998 ANDERSON, JERVIS. *A. Phillip Randolph: A Biographical Portrait.* New York: Harcourt Brace Jovanovich, 1972. 398 pages.
See entry 892.

999 BENNETT, LERONE, JR. *Confrontation Black and White.* Chicago: Johnson Publishing, 1965. 321 pages.
See entry 8.

1000 BERMAN, WILLIAM C. *The Politics of Civil Rights in the Truman Administration.* Columbus: Ohio State University Press, 1970. 261 pages.
See entry 658.

1001 BRISBANE, ROBERT H. *The Black Vanguard: Origins of the Negro Social Revolution, 1900–1960.* Valley Forge, PA: Judson Press, 1970. 285 pages.
Brisbane's historical account focuses on the black freedom struggle prior to the *Brown* decision. Only a brief final chapter covers events after 1954. This book is the prelude to Brisbane's *Black Activism* (1974, see entry 17).

1002 DALFIUME, RICHARD M. "The 'Forgotten Years' of the Negro Revolution." *Journal of American History* 55, no. 1 (1968): 90–106.
Dalfiume focuses on developments during World War II that contributed to the emergence of the modern civil rights movement in the 1950s.

1003 DAVIES, JAMES C. "The J-Curve of Rising and Declining Satisfactions as a Cause of Some Great Revolutions and a Contained Rebellion." In *The History of Violence in America: Historical and Comparative Perspectives,* edited by Hugh Davis Graham and Ted Robert Gurr, 690–

730. New York: Praeger Publishers, 1969. Reprinted in *Violence in America*, edited by Hugh Davis Graham and Ted Robert Gurr, 415–36. Beverly Hills, CA: Sage Publications, 1979.

Davis attempts to extend his theory of rising expectations as the cause of revolutions to apply it to the civil rights movement (the "contained rebellion" of his title). He maintains that revolution (or rebellion) is most likely to occur when the gap between a people's expected need satisfaction and actual need satisfaction becomes intolerably large.

1004   GESCHWENDER, JAMES A. "Social Structure and the Negro Revolt: An Examination of Some Hypotheses." *Social Forces* 43, no. 2 (1964): 248–56.

Geschwender uses a variety of data on the social and economic status of black Americans to test five hypotheses regarding the causes of the civil rights movement. He rejects the "Vulgar Marxist" and "Rise and Drop" hypotheses, and accepts the "Sophisticated Marxist," "Rising Expectations," and "Status Inconsistency" hypotheses. He finds one common denominator among the three that he accepts: "Changes in objective conditions cause feelings of relative deprivation, which, in turn, produce a tendency to protest and rebel."

1005   GRAVES, CARL R. "The Right to Be Served: Oklahoma City's Lunch Counter Sit-Ins, 1958–1964." In *We Shall Overcome*, edited by David J. Garrow, vol. 1, 283–97. Brooklyn, NY: Carlson Publishing, 1989. Orig. pub. in *Chronicles of Oklahoma* 59 (Summer 1981): 361–73.
See entry 480.

1006   JONES, BEVERLY W. "Before Montgomery and Greensboro: The Desegregation Movement in the District of Columbia, 1950–1953." *Phylon* 43, no. 2, (1982): 144–54.
See entry 464.

1007   LEWIS, DAVID L. "The Origins and Causes of the Civil Rights Movement." In *The Civil Rights Movement in America*, edited by Charles W. Eagles, 3–18. Jackson: University Press of Mississippi, 1986.

Lewis advances a demographic/political theory to explain the emergence of the civil rights movement. He stresses the importance of black migration to the North and the growing power of black voters in northern cities, which strengthened the urban liberal bloc of the Democratic party at the expense of Southern segregationists. Lewis also acknowledges the increasing support for the liberal position on race relations following the publication of Myrdal's *An American Dilemma* (1944). The *Brown* decision, according to Lewis, contributed to the movement's birth by creating a crisis in which rabid segregationists replaced "responsible" white leadership at the same time that moderate NAACP leaders were forced aside by more militant black leaders.

1008   MABEE, CARLETON. "Two Decades of Sit-Ins: Evolution of Non-Violence." *The Nation*, 12 August 1961, 78–81.
See entry 589.

1009 MCADAM, DOUG. *Political Process and the Development of Black Insurgency, 1930–1970.* Chicago: University of Chicago Press, 1982. 304 pages.

McAdam offers a political interpretation for the origin of the civil rights movement. The migration of southern blacks to the North and the growing political strength of northern black voting blocs are the key elements in this explanation. He argues that because of their dependence on black votes, Democratic presidents could no longer afford to ignore southern repression of blacks' constitutional rights.

1010 MCADAM, DOUG, and KELLY MOORE. "The Politics of Black Insurgency, 1930–1975." In *Violence in America: Protest, Rebellion, Reform,* 3d ed., edited by Ted Robert Gurr, vol. 2, 255–85. Newbury Park, CA: Sage Publications, 1989.

McAdam and Moore outline a "political process" model of social change to explain the growth and decline of the civil rights movement. They reject social-psychological theories such as "rising expectations" or "relative deprivation." Instead, they emphasize the existence of "significant structural changes" in American society that gave rise to "the increasing political leverage and greater organizational strength required to launch and sustain the modern civil rights movement." These themes are developed in more detail in McAdam's *Political Process and the Development of Black Insurgency* (1982, see entry 1009).

1011 MCCOY, DONALD, and RICHARD T. RUETTEN. "The Civil Rights Movement: 1949–1954." *Midwest Quarterly* 11, (October 1969): 11–34.

McCoy and Ruetten review the civil rights gains in the period between the beginning of World War II and the *Brown* decision. They maintain that if civil rights advances had continued at the same pace following 1954 as they had between 1940 and 1954, "the adjustment of the races . . . might have been a happier story." Lack of progress in the area of civil rights during the Eisenhower administration could not satisfy rising black aspirations, and this frustration, they argue, led to the emergence of the modern civil rights movement.

1012 MCNEIL, GENNA RAE. *Groundwork: Charles Hamilton Houston and the Struggle for Civil Rights.* Philadelphia: University of Pennsylvania Press, 1983. 308 pages.
See entry 617.

1013 MEIER, AUGUST, and ELLIOT RUDWICK. "The First Freedom Ride." *Phylon* 30 (1969): 213–22.
See entry 593.

1014 _____. "How CORE Began." *Social Science Quarterly* 49 (March, 1969): 789–99.
See entry 594.

1015 _____. "The Origins of Nonviolent Direct Action in Afro-American Protest: A Note on Historical Discontinuities." In *Along the Color Line: Explorations in the Black Experience,* edited by August Meier and Elliot Rudwick, 307–404. Urbana: University of Illinois Press, 1976. Reprinted in *We Shall Overcome*, edited by David J. Garrow, vol. 3, 833–930. Brooklyn, NY: Carlson Publishing, 1989.

Meier and Rudwick examine the antecedents of the nonviolent protests of the civil rights movement and the conditions that led to the widespread adoption of direct action against segregation. They describe numerous school boycotts, "don't buy where you can't work" campaigns, rent strikes during the Depression years, and postwar protests launched by CORE and other organizations. They maintain that of most immediate relevance for the emergence of the civil rights movement were successful boycotts in Baton Rouge, Orangeburg, Montgomery, Birmingham, Talahassee, Tuskegee, and Rock Hill, South Carolina. They conclude that "black direct action was essentially an indigenous creation of the Negro community . . . and was not inspired by outside models."

1016   MORRIS, ALDON D. *The Origins of the Civil Rights Movement: Black Communities Organizing for Change.* New York: Free Press, 1984. 354 pages.

Morris utilizes the resource mobilization theory to analyze the origins and development of the civil rights movement. He argues that "the urbanization of the southern black population during the first half of the twentieth century created the conditions that generated the resources needed to support a sustained movement against racial domination." First among these resources, according to Morris, was the black church, which not only provided the organizational framework for the movement, but also supplied the charismatic leadership that mobilized its supporters. Morris downplays the importance of outside elites and events in generating the movement, insisting that it was largely an indigenous protest.

1017   OPPENHEIMER, MARTIN. "The Movement—a Twenty-five Year Retrospective." *Monthly Review* 36 (1985): 49–55.

Oppenheimer reflects on the origins of the sit-in movement. The two most critical factors contributing to the emergence of the movement were, in his opinion, the urbanization and industrialization of the South and the growing power of black voters.

1018   PFEFFER, PAULA F. *A. Philip Randolph, Pioneer of the Civil Rights Movement.* Baton Rouge: Lousiana State University Press, 1990. 336 pages.
See entry 973.

1019   TUSHNET, MARK V. *The NAACP's Legal Strategy against Segregated Education. 1925–1950.* Chapel Hill: University of North Carolina Press, 1987. 222 pages.
See entry 629.

1020   WHITFIELD, STEPHEN J. *A Death in the Delta: The Story of Emmett Till.* New York: Free Press, 1988. 208 pages.
Whitfield describes the events surrounding the murder of Emmett Till in

1955. He contends that the national response to Till's lynching set the stage for the modern civil rights movement.

1021 WILLIAMS, ROBIN M., JR. "Social Change and Social Conflict: Race Relations in the United States, 1944–1964." *Sociological Inquiry* 35 (Winter 1965), 15–24. Reprinted in *The Black Revolt*, edited by James A. Geschwender, 24–33. Englewood Cliffs, NJ: Prentice Hall Press, 1971.

Williams examines the conditions giving rise to racial conflict and concludes that conflict is likely when relative deprivation and social humiliation are combined with (1) a high level of intragroup communication, (2) rapidly rising aspirations, (3) a strong sense of legitimacy, (4) the conviction that the blockage of these aspirations is immoral, (5) awareness of power, and (6) failure to remove the basic sources of grievance.

1022 WOODS, BARBARA A. "Modjeska Simkins and the South Carolina Conference of the NAACP, 1939–1957." In *Women in the Civil Rights Movement*, edited by Vicki L. Crawford, Jacqueline Anne Rouse, and Barbara Woods, 99–120. Brooklyn, NY: Carlson Publishing, 1990. See entry 497.

Sit-Ins

1023 CHAFE, WILLIAM. "The Greensboro Sit-Ins." *Southern Exposure* 6 (Fall, 1978): 78–87. See entry 432.

1024 FISHMAN, JACOB R., and FREDERIC SOLOMON. "Youth and Social Action: Perspectives on the Student Sit-In Movement." *American Journal of Orthopsychiatry* 33 (1963): 872–82. See entry 815.

1025 FORT, VINCENT D. "The Atlanta Sit-In Movement 1960–61: An Oral Study." In *Atlanta*, edited by David J. Garrow, 113–80. Brooklyn, NY: Carlson Publishing, 1989. M.A. thesis, Atlanta University, 1980. See entry 282.

1026 GAITHER, TOM. "Jailed-In." In *Nonviolence in America*, edited by Staughton Lynd, 399–415. Indianapolis: Bobbs-Merrill, 1966. Orig. pub. by League for Industrial Democracy, New York, 1961. See entry 478.

1027 GRAVES, CARL R. "The Right to Be Served: Oklahoma City's Lunch Counter Sit-Ins, 1958–1964." In *We Shall Overcome*, edited by David J. Garrow, vol. 1, 283–97. Brooklyn, NY: Carlson Publishing, 1989. Orig. pub. in *Chronicles of Oklahoma* 59 (Summer 1981): 361–73. See entry 480.

1028 LAWSON, JAMES M., JR. "We Are Trying to Raise the Moral Issue." In *Negro Protest Thought in the Twentieth Century*, edited by Francis L. Broderick and August Meier, 274–81. Indianapolis: Bobbs-Merrill, 1965. Address to SNCC conference, Raleigh, NC, April 1960.
See entry 522.

1029 LINCOLN, C. ERIC. "The Strategy of a Sit-In." In *Atlanta*, edited by David J. Garrow, 95–103. Brooklyn, NY: Carlson Publishing, 1989. Orig. pub. in *The Reporter* (5 January 1961): 20–23.
See entry 292.

1030 MABEE, CARLETON. "Two decades of Sit-Ins: Evolution of Non-Violence." *The Nation*, 12 August 1961, 78–81.
See entry 589.

1031 McDEW, CHARLES. "Spiritual and Moral Aspects of the Student Non-violent Struggle in the South." In *The New Student Left*, edited by Mitchell Cohen and Dennis Hale, 58–64. Boston: Beacon Press, 1966. Orig. pub. in *The Activist* 1 (1961). Speech given at Antioch College, October 1960.
McDew discusses the nature of the opposition to the student sit-in movement and the religious basis of the struggle for civil rights.

1032 MEIER, AUGUST. "The Successful Sit-Ins in a Border City: A Study in Social Causation." In *We Shall Overcome*, edited by David J. Garrow, vol. 2, 721–28. Brooklyn, NY: Carlson Publishing, 1989. Orig. pub. in *Journal of Intergroup Relations* 2 (Summer 1961): 230–37.
See entry 488.

1033 MORRIS, ALDON. "Black Southern Student Sit-In Movement: An Analysis of Internal Organization." *American Sociological Review* 46, no. 6 (1981): 744–67. Reprinted in *We Shall Overcome*, edited by David J. Garrow, vol. 3, 931–54. Brooklyn, NY: Carlson Publishing, 1989.
Morris argues that the student sit-in movement of 1960 was not a spontaneous uprising, but "grew out of pre-existing institutions and organizational forms." He shows that the spread of the sit-ins followed networks of pre-existing institutional relationships. He describes how black churches, colleges, protest organizations, and leaders nurtured and aided the movement's development. Morris expands on these themes in his *The Origins of the Civil Rights Movement* (1984, see entry 1016).

1034 NASH, DIANE. "Inside the Sit-Ins and Freedom Rides: Testimony of a Southern Student." In *We Shall Overcome*, edited by David J. Garrow, vol. 3, 955–74. Brooklyn, NY: Carlson Publishing, 1989. Orig. pub. in *The New Negro*, edited by Matthew Ahmann, 43–60. Notre Dame, IN: Fides Publishers, 1961.
See entry 448.

1035 OPPENHEIMER, MARTIN. "Institutions of Higher Learning and the 1960 Sit-Ins: Some Clues for Social Action." *Journal of Negro Education* 32 (Summer, 1963): 286–88.

Oppenheimer examines sit-ins occurring during 1960 in sixty-nine southern cities. He finds that communities experiencing these protests tend to be larger, located in the Upper South, and have a Negro college or university in the area. He maintains that sit-ins are more likely to be successful in cities where blacks constitute a lower percentage of the total population.

1036 _____. "The Movement—a Twenty-five Year Retrospective." *Monthly Review* 36 (1985): 49–55.

See entry 1017.

1037 _____. *The Sit-In Movement of 1960.* Brooklyn, NY: Carlson Publishing, 1989. 222 Pages. Ph.D. dissertation, University of Pennsylvania, 1963.

Oppenheimer focuses on the origins and spread of the student sit-in movement of 1960. He examines the attitudes of the participants and their interactions with local authorities in ten southern communities.

1038 _____. "The Southern Student Sit-Ins: Intra-Group Relations and Community Conflict." *Phylon* 27, no. 1 (1966): 20–26.

Oppenheimer applies several sociological concepts to the civil rights movement to illustrate their utility in expanding the understanding of protest activities.

1039 ORUM, ANTHONY M. *Black Students in Protest: A Study of the Origins of the Black Student Movement.* Washington, DC: American Sociological Association, 1972. 89 pages.

See entry 819.

1040 ORUM, ANTHONY M., and AMY W. ORUM. "The Class and Status Bases of Negro Student Protest." *Social Science Quarterly* 49, no. 3 (1968): 521–33.

See entry 820.

1041 PINARD, MAURICE, JEROME KIRK, and DONALD VON ESCHEN. "Processes of Recruitment in the Sit-In Movement." *Public Opinion Quarterly* 33 (Fall 1969): 355–69.

See entry 599.

1042 POLLITT, DANIEL H. "Dime Store Demonstrations: Events and Legal Problems of First Sixty Days." *Duke Law Journal* 10 (Summer 1960): 315–65.

See entry 789.

1043 PROUDFOOT, MERRILL. *Diary of a Sit-In.* New Haven: College and University Press, 1962. 204 pages.

See entry 448.

1044 REDDICK, L. D. "The State vs. the Student." *Dissent* 7 (Summer 1960): 219–28.
See entry 224.

1045 SEARLES, RUTH, and J. ALLEN WILLIAMS, JR. "Negro College Students: Participation in Sit-Ins." *Social Forces* 40 (March 1962): 215–20.
See entry 822.

1046 SESSIONS, JIM, and SUE THRASHER. "A New Day Begins: An Interview with John Lewis." *Southern Exposure* 4 (Fall 1976): 14–24.
See entry 538.

1047 SMITH, CHARLES U. "The Sit-Ins and the New Negro Student." *Journal of Intergroup Relations* 2 (1961): 223–29. Reprinted in *American Race Relations Today*, edited by Earl Raab, 69–75. Garden City, NY: Anchor Books, 1962.
See entry 273.

1048 SOLOMON, FREDERIC, and JACOB R. FISHMAN. "Youth and Social Action: II. Action Identity Formation in the First Student Sit-In Demonstration." *Journal of Social Issues* 29, no. 2 (1964): 36–47.
See entry 825.

1049 VON ESCHEN, DONALD, JEROME KIRK, and MAURICE PINARD. "The Organizational Substructure of Disorderly Politics." *Social Forces* 49 (1971): 529–43.
Von Eschen et al. use data from their study of sit-in participants (see Pinard [1969, entry 1041]) to argue against "mass society" theory. They maintain that organizational involvement may increase rather than inhibit participation in direct action movements. They claim that many protest organizations are needed to create and sustain a protest movement. Finally, they insist that the "role organizations play in disorderly politics is essentially the same as in routine politics."

1050 WALKER, JACK L. "Sit-Ins in Atlanta: A Study in the Negro Revolt." In *Atlanta*, edited by David J. Garrow, 59–93. Brooklyn, NY: Carlson Publishing, 1989. Orig. pub. as *Eagleton Institute Cases in Practical Politics no. 34*. New York: McGraw-Hill, 1964.
See entry 302.

1051 WALZER, MICHAEL. "A Cup of Coffee and a Seat." *Dissent* 7, no. 2 (1960): 111–20.
Walzer recounts his recent trip to North Carolina where he met with students involved in the sit-ins in Durham and Raleigh. He describes the excitement on the college campuses, the tactics used by the student demonstrators, and their religious convictions.

1052 WEHR, PAUL E. "A Southern Sit-In." In *Nonviolent Direct Action*, edited by A. Paul Hare and Herbert H. Blumberg, 100–106. Washington, DC: Corpus Books, 1968.
See entry 436.

1053 WOLFF, MILES. *Lunch at the 5 & 10: The Greensboro Sit-Ins, A Contemporary History.* 1970 Reprint. Chicago: Elephant Paperbacks, 1990. 204 pages.
See entry 439.

1054 ZINN, HOWARD. "Abolitionists, Freedom Riders, and the Tactics of Agitation." In *The Antislavery Vanguard,* edited by Martin Duberman, 417–51. Princeton: Princeton University Press, 1965.
Zinn compares contemporary civil rights activists with the abolitionists of the nineteenth century. He maintains that without the radical agitators and "extremists" of the civil rights movement, progress toward racial equality would not take place.

Freedom Rides

1055 GOLDMAN, ERIC F. "Progress—by Moderation and Agitation." *New York Times Magazine,* 18 June 1961. Reprinted in *Black Protest in the Sixties,* edited by August Meier and Elliot Rudwick, 29–36. Chicago: Quadrangle Books, 1970.
Goldman considers the question: "Should the legal processes be supplemented, and run ahead of, by the fire of dramatic agitation and direct action?" He compares the Freedom Rides with the protests by women's suffrage advocates and the UAW's sit-ins. He concludes that the civil rights movement seems "likely to prove one of those agitations which genuinely pushes ahead the cause."

1056 KAHN, THOMAS. "The Political Significance of the Freedom Rides." In *The New Student Left,* edited by Mitchell Cohen and Dennis Hale, 64–75. Boston: Beacon Press, 1966. Address given at the SDS Conference on Race and Politics at the University of North Carolina in 1962.
Kahn presents a radical critique of the civil rights movement, stressing the need to build a mass movement and not rely on outside activists as in the Freedom Rides. He is cautious in his assessment of the Kennedy administration, seeing it as "potentially helpful," but "dangerous" because of the influence of Dixiecrats within the Democratic party.

1057 LOMAX, LOUIS E. "The Freedom Rides." In *The Civil Rights Reader: Basic Documents of the Civil Rights Movement,* edited by Leon Friedman, 51–60. New York: Walker & Co. 1968. Orig. pub. in *The Negro Revolt* by Louis E. Lomax. New York: Harper & Row. 1962.
Lomax presents a detailed chronology of the Freedom Rides, which he describes as a major victory for James Farmer and CORE.

1058   _____. "The Unpredictable Negro." In *Freedom Now! The Civil Rights Struggle in America*, edited by Alan F. Westin, 22–24. New York: Basic Books, 1964. Orig. pub. in *New Leader*, 5 June 1961, 3–4.

Lomax links progress in civil rights to international relations. He writes: "the Negro's relief from injustice is . . . directly proportional to his ability to embarass and pressure the government during hours of international crisis."

1059   MAHONEY, WILLIAM. "In Pursuit of Freedom." In *Nonviolence in America*, edited by Staughton Lynd, 415–28. Indianapolis: Bobbs-Merrill, 1966. Orig. pub. in *Liberation* 6 (September 1961): 7–11.
See entry 590.

1060   MEIER, AUGUST, and ELLIOT RUDWICK. "The First Freedom Ride." *Phylon* 30, no. 3 (1969): 213–22.
See entry 593.

1061   NASH, DIANE. "Inside the Sit-Ins and Freedom Rides: Testimony of a Southern Student." In *We Shall Overcome*, edited by David J. Garrow, vol. 3, 955–74. Brooklyn, NY: Carlson Publishing, 1989. Orig. pub. in *The New Negro*, edited by Matthew Ahmann, 43–60. Notre Dame, IN: Fides Publishers, 1961.
See entry 448.

1062   PECK, JAMES. *Freedom Ride*. New York: Simon & Schuster, 1962. 160 pages.
See entry 597.

1063   _____. "Freedom Rides—1947 and 1961." In *Nonviolent Direct Action, American Cases: Social Psychological Analyses*, edited by A. P. Hare and Herbert H. Blumberg, 49–75. Washington, DC: Corpus Books, 1968.
See entry 598.

1064   SESSIONS, JIM, and SUE THRASHER. "A New Day Begins: An Interview with John Lewis." *Southern Exposure* 4 (Fall 1976): 14–24.
See entry 538.

Black Power and Decline

1065   ABERBACH, JOEL D., and JACK L. WALKER. "The Meanings of Black Power: A Comparison of White and Black Interpretations of a Political Slogan." *American Political Science Review* 64 (1970): 367–88.

Aberbach and Walker report on a 1967 survey of 394 whites and 461 blacks in Detroit. They measured the respondents' support for and understanding of Black Power. They found that 80 percent of whites had a negative reaction to the slogan while 42 percent of blacks expressed approval.

1066   ADLER, RENATA. "The Meredith Mississippi March." In *The Civil Rights Reader*, edited by Leon Friedman, 96–106. New York: Walker & Co. 1966. Orig. pub. in *New Yorker*, 16 July 1966, 21–25.
See entry 317.

1067   BARBOUR, FLOYD B., ed. *The Black Power Revolt: A Collection of Essays*. Boston: Porter Sargent, 1968. 287 pages.
See entry 116.

1068   BENSON, J. KENNETH. "Militant Ideologies and Organizational Contexts: The War on Poverty and the Ideology of 'Black Power.'" In *Social Movements and Social Change*, edited by R. J. Lauer, 107–20. Carbondale: Southern Illinois University Press, 1976.
Benson examines the relationship between the war on poverty and the emergence of the Black Power ideology in the late 1960s. He finds that "the poverty program provided an organizational setting which facilitated the emergence and consolidation of a coherent black power ideology." It also "provided a set of issues around which to mobilize low-income Negroes."

1069   CARMICHAEL, STOKELY. *Stokely Speaks: Black Power to Pan-Africanism*. New York: Random House, 1971. 229 pages.
Collected speeches and statements by a prominent spokesperson for Black Power.

1070   _____. "What We Want." *New York Review of Books*, 22 September 1966, 5–7.
An early formulation of the call for Black Power by its leading advocate.

1071   CARMICHAEL, STOKELY, and CHARLES V. HAMILTON. *Black Power: The Politics of Liberation in America*. New York: Random House, 1967. 198 pages.
This work is the result of a unique collaboration between a militant black activist (Carmichael) and a scholar (Hamilton). Together they advance the argument that black Americans are a colonial people who need to embrace Black Power to change their position in society. They offer examples of the Mississippi Freedom Democratic party, the Lowndes County Freedom Organization, and the Tuskegee Civic Association to illustrate the failure of traditional political solutions and the need for independent black political organizations.

1072   CARMICHAEL, STOKELY, and MIKE THELWELL. "Toward Black Liberation." *Massachusetts Review* 7, no. 4 (1966): 639–51.
Carmichael and Thelwell defend the concept of Black Power, identify the limitations of the liberal strategy of integration, and argue for the necessity of independent black political organization.

1073   CLARK, KENNETH B. "The Present Dilemma of the Negro." In *Black Protest Thought in the Twentieth Century*, edited by August Meier,

Elliot Rudwick, and Francis L. Broderick, 610–21. Indianapolis: Bobbs-Merrill, 1971. Orig. pub. in *Journal of Negro History* 53 (January 1968): 1–11.

Clark describes Black Power as "an anguished cry" born of desperation and fear. He warns that the demands of black separatists may crush all hopes for a racially integrated society.

1074　COOK, SAMUEL DUBOIS. "The Tragic Myth of Black Power." *New South* 21 (Summer 1966): 58–68.

Cook denounces the Black Power ideology as racist and separatist. He sees the origins of the concept in the "bitter disappointment, disgust, and despair over the pace, scope, and quality of social change" among young civil rights workers who have been struggling against "the grim and aching realities" of white racism in the Deep South.

1075　CRUSE, HAROLD. *Rebellion or Revolution?* New York: William Morrow & Co., 1968. 272 pages.
　　　See entry 124.

1076　DANZIG, DAVID. "In Defense of 'Black Power.'" *Commentary,* September 1966, 41–46.

Danzig defends the appeal to Black Power as an effort by blacks to build political strength that is "entirely in keeping with American minority politics." He contends that the new slogan signals the breakup of the liberal civil rights coalition following the realization of its major objectives. The problem of the Black Power movement, as Danzig sees it, is that by relying exclusively on self-interest, it may prevent the formation of a new coalition that is needed to attain its goals.

1077　DUBERMAN, MARTIN. "Black Power and the American Radical Tradition." In *Dissent: Explorations in the History of American Radicalism,* edited by Alfred F. Young, 301–17. DeKalb: Northern Illinois University Press, 1968. Orig. pub. in *Partisan Review,* 35 (Winter 1968): 34–68.

Duberman views the emergence of the Black Power ideology as an understandable, but potentially harmful development. He argues that "by concentrating on immediate prospects, the new doctrine may be jeopardizing larger possibilities for the future, those which could result from a national coalition with white allies." He then compares the Black Power advocates with the Abolitionists and anarchists of earlier periods. His analysis maintains that there is little hope that Black Power will result in meaningful change in American society.

1078　FAGER, CHARLES E. *Uncertain Resurrection: The Poor People's Washington Campaign.* Grand Rapids, MI: William B. Eerdmans Publishing Co., 1969. 142 pages.

Fager describes the events of the 1968 Poor People's Campaign in Washington, D.C., during the spring and summer of 1968. He concludes that it "never succeeded in bringing about the desired confrontation with the federal government over the issues of poverty and public responsibility. This failure was due at least as much to SCLC's own mistakes as it was to any Machiavellian machinations of the Administration."

1079 FELDMAN, PAUL. "The Pathos of 'Black Power.'" *Dissent* 14 (January-February 1967): 69–79.

Feldman rejects the ideology of Black Power, claiming that "any course leading to a prideful but damaging retreat into . . . the ghetto can only result in powerlessness." He criticizes Stokely Carmichael's analysis for its "paucity of economic thinking" because Carmichael's "refusal to work for coalitions that would cross economic lines is in practice a way of foregoing fundamental economic change." See Carmichael and Hamilton (1967, entry 1071).

1080 FORMAN, JAMES. *The Political Thought of James Forman.* Detroit: Black Star Publishing, 1970. 190 pages.
See entry 126.

1081 GESCHWENDER, JAMES A. "Civil Rights Protest and Riots: A Disappearing Distinction." In *The Black Revolt*, edited by James A. Geschwender, 300–11. Englewood Cliffs, NJ: Prentice Hall Press, 1971. Orig. pub. in *Social Science Quarterly* 49 (December 1968): 474–784.

Geschwender argues that "current urban disorders were a developing part of the civil rights movement."

1082 GESCHWENDER, JAMES, A. ed. *The Black Revolt: The Civil Rights Movement, Ghetto Uprisings, and Separatism.* Englewood Cliffs, NJ: Prentice Hall Press, 1971. 483 pages.
See entry 136.

1083 GOOD, PAUL. "The Meredith March." *New South* 21 (Summer 1966): 2–16.
See entry 351.

1084 ———. "A White Look at Black Power." *The Nation*, 8 August 1966, 112–17.

Good examines the tensions among civil rights organizations, especially between SNCC and the NAACP, which emerged during the 1966 Meredith march.

1085 GRAHAM, HUGH DAVIS. "The Storm over Black Power." *Virginia Quarterly Review* 43 (Autumn 1967): 545–65.

Graham views the civil rights movement of the early 1960s as a temporary alliance between white liberals whose goals were equality before the law and equality of individual opportunity and the Negro movement whose goal was the social and economic advancement of African Americans. He sees the Black Power controversy as the natural result of the inherent contradictions between the two ideologies.

1086 HAMILTON, CHARLES V. "An Advocate of Black Power Defines It." *New York Times Magazine*, 14 April 1968. Reprinted in *Black Protest in the*

Sixties, edited by August Meier and Elliot Rudwick, 154–68. Chicago: Quadrangle Books, 1970.

Hamilton defines Black Power as the "ability to organize independent bases of economic and political power." His arguement is addressed to white readers and seeks to persuade them that support of Black Power is a form of enlightened self-interest.

1087   HARDING, VINCENT. "Black Radicalism: The Road from Montgomery." In *Dissent: Explorations in the History of American Radicalism*, edited by Alfred F. Young, 319–54. DeKalb: Northern Illinois University Press, 1968. Reprinted in *We Shall Overcome*, edited by David J. Garrow, vol. 1, 335–70. Brooklyn, NY: Carlson Publishing, 1989.

Harding discusses the reasons for the growing radicalization within the civil rights movement between the March on Washington in 1963 and the assassination of Martin Luther King in 1968.

1088   ———. "The Religion of Black Power." In *We Shall Overcome*, edited by David J. Garrow, vol. 1, 371–406. Brooklyn, NY: Carlson Publishing, 1989. Orig. pub. in *The Religious Situation 1968*, edited by Donald R. Cutler, 3–38. Boston: Beacon Press, 1968.

Harding examines religious elements of the Black Power ideology including self-love, the search for community, messianism, and resurrection.

1089   ———. "Where Have All the Lovers Gone?" In *We Shall Overcome*, edited by David J. Garrow, vol. 1, 323–34. Brooklyn, NY: Carlson Publishing, 1989. Orig. pub. in *New South* 21 (Winter 1966): 27–38.

Harding reflects on the demise of the nonviolent civil rights movement and the paradox of nonviolence in the movement.

1090   HERBERS, JOHN. *The Black Dilemma*. New York: John Day, 1973. 116 pages.

Herbers views the development of black nationalism in the 1960s as an outgrowth of the civil rights movement. He argues that the movement raised black hopes across the nation, but was only able to deliver tangible progress in the South. According to Herbers, the movement's inability to address the problems of urban blacks sparked the rise of black nationalism.

1091   ———. *The Lost Priority: What Happened to the Civil Rights Movement in America?* New York: Funk & Wagnalls, 1970. 236 pages.

Herbers covered the civil rights movement for *The New York Times*. He examines events in Washington during the spring and summer of 1965 that, in his opinion, resulted in the loss of faith in the federal government and the rejection of nonviolence by militant blacks. He argues that the escalation of the Vietnam War, the handling of the Moynihan report, the White House conference on civil rights, and the lack of civil rights enforcement "encouraged the trend away from nonviolence." Herbers contends that, as blacks in increasing numbers adopted the tactic of violence, white reaction further widened the gap between the races.

1092 HOUGH, JOSEPH C., JR. *Black Power and White Protestants: A Christian Response to the New Negro Pluralism*. New York: Oxford University Press, 1968. 228 pages.

Hough examines the factors which contributed to the emergence of Black Power as well as the significance of the term. He views Black Power as "a call for self-determination, equal opportunity, and full appreciation for black men in a white man's nation."

1093 HUBBARD, HOWARD. "Five Long Hot Summers and How They Grew." In *We Shall Overcome*, edited by David J. Garrow, vol. 2, 461–82. Brooklyn, NY: Carlson Publishing, 1989. Orig. pub. in *Public Interest* 12 (Summer 1968): 3–24.

Hubbard applies the insights of game theory to examine the escalation of violence in racial protests between 1963 and 1968. He concludes that the lesson of the summer of 1968 is "that there are stringent limits on what one can accomplish politically with violence."

1094 JACK, HOMER A. "Black Power and the Meredith March." *Gandhi Marg* 10 (October 1966): 285–302.

Jack compares the 1966 Meredith march with the 1965 Selma to Montgomery march and defends the Black Power slogan which emerged during the march. He concludes that "Black Power may be a concept which may be psychologically and politically useful at this difficult stage in the civil rights movement."

1095 KILLIAN, LEWIS M. *The Impossible Revolution?: Black Power and the American Dream*. New York: Random House, 1968. 198 pages.

Killian offers a sociohistorical analysis of the rise of the Black Power movement. "The theme of Black Power" he argues, "reflects the growing disillusionment of Negro Americans with the white man's willingness to give up his position of supremacy."

1096 _____. *The Impossible Revolution, Phase II: Black Power and the American Dream*. New York: Random House, 1975. 197 pages.

This revision of Killian's 1968 analysis of Black Power (see entry 1095) includes one chapter which examines the subsidence of militant black protest. He claims that the revolutionary spirit remains strong nonetheless, and that "a violent revolutionary phase will arise again."

1097 _____. "The Significance of Extremism in the Black Revolution." *Social Problems* 20, no. 1 (1972): 41–48.

Killian examines the role of civil rights leaders identified by the press as "extremists." He advances five propositions regarding the role of extremists in the civil rights movement: (1) they make moderate leaders seem more reasonable, (2) their pessimism serves as a corrective to "illusions of progress," (3) they help identify unresolved issues facing the movement, (4) they may radicalize a segment of the movement and thus increase the polarization between the movement and its opposition, and (5) they may evoke repression of the whole movement.

1098   KOPKIND, ANDREW. "Soul Power." *New York Review of Books,* 24 August 1967, 3–6.

Kopkind analyzes the "failure" of the civil rights movement to make meaningful changes in the lives of the black masses. He claims that victories over segregation in the Deep South were relatively easy because its anachronistic feudal system was unsupportable. When the movement began to attack racism outside the South, however, he maintains that it discovered that "the national system of industrial and technological capitalism was practically invulnerable."

1099   LADNER, JOYCE. "What 'Black Power' Means to Negroes in Mississippi." *Trans-action* 5 (November 1967): 7–15.
See entry 377.

1100   LAWSON, JAMES. "The Meredith March and Tomorrow." *Concern,* 15 July 1966, 4–13.

Lawson, a Memphis minister, describes his involvement in the Meredith march and discusses the objectives of the march, disagreements that arose during the march, and the need for a more revolutionary use of nonviolent direct action against racism.

1101   LEONARD, EDWARD A. "Nonviolence and Violence in American Racial Protest, 1942–1967." *Rocky Mountain Social Science Journal* 6 (1969): 10–22.

Leonard examines violence and nonviolence in civil rights protests from the early demonstrations by CORE in Chicago in 1942 to the growth of the Black Power doctrine and the urban riots of 1967. He identifies three causes of the turn toward violence: (1) frustration that the movement "did not produce appreciable changes" in the lives of many blacks, (2) "the violence suffered by Negroes at the hands of whites," and (3) the escalation of the war in Vietnam.

1102   LESTER, JULIUS. "The Angry Children of Malcolm X." In *We Shall Overcome,* edited by David J. Garrow, vol. 2, 589–602. Brooklyn, NY: Carlson Publishing, 1989. Orig. pub. in *Sing Out* 17 (October 1966): 20–25.

Lester describes the growing impatience of young blacks involved in the civil rights movement. He writes: "More than any other person Malcolm X was responsible for the new militancy that entered The Movement in 1965."

1103   _____. *Look Out Whitey! Black Power's Goin' Get Your Mama.* New York: Dial Press, 1968. 152 pages.

Lester offers an angry justification for Black Power.

1104   _____. *Revolutionary Notes.* New York: Grove Press, 1969. 209 pages.

This collection of columns written for *The Guardian,* a leftist newspaper, between October 1967 and January 1969 contains Lester's reflections on many political issues, most of which are related to civil rights.

1105   MCADAM, DOUG. "The Decline of the Civil Rights Movement." In *Social Movements of the Sixties and Seventies*, edited by Jo Freeman, 279–329. New York: Longman, 1983.

McAdam uses the case of the civil rights movement in the late 1960s to evaluate three theoretical perspectives on social movement decline: classical, resource mobilization, and political process. He finds that the growing radicalism of the black movement does not correspond to the stages of organization, conservatization, and institutionalization predicted by the classical model. He also rejects the resource mobilization model based on his observation that financial support for the movement organizations followed, rather than preceded, peaks of movement activity. He favors the political process model which stresses the importance of the internal strength of movement forces, the external "structure of political opportunities," and the response of other groups, especially repressive measures of the federal government.

1106   MATUSOW, ALLEN J. "From Civil Rights to Black Power: The Case of SNCC, 1960–1966." In *Twentieth Century America: Recent Interpretations*, edited by Barton J. Bernstein and Allen J. Matusow, 531–36. New York: Harcourt, Brace and World, 1969.

See entry 526.

1107   MEIER, AUGUST, ed. *The Transformation of Activism: Black Experience*. Chicago: Aldine Publishing Co, 1970. 178 pages.

See entry 146.

1108   MUSE, BENJAMIN. *The American Negro Revolution: From Nonviolence to Black Power, 1963–1967*. Bloomington: University of Indiana Press, 1968. 406 pages.

See entry 72.

1109   PECK, JAMES. "Black Racism." *Liberation* 11 (October 1966): 31–32.

Peck, a veteran CORE activist and Freedom Rider, denounces Black Power as "a racist slogan" following his ouster from CORE. He argues that the civil rights movement must not abandon the goal of racial integration and the tactics of nonviolence.

1110   POUSSAINT, ALVIN F. "How the 'White Problem' Spawned 'Black Power.'" *Ebony*, August 1967, 88–94.

Movement psychiatrist Poussaint traces the origins of the Black Power ideology to "the unresolved psychological difficulties in 'black-white relations' within the southern civil rights movement." Based on his interviews with black civil rights workers, he documents many negative facets of the Mississippi Summer Project of 1964. These included whites with a need for self-glorification, examples of white paternalism and superiority, unnecessary risk-taking and provocative behavior, white guilt, and sexual rivalry.

1111 　　　. "A Negro Psychiatrist Explains the Negro Psyche." *New York Times Magazine*, 20 August 1967, 55.

Poussaint argues that nonviolent protestors against segregation were "struggling with suppressed rage toward whites." With the emergence of Black Power these civil rights "workers appeared to be seeking a sense of inner psychological emancipation from racism through self-assertion and release of aggressive, angry feelings."

1112 POWLEDGE, FRED. *Black Power, White Resistance: Notes on the New Civil War*. Cleveland: World Publishing, 1967. 282 pages.

Powledge discusses the changes that the civil rights movement underwent in the North and South between 1964 and 1966.

1113 RADOSH, RONALD. "From Protest to Black Power: The Failure of Coalition Politics." In *The Great Society Reader*, edited by Marvin Gettleman and David Mermelstein, 278–93. New York: Random House, 1967.

Radosh presents a radical critique of Bayard Rustin's essay "From Protest to Politics" (1965, see entry 1116). He rejects Rustin's proposal for a coalition between the civil rights movement and other liberal forces within the Democratic party, claiming it "has actually directed one segment of the movement into co-operation with the dominant system of oppression."

1114 RUDWICK, ELLIOT, and AUGUST MEIER. "Integration vs. Separatism: The NAACP and CORE Face Challenge from Within." In *Along the Color Line*, edited by August Meier and Elliot Rudwick, 238–64. Urbana: University of Illinois Press, 1976.

See entry 603.

1115 RUSTIN, BAYARD. "Black Power and Coalition Politics." *Commentary* 42 (September 1966): 35–40. Reprinted in *We Shall Overcome*, edited by David J. Garrow, vol. 3, 1011–16. Brooklyn, NY: Carlson Publishing, 1989.

Rustin discusses the factors contributing to the popularity of the Black Power ideology and the consequences of its widespread adoption. He views the concept as both "utopian and reactionary," and claims it is "more likely to bring hostility to the surface than respect." He accuses the advocates of Black Power of diverting "the entire civil rights movement from the hard task of developing strategies to realign the major parties" and of embroiling it "in a debate that can only lead more and more to politics by frustration."

1116 　　　. "From Protest to Politics: The Future of the Civil Rights Movement." *Commentary* 39, no. 2 (1965): 25–31. Reprinted in *We Shall Overcome*, edited by David J. Garrow, vol. 3, 997–1010. Brooklyn, NY: Carlson Publishing, 1989.

Rustin argues that the passage of the 1964 Civil Rights Act means that the goals of the movement must change from gaining individual civil rights to achieving equality through economic reforms. He feels that this can only be accomplished through political change. Rustin also insists that blacks must continue to work with white allies in union, liberal, and religious groups within the Democratic party.

1117 THOMAS, CURLEW O., and BARBARA BOSTON THOMAS. "Blacks' Socioeconomic Status and the Civil Rights Movement's Decline, 1970–1979: An Examination of Some Hypotheses." *Phylon* 45, no. 1 (1984): 40–51.

The authors examine data on black income, occupations, and education to determine if changes in these variables can explain the decline of the civil rights movement during the 1970s. They find that none of their five hypotheses are supported because the "objective living conditions of blacks were neither worsened nor reversed during the 1970s."

1118 VIVIAN, C. T. *Black Power and the American Myth*. Philadelphia: Fortress Press, 1970. 135 pages.

Vivian interprets the civil rights movement in light of the violent confrontations and Black Power rhetoric of the late 1960s. He describes the movement as both a success and a failure. He feels that it was successful in raising expectations of black people, but it was also a failure because it did not change the material conditions of life in the black community.

1119 VON ESCHEN, DONALD, JEROME KIRK, and MAURICE PINARD. "The Disintegration of the Negro Non-Violent Movement." In *Social Movements and Social Change*, edited by R. H. Lauer, 203–26. Carbondale: Southern Illinois University Press, 1976. Orig. pub. in *Journal of Peace Research* 6, no. 3 (1969): 215–34.

Von Eschen and associates draw upon studies of local movements in Tennessee, Florida, and Maryland to explain why the civil rights movement abandoned the practice of nonviolence after 1966 in spite of its previous successes. They maintain this happened because "blacks concluded correctly that disorder works" and because the expansion of the movement "brought in people whose life styles were inconsistent with nonviolent action." Equally important in their view was the movement's shift to new goals that did not pose as strong a moral dilemma for whites as did the initial goals of open public accommodations and voting rights.

1120 WEHR, PAUL E. "Nonviolence and Differentiation in the Equal Rights Movement." *Sociological Inquiry* 38 (Winter 1968): 65–76.

Wehr argues that if the civil rights movement is to regain lost momentum it must develop "an extremely militant but basically nonviolent tactic of social disruption, combining all but the most violent techniques used to date by equal rights activists."

1121 WILSON, C. E. "Black Power and the Myth of Black Racism." *Liberation* 11 (September 1966): 27–29.

Wilson claims that the notion that Black Power constitutes "black racism" is a creation of white liberals whose "favored place in the civil-rights movement is being threatened." He maintains that the myth of black racism helps white liberals "explain the growing open hostility of Negroes toward them" and serves as an excuse for them to isolate the Black Power advocates.

1122   WOODWARD, C. VANN. "After Watts—Where Is the Negro Revolution Headed?" *New York Times Magazine*, 29 August 1965. Reprinted in *Black Protest in the Sixties*, edited by August Meier and Elliot Rudwick, 116–26. Chicago: Quadrangle Books, 1970.

In the wake of the "mounting Negro impatience, bitterness, and anger" that surfaced in the Watts riot, Woodward assesses the future of the civil rights movement. He states that the movement is at a turning point, but the black leaders "are not agreed on which way it should turn." He compares leftist programs such as the MFDP with the more moderate coalition politics advocated by Bayard Rustin.

1123   WRIGHT, NATHAN, JR. *Black Power and Urban Unrest*. New York: Hawthorn Books, 1967. 200 pages.

Wright outlines an agenda for the Black Power movement. He maintains there is a need for both the Black Power movement, which he defines in terms of black self-development, and the civil rights movement, which he sees as being primarily concerned with rights due to black people as American citizens.

9

Other Topics

Public Opinion

1124 ABERBACH, JOEL D., and JACK L. WALKER. "The Meanings of Black Power: A Comparison of White and Black Interpretations of a Political Slogan." *American Political Science Review* 64 (1970): 367–88. See entry 1065.

1125 BRINK, WILLIAM, and LOUIS HARRIS. *Black and White: A Study of U.S. Racial Attitudes Today.* New York: Simon & Schuster, 1967. 285 pages.

Brink and Harris report on a national survey of the attitudes of black and white Americans conducted in 1966. Also included in their report is a survey of 100 black leaders. This study complements their previous work, *The Negro Revolution in America* (1964, see entry 1126). They find that white attitudes toward blacks arc more favorable than in 1963, but that many are also "deeply upset by the disturbing course the Negro's struggle has taken." Among blacks, they report that the majority remains committed to integration and nonviolence, but "they are somewhat less optimistic" about their chances for further progress.

1126 ———. *The Negro Revolution in America.* New York: Simon & Schuster, 1964. 249 pages.

This is the report of a 1963 national survey of black and white attitudes on racial issues, especially those issues arising out of the civil rights movement. Also interviewed in the survey were 100 black leaders. According to the authors, blacks express strong support for the objectives and leaders of the movement. They also maintain that while a majority of whites express support for black civil rights, many object to close social contact between the two races.

1127   BURSTEIN, PAUL. "Public Opinion, Demonstrations, and the Passage of Anti-Discrimination Legislation." *Public Opinion Quarterly* 43 (Summer 1979): 157–73.
    See entry 713.

1128   CAMPBELL, ANGUS. *White Attitudes Toward Black People.* Ann Arbor, MI: Institute for Social Research, 1971. 177 pages.
    The first six chapters of this book present the results of a survey of racial attitudes in fifteen major U.S. cities, which was commissioned by the National Advisory Commission on Civil Disorders. Included are questions on support for black protest and support for civil rights legislation. Chapter 7 uses data from national surveys conducted in 1964, 1968 and 1970 to measure changes in white attitudes over time. Campbell finds little support for a "white backlash." Instead, he reports growing support for black civil rights among all segments of the white population. He states: "We find no instances in which a specific group moves in opposition to a general positive change in the larger population."

1129   ERSKINE, HAZEL. "The Polls: Demonstrations and Race Riots." *Public Opinion Quarterly* 31 (Winter 1967): 655–77.
    This article includes answers to questions asked by several polling organizations on opinions of civil rights demonstrations, the effectiveness of civil rights demonstrations and black leaders, and presidents' handling of civil rights crises.

1130   _____. "The Polls: Negro Employment." *Public Opinion Quarterly* 32 (Spring 1968): 132–53.
    Erskine summarizes responses to questions about black employment asked by several national polling organizations. Among the topics she covers are: willingness to work with blacks, prejudice toward blacks in specific occupations, fair employment legislation, and possible solutions to black employment problems.

1131   _____. "The Polls: Negro Housing." *Public Opinion Quarterly* 31 (Fall 1967): 482–98.
    This article includes answers to questions dealing with housing segregation and integration that were asked in national surveys conducted by several polling organizations. Some questions date from the 1940s, but most of the studies were conducted during the 1960s.

1132   _____. "The Polls: Race Relations." *Public Opinion Quarterly* 26 (Spring 1962): 137–48.
    This article presents the results of studies of racial integration conducted by various polling organizations from 1942 to 1961. Specific topics include integration of schools, segregation in public places, Freedom Rides, and segregation in housing.

1133   _____. "The Polls: Recent Opinion on Racial Problems." *Public Opinion Quarterly* 32 (Winter 1968): 696–703.
    Erskine presents answers to eight questions asked in a Gallop poll deal-

ing with the prospects of "serious racial trouble," and with police response to looters, Kerner Commission findings, treatment of Negroes, who is "to blame" for blacks' problems, prevalence of employment discrimination, labor union discrimination, and the pace of government efforts to promote integration.

1134 _____. "The Polls: Speed of Racial Integration." *Public Opinion Quarterly* 32 (Fall 1968): 513–24.

Erskine reports results of several Gallup polls asking whether or not the "administration is pushing racial integration too fast." Also included are results of several Harris and Survey Research Center (SRC) polls dealing with the pace of integration.

1135 _____. "The Polls: World Opinion on U.S. Racial Problems." *Public Opinion Quarterly* 32 (Summer 1968): 299–312.

This article includes opinions of U.S. racial problems from people of various foreign nations. Most data were collected by the U.S. Information Agency in the late 1950s and early 1960s.

1136 GOLDMAN, PETER. *Report from Black America.* New York: Simon & Schuster, 1970. 282 pages.

Newsweek senior editor Goldman reports on a 1969 national survey of black attitudes, using many of the same questions that Brink and Harris used in their surveys of 1963 (see entry 1126) and 1966 (see entry 1125). He reports that although "dissatisfaction remains the norm in the black community," most black Americans "are not *that* angry." They want their rightful place in American society, but according to Goldman "their choice of weapons runs to politics, diplomacy and nonviolent action."

1137 HYMAN, HERBERT H., and PAUL B. SHEATSLEY. "Attitudes Toward Desegregation." *Scientific American* 211, no. 1 (1964): 16–23.

Hyman and Sheatsley trace changes in white attitudes toward racial integration between 1956 and 1963. Analysis of survey data gathered by the National Opinion Research Center (NORC) leads them to conclude that "the attitudes of white Americans of both the North and South are continuing to shift toward greater acceptance of integration."

1138 LEMON, RICHARD. *The Troubled Americans.* New York: Simon & Schuster, 1970. 255 pages.

Lemon reports the results of a 1969 survey of the attitudes of "middle Americans." Chapter 4 ("The Troublemakers") covers several questions dealing with race relations and reveals considerable resentment of supposed favorable treatment given blacks and lenient treatment of black militants. Much of this data was first published in *Newsweek*, 6 October 1969.

1139 LUBELL, SAMUEL. *Black and White: Test of a Nation.* New York: Harper & Row, 1964. 210 pages.

Lubell is a political analyst who examines the debate over civil rights for blacks with an eye on white public opinion. The most interesting section is chapter 6 ("The Second Civil War"), which probes the attitudes of southern whites following the Freedom Rides of 1961. He is amazed at "how prodigious has been the psychological turmoil over so small a degree of actual change."

1140   MARX, GARY T. *Protest and Prejudice: A Study of Belief in the Black Community.* New York: Harper & Row, 1967. 228 pages.

Marx reports the results of a 1964 survey of urban blacks. He finds that although "there is deep anger and frustration, as well as varying degrees of suspicion and resentment of whites," there is "still optimism about the possibility of change within the system."

1141   _____. "Religion: Opiate or Inspiration of Civil Rights Militancy among Negroes?" *American Sociological Review* 32, no. 1 (1969): 64–72.

Marx studied support for civil rights protests among a national sample of blacks. He reports here that people with greater religious involvement had less militant views, but church members with a strong "temporal" orientation were also militant on civil rights issues.

1142   SCHWARTZ, MILDRED. *Trends in White Attitudes toward Negroes.* Report no. 119. Chicago: National Opinion Research Center, 1967. 134 pages.

Drawing upon ten NORC surveys conducted between 1942 and 1965 and supplemented with data from surveys conducted by other organizations, Schwartz traces changes in white attitudes toward African Americans. Specific chapters focus on issues of education, housing, and discrimination in "other areas." Of particular interest is chapter 5, which examines attitudes toward the civil rights movement, including its goals and tactics, various civil rights organizations, and future prospects for race relations. She concludes: "Among white Americans the trend has been to greater favorability to integration and to positive assessment of the goals of the civil rights movement." She also acknowledges, however, that there is "evidence of fear, suspicion, and serious reservation" on the issue of black civil rights among many whites.

1143   SHEATSLEY, PAUL B. "White Attitudes toward the Negro." In *The Negro American,* edited by Talcott Parsons and Kenneth B. Clark, 303–23. Boston: Beacon Press, 1966.

Sheatsley reviews public opinion data from 1942 to 1963 that show a steady increase in white support for racial integration in schools, housing, and transportation. He uses the results of a 1963 National Opinion Research Center (NORC) survey to examine the effect of various demographic variables on support for integration and attitudes toward the civil rights movement. He concludes that while most whites are "more comfortable in a segregated society . . . most of them know . . . that racial discrimination is morally wrong and recognize the legitimacy of the Negro protest." He presents evidence that suggests that white support for black civil rights increases "when acts of discrimination become contrary to the law of the land."

1144 TAYLOR, D. GARTH, PAUL B. SHEATSLEY, and ANDREW M. GREELEY. "Attitudes toward Racial Integration." *Scientific American* 238, no. 6 (1978): 42–49.

Taylor and associates trace changes in attitudes of white Americans toward racial integration between 1963 and 1978 as measured by the National Opinion Research Center. They find a steady increase in favorable attitudes towards integration with a large spurt of acceptance occurring between 1970 and 1972.

1145 WIEBE, ROBERT H. "White Attitudes and Black Rights from *Brown* to *Bakke.*" In *Have We Overcome? Race Relations Since Brown*, edited by Michael V. Namorato, 147–71. Jackson: University Press of Mississippi, 1979.

Wiebe traces changes in white public opinion toward black rights in the years following the *Brown* decision. He finds a fundamental change in white attitudes towards blacks as human beings and as equals. He maintains that while whites are much more supportive of the principle of racial equality, they falter where black rights blend with the needs of poor Americans generally. Wiebe points out that it is class, not race, which lies at the base of the blacks' problems.

Leadership

1146 BRISBANE, ROBERT H. *Black Activism: Racial Revolution in the United States, 1954–1970.* Valley Forge, PA: Judson Press, 1974. 332 pages. See entry 17.

1147 CAPECI, DOMINIC J., JR. "From Harlem to Montgomery: The Bus Boycott and Leadership of Adam Clayton Powell, Jr., and Martin Luther King, Jr." In *The Walking City*, edited by David J. Garrow, 303–22. Brooklyn, NY: Carlson Publishing, 1989. Orig. pub. in *Historian* 41 (August 1979): 721–37. See entry 176.

1148 CLARK, KENNETH B. "The Management of the Civil Rights Struggle." In *Freedom Now! The Civil Rights Struggle in America*, edited by Alan F. Westin, 30–40. New York: Basic Books, 1964. Transcript of a televised panel discussion, WGBH TV, Boston, 23 July 1963.

In this transcript, Clark moderates a discussion in which the leaders of the five major civil rights organizations are the panelists. The panelists include Roy Wilkins, Whitney Young, Jr., James Farmer, James Forman, and Martin Luther King, Jr.

1149 GARROW, DAVID J. "Black Ministerial Protest Leadership, 1955–1970." In *Encyclopedia of Religion in the South*, edited by Samuel S. Hill, 106–8. Macon, GA: Mercer University Press, 1984.

Garrow credits "young black ministers, often new to their pastorates but with solid collegiate training" with "starting many of the local protests against segregation that sprang up across the South throughout the 1950s and early 1960s."

1150   HINES, RALPH H., and JAMES E. PIERCE. "Negro Leadership after the Social Crisis: An Analysis of Leadership Changes in Montgomery, Alabama." *Phylon* 26, no. 2 (1965): 162–72.
See entry 205.

1151   KILLIAN, LEWIS M. "Leadership in the Desegregation Crisis: An Institutional Analysis." In *Intergroup Relations and Leadership*, edited by Muzafer Sherif, 142–66. New York: John Wiley & Sons, 1962.
Killian reviews research on Negro leadership since the *Brown* decision, including his own study of Tallahassee, and concludes that there has been a sweeping change. He maintains that old accommodating leaders have been replaced by new protest leadership, and that this change has come about primarily due to "the altered temper of the Negroes of the South."

1152   KILLIAN, LEWIS M., and CHARLES M. GRIGG. *Racial Crisis in America: Leadership in Conflict.* Englewood Cliffs, NJ: Prentice Hall Press, 1964. 144 pages.
See entry 268.

1153   KILLIAN, LEWIS M., and CHARLES U. SMITH. "Negro Protest Leaders in a Southern Community." *Social Forces* 38 (March 1960): 253–57. Reprinted in *Conflict and Competition: Studies in the Recent Black Protest Movement*, edited by John Bracey, August Meier, and Elliot Rudwick, 34–41. Belmont, CA: Wadsworth, 1970.
See entry 269.

1154   LADD, EVERETT CARLL, JR. *Negro Political Leadership in the South.* Ithaca, NY: Cornell University Press, 1966. 348 pages.
See entry 435.

1155   LOMAX, LOUIS E. "The Negro Revolt against 'the Negro Leaders.'" In *We Shall Overcome*, edited by David J. Garrow, vol. 2, 603–10. Brooklyn, NY: Carlson Publishing, 1989. Orig. pub. in *Harper's*, June 1960, 41–48.
See entry 615.

1156   McWHORTER, GERALD, and ROBERT CRAIN. "Subcommunity Gladitorial Competition: Civil Rights Leadership as a Competitive Process." *Social Forces* 46 (September 1967): 8–21. Reprinted in *Conflict and Competition*, edited by John H. Bracey, Jr., August Meier, and Elliot Rudwick, 65–83. Belmont, CA: Wadsworth, 1971.
Based on a 1965 National Opinion Research Center (NORC) study of school integration in fifteen cities—eight northern and seven southern—McWhorter and Crain examine the factors "causing variation in the degree and character of civil rights leadership competition." They find that organized

competition exists in cities where there are multiple, independent bases of support. Independent competition is found where there is a weak or ambiguous prestige structure in the black community. They also find that organized competition stimulates the most intense civil rights activity, while individual competition is better for "sustained activity over a period of years." The city without leadership competition, however, they claim "is probably best able to carry out a tightly planned campaign to achieve specific goals."

1157 MORRISON, MINION K. C. *Black Political Mobilization: Leadership, Power, and Mass Behavior.* Albany: State University of New York Press, 1987. 303 pages.
See entry 392.

1158 NELSON, HAROLD A. "Leadership and Change in an Evolutionary Movement: An Analysis of Change in the Leadership Structure of the Southern Civil Rights Movement." *Social Forces* 49 (1971): 353–71.
Nelson examines changes in leadership within the southern civil rights movement. He argues that the achievement of the movement's short-term goal of destroying legally sanctioned segregation required charismatic leadership. Its success in achieving this goal he feels led to the emergence of more specialized, noncharismatic leaders as the movement shifted its energies to accomplishing the long-range goal of integration.

1159 ROGERS, KIM LACY. "Organizational Experience and Personal Narrative: Stories of New Orleans' Civil Rights Leadership." *Oral History Review* 13 (1985): 23–54.
See entry 314.

1160 WALKER, JACK L. "The Functions of Disunity: Negro Leadership in a Southern City." In *Racial Conflict*, edited by Gary T. Marx, 379–87. Boston: Little, Brown & Co., 1971. Orig. pub. in *Journal of Negro Education* 32 (Summer 1963), 227–36.
See entry 300.

1161 ———. "Protest and Negotiation: A Case Study of Negro Leadership in Atlanta, Georgia." In *Atlanta*, edited by David J. Garrow, 31–58. Brooklyn, NY: Carlson Publishing, 1989. Orig. pub. in *Midwest Journal of Political Science* 7 (May 1963): 99–124.
See entry 301.

1162 WALZER, MICHAEL. "The politics of the New Negro." *Dissent* 7, no. 3 (1960): 235–43.
Walzer describes his observations of the early movement and the conflict between older, established black leaders and the student protestors. He sees the origins of the movement in "the increasing number of talented, aggressive young men" who could not find opportunities for themselves as part of the "limited Negro middle class." He points out that the young blacks reject the accommodationist middle class leaders and form alliances with "the best of the preachers, who are the real leaders of the Negro masses."

This conflict, according to Walzer, is therefore as much a matter of class as of generation.

1163 WARREN, ROBERT PENN. *Who Speaks for the Negro?* New York: Random House, 1965. 454 pages.
See entry 162.

1164 WEISS, NANCY J. "Creative Tensions in the Leadership of the Civil Rights Movement." In *The Civil Rights Movement in America*, edited by Charles W. Eagles, 39–64. Jackson: University Press of Mississippi, 1986.
Weiss points to the positive consequences of the often-noted differences between leaders of the major civil rights organizations. The variety of approaches, she argues, gave the movement the ability to attack a complex problem from many perspectives. She examines the Council for United Civil Rights Leadership as an example of formal cooperation among the seven major civil rights organizations. She uses Whitney Young to illustrate how more conservative black leaders benefitted from the demands of their more radical brethren. After 1965, however, Weiss observes that the widening disagreement over strategies and tactics reduced the amount of informal cooperation among civil rights leaders.

White Reaction

1165 BARTLEY, NUMAN V. *The Rise of Massive Resistance: Race and Politics in the South During the 1950's*. Baton Rouge: Louisiana State University Press, 1969. 390 pages.
This describes the political reaction against racial integration in the South during the 1950s. Bartley focuses on the rise (and eventual decline) of "neobourbon" political leaders who attempted to preserve segregation following the *Brown* decision. He documents the growing racial polarization in the Deep South which preceded the civil rights movement.

1166 BELKNAP, MICHAEL R. "The Legal Legacy of Lemuel Penn." *Howard Law Journal* 25 (1982): 457–524.
See entry 739.

1167 BLASI, ANTHONY J. *Segregationist Violence and Civil Rights Movements in Tuscaloosa*. Washington, DC: University Press of America, 1980. 168 pages.
See entry 171.

1168 BRADEN, WALDO W. "The Rhetoric of a Closed Society." *Southern Speech Communication Journal* 45 (Summer 1980): 333–51.
See entry 321.

1169 BRADY, TOM. *Black Monday*. Winona, MS: Citizens' Councils of America, 1955. 92 pages.
Brady, a Yale-educated Mississippi circuit judge, is described as the

"intellectual leader" of the anti-desegregation movement. *Black Monday* is
an expanded version of a speech he delivered in 1954 in which he defends
racial segregation, attacks the Supreme Court's *Brown* decision, and calls for
organized resistance to its implementation.

1170   CANZONERI, ROBERT. *"I Do So Politely": A Voice from the South.* Bos-
       ton: Houghton Mifflin Co., 1965. 182 pages.
       See entry 326.

1171   CARTER, HODDING. *So the Heffners Left McComb.* New York: Double-
       day, 1965. 142 pages.
       See entry 327.

1172   COOK, JAMES GRAHAM. *The Segregationists.* New York: Appleton-
       Century Crofts, 1962. 376 pages.
       Cook profiles a variety of segregationists and their organizations. Al-
though he does not sympathize with their objectives, he does respect their
dedication and intelligence. Cook claims that the segregationists "have some
very resourceful people" on their side.

1173   EAST, P. D. 1960. *The Magnolia Jungle: The Life, Times and Educa-
       tion of a Southern Editor.* New York: Simon & Schuster, 1960. 243
       pages.
       See entry 341.

1174   FRADY, MARSHALL. *Wallace.* Cleveland: World Publishing, 1970. 246
       pages.
       See entry 929.

1175   GORDON, BUD. *Nightriders: The Inside Story of the Liuzzo Killing.*
       Birmingham: BRALGO Publications, 1966. 64 pages.
       See entry 199.

1176   HALBERSTAM, DAVID. "A County Divided against Itself." *The Reporter*,
       15 December 1955, 30–32.
       See entry 356.

1177   HARKEY, IRA B., JR. *The Smell of Burning Crosses: An Autobiography
       of a Mississippi Newspaperman.* Jacksonville, IL: Harris, Wolfe & Co.,
       1967. 207 pages.
       See entry 360.

1178   HAYS, BROOKS. *A Southern Moderate Speaks.* Chapel Hill: University
       of North Carolina Press, 1959. 231 pages.
       See entry 251.

1179   HOROWITZ, DAVID ALLEN. "White Southerners, Alienation, and Civil
       Rights: The Response to Corporate Liberalism, 1956–1965." *Journal of
       Southern History* 54, no. 2 (1988): 173–203.
       Horowitz draws upon letters to Lyndon Johnson, editorials in southern
newspapers, and statements by southern politicians to examine the reasons

for opposition to federal civil rights measures. The objections of working and middle class whites cannot be dismissed as mere racism, he argues. He shows that included in their criticism was a feeling of "helplessness concerning increased government jurisdiction over personal life" and a rejection of liberal modernism.

1180 KALLAL, EDWARD W., JR. "St. Augustine and the Ku Klux Klan: 1963 and 1964." In *St. Augustine*, edited by David J. Garrow, 93–176. Brooklyn, NY: Carlson Publishing, 1989. Senior thesis, University of Florida, 1976.
       See entry 266.

1181 KILPATRICK, JAMES J. *The Southern Case for School Segregation*, New York: Crowell-Collier Press, 1962. 220 pages.
       Kilpatrick argues against "compulsory integration" of public educational facilities. He urges white Southerners to accept the inevitability of the *Brown* decision, but advocates "freedom of choice" plans and private education as acceptable methods for preserving the tradition of racial separation in the schools.

1182 MCMILLEN, NEIL R. *The Citizens' Council: Organized Resistance to the Second Reconstruction, 1954–1964*. Urbana: University of Illinois Press, 1971. 397 pages.
       McMillen has written the definitive history of the White Citizens' Council, the organization that led southern resistance to the civil rights movement in the late 1950s and early 1960s. He surveys the various council affiliates on a state-by-state basis, deliniates their ideology of racial superiority, and traces their activities and decline. Much of his account focuses on Mississippi, where the council was strongest. He claims that the council managed "to slow the processes of change, but not to still them." Despite its promises to defend the racial status quo, the council "was frail protection against the leveling force of the Second Reconstruction."

1183 _____. "Development of Civil Rights, 1956–1970." In *A History of Mississippi*, edited by Richard Aubrey McLemore, vol. 2, 154–76. Hattiesburg: University and College Press of Mississippi, 1973.
       See entry 386.

1184 _____. "Organized Resistance to School Desegregation in Tennessee." *Tennessee Historical Quarterly* 30 (Fall 1971): 315–28.
       See entry 447.

1185 _____. "White Citizens' Council and Resistance to School Desegregation in Arkansas." *Arkansas Historical Quarterly* 30 (Spring 1971): 95–122.
       See entry 254.

1186 MARTIN, JOHN BARTLOW. *The Deep South Says Never.* New York: Ballantine Books, 1957. 181 pages.

Martin describes reaction to the 1954 *Brown* decision in several southern states. Most of his reporting focuses on the White Citizens' Council and several of its leaders, although he also presents the cases of the black plaintiffs in Clarendon County, South Carolina, and the relatively successful desegregation of schools in the border states. Martin maintains that the massive white reaction against the *Brown* decision came about "because the people of the Deep South were not prepared to abandon what they consider their way of life. To Southerners the Court's decision seemed to do far more than break down segregation in the schools; it rent the seamless garment of apartness."

1187 MUSE, BENJAMIN. *Virginia's Massive Resistance.* Bloomington: Indiana University Press, 1961. 184 pages.

See entry 459.

1188 ROWAN, CARL T. *Go South to Sorrow.* New York: Random House, 1957. 246 pages.

Rowan reports on his trip through the South in 1956. He finds that reaction to the *Brown* decision has stimulated intense resistance to desegregation and that there are only isolated pockets of acceptance.

1189 ROWE, GARY THOMAS., JR. *My Undercover Years with the Ku Klux Klan.* New York: Bantam Books, 1976. 216 pages.

Rowe was a member of the Alabama Klan who participated in the 1961 attack on the Freedom Riders in Birmingham and the 1965 shooting of Viola Liuzzo after the Selma march. He was subsequently recruited as an undercover informant by the FBI and testified against Klansmen arrested for Liuzzo's murder. His autobiography exposes the Klan's inner workings and its close ties with southern law officers.

1190 RUSTIN, BAYARD. "Fear in the Delta." In *Down the Line*, edited by Bayard Rustin, 62–87. Chicago: Quadrangle Books, 1971. Orig. pub. in *Liberation* 1 (December 1956), 17–19.

See entry 404.

1191 SCHAEFER, RICHARD T. "The Ku Klux Klan: Continuity and Change." *Phylon* 32, no. 2 (1971): 143–57.

Schaefer views the modern Klan from a historical perspective. He contends that the Klan has ceased to be a viable social movement, but that the mentality behind it continues to thrive.

1192 SHIPP, BILL. *Murder at Broad River Bridge: The Slaying of Lemuel Penn by Members of the Ku Klux Klan.* Atlanta: Peachtree Publishers, 1981. 91 pages.

See entry 298.

1193　SIKORA, FRANK. *Until Justice Rolls Down: The Birmingham Church Bombing Case.* Tuscaloosa: University of Alabama Press, 1991. 192 pages.
　　　See entry 233.

1194　SITTON, CLAUDE. "Bullets and Ballots in Greenwood, Mississippi." In *Freedom Now! The Struggle for Civil Rights in America,* edited by Alan F. Westin, 87–94. New York: Basic Books, 1964. Orig. pub. in the *New York Times,* 6 April 1963, 20.
　　　See entry 412.

1195　SMITH, BOB. *They Closed Their Schools: Prince Edward County, Virginia, 1951–1964.* Chapel Hill: University of North Carolina Press, 1965. 281 pages.
　　　See entry 460.

1196　SMITH, FRANK. *Congressman from Mississippi.* New York: Capricorn Books, 1964. 338 pages.
　　　Smith, a member of Congress from Mississippi between 1950 and 1962, was defeated when his opponents successfully branded him a "liberal" despite the fact that he never openly challenged the segregationist orthodoxy of his home state. His book contains valuable insights on the growth of the White Citizens' Council and the white reaction against the civil rights movement.

1197　VANDER ZANDEN, JAMES W. "The Klan Revival." *American Journal of Sociology* 65 (March 1960): 456–62.
　　　Vander Zanden examines the occupational status of 153 Klan members. He finds that ninety-eight could be classified as skilled workers, marginal businessmen, or marginal white-collar workers. He claims that their economic "status is insecure and anxious" and they "lack the resources, skills, or education necessary to improve their life-chances." He argues that their insecurity and thwarted aspirations explain the attraction of Klan membership.

1198　———. *Race Relations in Transition: The Segregation Crisis in the South.* New York: Random House, 1965. 135 pages.
　　　Most of the material in this book appeared previously in various sociological journals. The major focus is on white resistance to desegregation efforts in the South. Also included are analyses of the White Citizens' Council and the Ku Klux Klan.

1199　———. "Seven Years of Southern Resistance.: *Midwest Quarterly* 2 (1961): 273–84.
　　　Vander Zanden reviews here the attempts by southern politicians to evade the 1954 *Brown* decision. He concludes that "despite continuing southern efforts to stall and resist . . . the chief battlements in defense of

segregation have been seriously and irredeemably breached." He considers the 1957 Little Rock crisis as "the turning point in the struggle."

1200 _____. "Voting on Segregationist Referenda." *Public Opinion Quarterly* 25 (Spring 1961): 92–105.

Vander Zanden examines the relationship between socio-economic status and support for segregationist referenda in six southern states between 1954 and 1956. He finds that the evidence is "inconsistent and even contradictory." Despite opinion polls indicating an inverse relationship between social class and segregationist sentiments, he failed to find any definitive pattern in the election returns.

1201 WAKEFIELD, DAN. *Revolt in the South.* New York: Grove Press, 1960. 128 pages.

Wakefield describes the first phase of the civil rights movement between 1954 and 1960, which he covered for *The Nation* magazine. Among the topics he reports on are the growth of the White Citizens' Council in Mississippi, the plight of white moderates, and the growing militance of young blacks.

1202 WHITEHEAD, DON. *Attack on Terror: The FBI against the Ku Klux Klan in Mississippi.* New York: Funk & Wagnalls, 1970. 321 pages. See entry 423.

1203 WILHOIT, FRANCIS M. *The Politics of Massive Resistance.* New York: George Braziller, 1973. 320 pages.

Wilhoit provides an interpretive analysis of the origins, politics, and ideology of the massive resistance movement—the white South's response to the Supreme Court's desegregation decision. He hypothesizes that the "chief proximate causes of Massive Resistance racism were political oligarchicalism, economic underdevelopment, the Calvinist-Bacchus syndrome, and evangelical Protestantism."

1204 WORKMAN, WILLIAM D., JR. *The Case for the South.* New York: Devin-Adair Publishers, 1960. 309 pages.

Workman presents a defense of the white South and its desire to preserve segregation. He views the South as "being scourged by four pestential forces," which include the Supreme Court, the NAACP, northern politicians and propagandists, and the Ku Klux Klan.

Music of the Movement

1205 CARAWAN, GUY, and CANDIE CARAWAN. *Freedom Is A Constant Struggle.* New York: Oak Press, 1968. 224 pages.

This collection of Freedom Songs from the civil rights movement takes up where *We Shall Overcome* (1962, see entry 1207) left off. Each song is accompanied by a brief introduction and compelling photography.

1206 _____. *Sing for Freedom: The Story of the Civil Rights Movement Through Its Songs.* Bethlehem, PA: Sing Out Publications, 1990. 312 pages.

This book contains words and music to more than 100 Freedom Songs collected by the Carawans during the 1960s while they were active participants in the movement as staff members of the Highlander Folk School. In addition, there are comments on the origins of each song and many compelling photographs of movement activists. This volume is a combination of two works previously published by the Carawans: *We Shall Overcome* (1962, see entry 1207) and *Freedom Is A Constant Struggle* (1968, see entry 1205).

1207 _____. *We Shall Overcome.* New York: Oak Press, 1962. 122 pages.

This book includes music and lyrics to Freedom Songs collected by the Carawans during their work for the Highlander Folk Center. Each song has a brief introduction describing its origins. The book is richly illustrated with photographs of the movement.

1208 CLUSTER, DICK. "The Borning Struggle: An Interview with Bernice Johnson Reagon." *Radical America* 12 (November/December 1978): 8–25.

See entry 280.

1209 DUNSON, JOSH. *Freedom in the Air: Song Movements of the Sixties.* New York: International Publishers, 1965. 127 pages.

Dunson examines two sources of politically oriented folk songs of the early 1960s—the topical protest songs from the North and the Freedom Songs from the southern civil rights movement. He traces the influences on the development of each type of song and describes how they influenced each other. Of particular interest are chapter 3, "The Students Move," and chapter 6, "The South Spreads Its Songs."

1210 REAGON, BERNICE JOHNSON. "Let the Church Sing 'Freedom.'" *Black Music Research Journal* 7 (1987): 105–18.

Reagon examines the importance of music in the civil rights movement. She uses the case of a 1963 meeting in Greenwood, Mississippi, to illustrate the ways in which Freedom Songs were used to communicate the message of the movement.

1211 SEEGER, PETE, and BOB REISER. *Everybody Says Freedom.* New York: W. W. Norton & Co., 1989. 266 pages.

See entry 86.

1212 SPENCER, JON MICHAEL. "Freedom Songs of the Civil Rights Movement." *Journal of Black Sacred Music* 1 (Fall 1987): 1–16.

Spencer examines the origins, content, and functions of the Freedom

Songs. He finds that eighty-eight of 145 songs incorporated biblical language and that most had their origins in the black church. He contends that singing together helped link divergent groups within the civil rights movement, but when their differences became too great the singing stopped and the movement disintegrated.

1213 WATTERS, PAT. *Down to Now: Reflections on the Southern Civil Rights Movement.* New York: Pantheon Books, 1971. 426 pages.
See entry 100.

Consequences

1214 BALL, HOWARD, DALE KRANE, and THOMAS P. LAUTH. *Compromised Compliance: Implementation of the 1965 Voting Rights Act.* Westport, CT: Greenwood Press, 1982. 300 pages.
See entry 656.

1215 BARTLEY, NUMAN V., and HUGH D. Graham. *Southern Politics and the Second Reconstruction.* Baltimore: Johns Hopkins University Press, 1975. 233 pages.
Bartley and Graham survey southern politics from the end of World War II to 1972. They see four major political consequences of the civil rights movement: (1) growing antagonism between blacks and less affluent whites, (2) alliances between blacks and more affluent whites, (3) the growth of two-party politics, and (4) an increase of six million registered voters, 70 percent of them white.

1216 BENNETT, LERONE, JR. "Have We Overcome?" In *Have We Overcome? Race Relations Since Brown,* edited by Michael V. Namorato, 189–200. Jackson: University Press of Mississippi, 1979.
Answering the question "Have we overcome?" Bennett says, "No, a thousand times no." This does not mean that he feels the civil rights movement was a failure, but that there is much work to be done before the goal of equality is reached.

1217 BLACKWELL, JAMES E. "Persistence and Change in Intergroup Relations: The Crisis upon Us." *Social Problems* 29, no. 4 (1982): 325–45.
Blackwell assesses the consequences of the civil rights movement for African Americans. He finds that despite many profound changes, the movement has not affected the lives of millions of minority group members who are "almost hopelessly mired in poverty and alienation."

1218 BROOKS, GARY H., and WILLIAM CLAGGETT. "Black Electoral Power, White Resistance, and Legislative Behavior." *Political Behavior* 3, no. 1 (1981): 49–68.
Brooks and Claggett examine the roll call votes of white members of the Mississippi House of Representatives during 1977. They report little evi-

dence to support the hypothesis that white legislators' willingness to support pro-black legislation is influenced by the size of the black electorate in their districts.

1219   BULLOCK, CHARLES S., III. "Congressional Voting and the Mobilization of a Black Electorate in the South." *Journal of Politics* 43 (August 1981): 662–82.

Bullock examines roll call votes made by southern members of Congress to determine whether their votes were influenced by the growing number of black voters in their districts. He reports an "increased responsiveness of legislators from districts with large black populations." He points out that whereas these representatives were once the staunchest opponents of legislation favored by civil rights organizations, they shifted to a position that is slightly more liberal that most other southern members of Congress.

1220   BUTTON, JAMES W. *Blacks and Social Change: Impact of the Civil Rights Movement in Southern Communities.* Princeton: Princeton University Press, 1989. 326 pages.
See entry 257.

1221   _____. "The Outcomes of Contemporary Black Protest and Violence." In *Violence in America: Protest, Rebellion, Reform,* 3d ed., edited by Robert Ted Gurr, vol. 2, 286–306. Newbury Park, CA: Sage Publications, 1989.

Button examines the short- and long-term consequences of the civil rights movement of the early 1960s and the urban riots of the late 1960s. He finds that the early protests were effective for several reasons: a "significant portion of the authorities and the public" were sympathetic to their goals; the protests were not so severe that they threatened "to cause massive societal and political instability"; the demands of the protestors were "relatively limited, specific, and clear"; the protests took place at a time when resources were relatively abundant; and the protests were coupled with "other more conventional strategies."

1222   CHAFE, WILLIAM H. "The End of One Struggle, the Beginning of Another." In *The Civil Rights Movement in America,* edited by Charles W. Eagles, 121–56. Jackson: University Press of Mississippi, 1986.

In assessing the accomplishments of the civil rights movement, Chafe stresses the distinction between the individual goal of attaining greater personal freedom and the collective goals of achieving racial equality. With respect to the first, he feels that the movement was undoubtedly successful. The second, however, he believes remains far from realization. He points out that ironically, increased opportunities for middle class blacks have helped widen the gap between the rich and the poor. Chafe credits the movement with clarifying the linkage between class, race, and gender in American society. Where it failed, he contends, is in not providing an effective political strategy for addressing the persistent problems of poverty and inequality.

1223   COLBY, DAVID C. "Black Power, White Resistance, and Public Policy: Political Power and Poverty Program Grants in Mississippi." *Journal of Politics* 47, no. 2 (1985): 579–95.
See entry 330.

1224   COUTO, RICHARD A. *Ain't Gonna Let Nobody Turn Me Round: The Pursuit of Racial Justice in the Rural South.* Philadelphia: Temple University Press, 1991. 310 pages.
Couto focuses on federally funded community health centers in four rural southern communities: Haywood County, Tennessee; Lee County, Arkansas; Lowndes County, Alabama; and Sea Islands, South Carolina. He describes how these projects came about as a result of the civil rights movement and explains how local leaders, civil rights activists, and community organizers worked against considerable odds to make real progress on basic issues of land reform, education, voter registration, and health care.

1225   DORSEY, L. C. *Freedom Came to Mississippi.* New York: Field Foundation, 1977. 44 pages.
See entry 340.

1226   EDDS, MARGARET. *Free at Last: What Really Happened When Civil Rights Came to Southern Politics.* Bethesda, MD: Adler & Adler, 1987. 277 pages.
Edds, a Virginia journalist, traveled throughout the South twenty years after the passage of the Voting Rights Act to assess its impact on the lives of southern blacks. She reports on eight communities as well as two specific politicians—Harvey Gantt and Douglas Wilder. She found that in some areas blacks had "progressed no further than the threshold of political influence." Even in places where blacks had been successful in gaining political power, she notes that there is little evidence that they have been able to improve the lives of their constituents. Edds concludes: "Achieving concrete gains from voting, and even from electing black officials, was proving to be a slower, more evolutionary process than many had hoped."

1227   FARLEY, REYNOLDS. *Blacks and Whites: Narrowing the Gap?* Cambridge: Harvard University Press, 1984.
Farley offers abundant statistical data comparing the status of blacks and whites in areas such as education, employment, occupation, income, and earnings. He reports evidence of both progress toward racial equality and the persistence of wide gaps between the statuses of black and white Americans.

1228   ———. "Trends in Racial Inequalities: Have the Gains of the 1960s Disappeared in the 1970s?" *American Sociological Review* 42, no. 2 (1977): 189–208.
Farley reviews comparative statistics on the education, employment,

occupations, family incomes and personal earnings of blacks and whites, and concludes that the gains made by blacks in the 1960s did not disappear during the 1970s. Despite continued progress in some areas, however, he finds that "reductions in inequality are small when compared to the remaining differences on many indicators."

1229 FENDRICH, JAMES M. "Keeping the Faith or Pursuing the Good Life: A Study of the Consequences of Participation in the Civil Rights Movement." *American Sociological Review* 42, no. 1 (1977): 144–57.
See entry 809.

1230 FENDRICH, JAMES M., and ELLIS S. KRAUSS. "Student Activism and Adult Left-Wing Politics: A Causal Model of Political Socialization for Black, White, and Japanese Students of the 1960's Generation." In *Research in Social Movements, Conflict and Change*, edited by Lewis Kriesberg, vol. 1, 231–55. Greenwich, CT: JAI Press, 1978.
See entry 812.

1231 FENDRICH, JAMES M., and KENNETH M. LOVOY. "Back to the Future: Adult Political Behavior of Former Student Activists." *American Sociological Review* 52 (December 1988): 780–84.
See entry 813.

1232 FENDRICH, JAMES M., and ALLISON T. TARLEAU. "Marching to a Different Drummer: Occupational and Political Correlates of Former Student Activists." *Social Forces* 53 (December 1973): 245–52.
See entry 810.

1233 FOSTER, E. C. "A Time of Challenge: Afro-Mississippi Political Developments since 1965." *Journal of Negro History* 68 (Spring 1983): 185–200.
See entry 347.

1234 GREENE, MELISSA FAY. *Praying for Sheetrock*. Reading, MA: Addison-Wesley Publishing Co., 1991. 337 pages.
See entry 285.

1235 HANKS, LAWRENCE J. *The Struggle for Black Political Empowerment in Three Georgia Counties*. Knoxville: University of Tennessee Press, 1987. 227 pages.
See entry 286.

1236 JACKSON, MAURICE. "The Civil Rights Movement and Social Change." In *Social Movements and Social Change*, edited by R. L. Lauer, 174–89. Carbondale: Southern Illinois University Press, 1976. Orig. pub. in *American Behavioral Scientist* 12 (March/April 1969): 8–17.
In this preliminary examination of the effect of the civil rights movement on American society, Jackson finds sufficient evidence to conclude that "the civil rights movement has resulted in a large measure of change"

both in basic social institutions and in the amount of self-respect of blacks and other ethnic groups.

1237   JONES, MACK. "Black Political Officeholding and Political Development in the Rural South." *Review of Black Political Economy* 6 (Summer 1976): 375–407.

Jones examines the relationships among increased black voter registration, the election of black officials, and improvements in the well-being of black constituents in mainly black southern counties. He concludes that "black officeholders in local governments in the rural South have not had significant success in reordering the priorities of the bodies on which they serve and they have enjoyed only limited success in increasing the black community's share of benefits and services."

1238   KLEIN, JOE. "The Emancipation of Bolton, Mississippi." *Esquire*, December 1985, 258–62.

See entry 374.

1239   LAUE, JAMES H. "The Movement: Discovering where It's at and How to Get It." In *Social Movements and Social Change*, edited by Robert H. Lauer, 190–96. Carbondale: Southern Illinois University Press, 1976. Orig. pub. in *Urban and Social Change Review* 3 (Spring 1970): 6–11.

Laue assesses the consequences of the civil rights movement and finds its legacy in "a politicized society in which the decision-making process at all levels is fair game for exposing and influencing."

1240   LAWSON, STEVEN F. *In Pursuit of Power: Southern Blacks and Electoral Politics, 1965–1982.* New York: Columbia University Press, 1985. 391 pages.

This book picks up in 1965 where *Black Ballots* (1976, see entry 722) left off, and traces the implementation and enforcement of the 1965 Voting Rights Act in the South. Lawson "closely charts the efforts of civil rights forces to redress grievances through federal action." He describes the "imaginative enforcement strategies" devised by the Justice Department and assesses their effectiveness.

1241   LEVIN, HENRY M. "Education and Earnings of Black Americans and the *Brown* Decision." In *Have We Overcome? Race Relations Since Brown*, edited by Michael V. Namorato, 79–120. Jackson: University Press of Mississippi, 1979.

Levin reviews data on education and income of black and white Americans to measure progress towards equality since the *Brown* decision.

1242   LINCOLN, C. ERIC. "The New Black Estate: The Coming of Age of Blackamerica." In *Have We Overcome? Race Relations Since Brown*, edited by Michael V. Namorato, 3–30. Jackson: University Press of Mississippi, 1979.

Lincoln reviews the changes that have occurred among black Americans as a result of the civil rights movement.

1243   MCADAM, DOUG. *Freedom Summer.* New York: Oxford University
       Press, 1988. 322 pages.
       See entry 382.

1244   MORRISON, MINION K. C. *Black Political Mobilization: Leadership,
       Power, and Mass Behavior.* Albany: State University of New York
       Press, 1987. 303 pages.
       See entry 392.

1245   NAMORATO, MICHAEL V., ed. *Have We Overcome? Race Relations Since
       Brown.* Jackson: University Press of Mississippi, 1979. 232 pages.
       See entry 151.

1246   PARKER, FRANK R. *Black Votes Count: Political Empowerment in Mis-
       sissippi After 1965.* Chapel Hill: University of North Carolina Press,
       1990. 254 pages.
       See entry 398.

1247   RODGERS, HARRELL R. JR., and CHARLES S. BULLOCK III. *Law and Social
       Change: Civil Rights Laws and Their Consequences.* New York:
       McGraw-Hill, 1972. 230 pages.
       See entry 791.

1248   ROLLINS, JUDITH. "Part of a Whole: The Interdependence of the Civil
       Rights Movement and other Social Movements." *Phylon* 47, no. 1
       (1986): 61–70.
       Rollins examines the links between the civil rights movement and other
national and international social movements. Her thesis is that the U.S. civil
rights movement was an essential part of a worldwide movement that involved the liberation of peoples of color and the weakening of capitalist
controls. She credits the movement with awakening other people of color
within the United States as well as other groups such as women and gays.

1249   WALTON, HANES, JR. *When the Marching Stopped: The Politics of Civil
       Rights Regulatory Agencies.* Albany: State University of New York
       Press, 1988. 263 pages.
       See entry 706.

1250   WILLIAMS, JUAN. "Have We Forgotten the Dream?" *Public Welfare* 46
       (Winter 1988): 35–39.
       Williams examines popular impressions of the civil rights movement
and finds that for many Americans "a popular mythology of the movement
has replaced the reality of the movement." He also finds that "despite the
glorious successes of the civil rights movement, race remains a major disad-
vantage in America from infancy to death."

1251   WIRT, FREDERICK M. *The Politics of Southern Equality: Law and
       Change in a Mississippi County.* Westport, CT: Greenwood Press,
       1970. 335 pages.
       See entry 425.

1252 ZASHIN, ELLIOT. "The Progress of Black Americans in Civil Rights: Two Decades Assessed." *Daedalus* 107 (Winter 1978): 239–62.

Zashin examines changes since the 1954 *Brown* decision in four areas: public education, voting and political power, occupational status and income, and housing conditions and residential segregation. He concludes that blacks in general are "much closer to equality . . . than ever before in our history," but that one cannot assume that black inequality will soon disappear from American society.

Politics

1253 ABNEY, GLENN F. "Factors Related to Negro Voter Turnout in Mississippi." *Journal of Politics* 36 (November 1974): 1057–63.
See entry 316.

1254 BARTLEY, NUMAN V. *The Rise of Massive Resistance: Race and Politics in the South During the 1950's.* Baton Rouge: Louisiana State University Press, 1969. 390 pages.
See entry 1165.

1255 BARTLEY, NUMAN V., and HUGH D. GRAHAM. *Southern Politics and the Second Reconstruction.* Baltimore: Johns Hopkins University Press, 1975. 233 pages.
See entry 1216.

1256 BASS, JACK, and WALTER DEVRIES. *The Transformation of Southern Politics: Social Change and Political Consequences Since 1945.* New York: Basic Books, 1976. 527 pages.

This state-by-state review of southern politics devotes one chapter to "Black Politics."

1257 BLACK, EARL. *Southern Governors and Civil Rights: Racial Segregation as a Campaign Issue in the Second Reconstruction.* Cambridge: Harvard University Press, 1976. 408 pages.

Black examines the issue of racial segregation in campaigns for governor in eleven southern states between 1950 and 1973. His analysis of political rhetoric demonstrates "that one important consequence of federal intervention in southern race relations has been the cumulative abandonment of old-fashioned segregationist oratory by white politicians." Although this change had begun prior to 1964 in the "peripheral South" (i.e., Texas, Tennessee, and Virginia), Black declares that it was not until the Kennedy and Johnson administrations secured the passage of strong civil rights legislation that politicians in the Deep South adopted nonsegregationist rhetoric.

1258 BLACK, EARL, and MERLE BLACK. *Politics and Society in the South.* Cambridge: Harvard University Press, 1987. 363 pages.

Black and Black examine the changes in southern politics from 1950 to

1980. Two major components of their analysis are black enfranchisement and the decline of the Democratic party. They contend that "the central tendencies in southern politics are primarily established by the values, beliefs, and objectives of the expanding white urban middle class."

1259 BROOKS, GARY H., and WILLIAM CLAGGETT. "Black Electoral Power, White Resistance, and Legislative Behavior." *Political Behavior* 3, no. 1 (1981): 49–68.
See entry 1218.

1260 BULLOCK, CHARLES S., III. "Congressional Voting and the Mobilization of a Black Electorate in the South." *Journal of Politics* 43 (August 1981): 662–82.
See entry 1219.

1261 BULLOCK, CHARLES S., III, and CHARLES M. LAMB, eds. *Implementation of Civil Rights Policy.* Monterey, CA: Brooks/Cole Publishing Co., 1984. 223 pages.
See entry 662.

1262 CAMPBELL, DAVID, and JOE R. FEAGIN. "Black Politics in the South: A Descriptive Analysis." *Journal of Politics* 37 (February 1975): 129–62.
Campbell and Feagin examine the political gains made by southern blacks as a result of the civil rights movement. They conclude that "black southerners have made important gains in regard to [voter] registration and turnout and some . . . important gains in regard to political organization and cohesion." According to the authors, this has led to a growing number of black elected officials who "are bringing new and important benefits to their black constituencies."

1263 CARMINES, EDWARD G., and JAMES A. STIMSON. *Issue Evolution: Race and the Transformation of American Politics.* Princeton: Princeton University Press, 1989. 217 pages.
Carmines and Stimson trace the evolution of race as a political issue from the time of Roosevelt to the Reagan administration. They argue that fifty years ago an American politician could be both a liberal and a racist and that conservatives were often advocates of racial equality. They maintain that since 1960, however, the issue of race has been transformed so that "racial attitudes are now tightly linked to prevailing political ideology." This change occurred, according to the authors, when the New Deal Democratic coalition fell apart because "all the sources of issue competition were favorably disposed toward race."

1264 COLBY, DAVID C. "Black Power, White Resistance, and Public Policy: Political Power and Poverty Program Grants in Mississippi." *Journal of Politics* 47, no. 2 (1985): 579–95.
See entry 330.

1265   COOMBS, DAVID, M. H. ALSIKAFI, C. HOBSON BRYAN, and IRVING WEB-
       BER. "Black Political Control in Greene County, Alabama." *Rural So-
       ciology* 42, no. 3 (1977): 398–406.
       See entry 179.

1266   CRAIN, ROBERT L. *The Politics of School Desegregation: Comparative
       Case Studies of Community Structure and Policy-Making.* National
       Opinion Research Center Monographs in Social Research, vol. 14.
       Chicago: Aldine Publishing Co., 1968. 390 pages.
       This comparative study focuses on the school desegregation process in
fifteen American cities—eight in the North where a variety of voluntary
plans were debated and implemented, and seven in the South where federal
courts provided the direction for school integration efforts. One-fourth of
the book is devoted to an analysis of the 1960 school desegregation controversy in New Orleans and the failure of that city's civic and business elite to
exercise leadership and prevent prolonged community conflict. Two chapters examine the relationship between the civil rights movement and the
desegregation process in northern and other southern cities, with the main
focus on the decision-making process. Crain identifies two main reasons
why school integration generated more conflict than other areas of racial
change. The first is the relative autonomy of local school boards, which have
less to lose from social conflict than the mayor or other political leaders. The
second is the "symbolic orientation" of the civil rights movement, which
increases pressure on school boards to make decisions based on ideology
rather than pragmatism.

1267   DYE, THOMAS R. *The Politics of Equality.* Indianapolis: Bobbs-Merrill,
       1971. 241 pages.
       Dye reviews the political dimension of American race relations. He em-
phasizes the distinction between equality of opportunity and "equalization
of life chances." He points out that while most white politicians endorse the
concept of equal opportunity, few support "the massive public effort in re-
distributing income, education, jobs, and other resources" that would be
necessary to create full equality between blacks and whites.

1268   EDDS, MARGARET. *Free at Last: What Really Happened When Civil
       Rights Came to Southern Politics.* Bethesda, MD: Adler & Adler, 1987.
       277 pages.
       See entry 1226.

1269   FEAGIN, JOE R., and HARLAN HAHN. "The Second Reconstruction: Black
       Political Strength in the South." *Social Science Quarterly* 51 (June
       1970): 42–56.
       Feagin and Hahn identify conditions that have contributed to greater
black political strength in the South. They observe that black political gains
have been closely tied to the size of the black population and increased
voter registration following the Voting Rights Act of 1965. They maintain that

a high degree of cohesion among black voters and a divided vote among whites strengthens the prospect of enduring black political power in the South.

1270   FINDLAY, JAMES F. "Religion and Politics in the Sixties: The Churches and the Civil Rights Act of 1964." *Journal of American History* 77 (June 1990): 69–70.
       See entry 718.

1271   GUYOT, LAWRENCE, and MIKE THELWELL. "The Politics of Necessity and Survival in Mississippi." *Freedomways* 6, no. 2 (1966): 120–32.
       See entry 354.

1272   _____. "Toward Independent Political Power." *Freedomways* 6, no. 3 (1966): 246–54.
       See entry 355.

1273   HAMER, FANNIE LOU. "Sick and Tired of Being Sick and Tired." *Katallagete*, Fall 1968, 19–26.
       See entry 358.

1274   HAMILTON, CHARLES V. *Minority Politics in Black Belt Alabama.* Eagleton Institute: Cases in Practical Politics, no. 19. New York: McGraw-Hill, 1962. 32 pages.
       See entry 202.

1275   HANKS, LAWRENCE J. *The Struggle for Black Political Empowerment in Three Georgia Counties.* Knoxville: University of Tennessee Press, 1987. 227 pages.
       See entry 286.

1276   HOLLOWAY, HARRY. *The Politics of the Southern Negro: From Exclusion to Big City Organization.* New York: Random House, 1969. 374 pages.
       Holloway describes the changes in Southern politics that resulted from the civil rights movement. Subjects of his eight case studies are: Mississippi; Fayette County, Tennessee; Macon County, Alabama; Marion County, Texas; Birmingham; Atlanta; Houston; and Memphis.

1277   HUMPHREY, HUBERT H. *Beyond Civil Rights: A New Day of Equality.* New York: Random House, 1968. 193 pages.
       See entry 676.

1278   JONES, MACK. "Black Political Officeholding and Political Development in the Rural South." *Review of Black Political Economy* 6 (Summer 1976): 375–407.
       See entry 1237.

1279   KEECH, WILLIAM R. *The Impact of Negro Voting: The Role of the Vote in the Quest for Equality.* Chicago: Rand McNally & Co., 1968. 113 pages.
       See entry 211.

1280 KLEIN, JOE. "The Emancipation of Bolton, Mississippi." *Esquire*, December 1985, 258–62.
See entry 374.

1281 LADD, EVERETT CARLL., JR. *Negro Political Leadership in the South.* Ithaca, NY: Cornell University Press, 1966. 348 pages.
See entry 435.

1282 LAWSON, STEVEN F. *Black Ballots: Voting Rights in the South, 1944–1969.* New York: Columbia University Press, 1976. 474 pages.
See entry 722.

1283 _____. *In Pursuit of Power: Southern Blacks and Electoral Politics, 1965–1982.* New York: Columbia University Press, 1985. 391 pages.
See entry 1240.

1284 _____. *Running for Freedom: Civil Rights and Black Politics since 1941.* New York: McGraw-Hill, 1991. 306 pages.
A short synthesis of Lawson's previous research on voting rights and the politics of the civil rights movement.

1285 LEVESQUE, RUSSELL J. "White Response to Nonwhite Voter Registration in the Southern States." *Pacific Sociological Review* 15 (April 1972): 245–55.
Levesque examines 1968 voter registration data for 440 southern counties. He finds that following the passage of the 1965 Voting Rights Act, southern whites "perceived a nonwhite threat to their voting supremacy" and responded by substantially increasing their registration. In ninety counties, he points out, 100 percent or more of the eligible whites were registered.

1286 LOEVY, ROBERT D. *To End All Segregation: The Politics of the Passage of the Civil Rights Act of 1964.* Lanham, MD: University Press of America, 1990. 373 pages.
See entry 723.

1287 MARTIN, JOHN F. *Civil Rights and the Crisis of Liberalism: The Democratic Party, 1945–1976.* Boulder: Westview Press, 1979. 301 pages.
Martin examines the civil rights issue in Democratic politics from 1945 to 1976. He argues that liberals within the party redefined the notion of liberalism to mean civil rights and federal power. He also describes how during the Kennedy and Johnson administrations liberals wielded unprecedented power, but when attacked by both the left and the right they retreated from their positions.

1288 MATTHEWS, DONALD R., and JAMES W. PROTHRO. *Negroes and the New Southern Politics.* New York: Harcourt, Brace and World, 1966. 551 pages.
This detailed study conducted in 1961 of black political participation is based on interviews with samples of black and white southerners. Of special interest are their observations of the impact of black voters and the civil rights movement on southern politics.

1289   MATUSOW, ALLEN J. *The Unraveling of America: A History of Liberal-
       ism in the 1960s.* New York: Harper & Row, 1984. 542 pages.
       See entry 691.

1290   MORRISON, MINION K. C. *Black Political Mobilization: Leadership,
       Power, and Mass Behavior.* Albany: State University of New York
       Press, 1987. 303 pages.
       See entry 392.

1291   MORRISON, [MINION] K. C., and JOE C. HUANG. "The Transfer of Power
       in a Mississippi Town." *Growth and Change* 4 (April 1973): 25–29.
       See entry 393.

1292   PARKER, FRANK R. *Black Votes Count: Political Empowerment in Mis-
       sissippi After 1965.* Chapel Hill: University of North Carolina Press,
       1990. 254 pages.
       See entry 398.

1293   ROZIER, JOHN. *Black Boss: Political Revolution in a Georgia County.*
       Athens: University of Georgia Press, 1982. 220 pages.
       See entry 297.

1294   STEWART, JOSEPH, JR., and JAMES F. SHEFFIELD, JR. "Does Interest Group
       Litigation Matter? The Case of Black Political Mobilization in Missis-
       sippi." *Journal of Politics* 49 (August 1987): 780–98.
       See entry 414.

1295   THERNSTROM, ABIGAIL. *Whose Votes Count? Affirmative Action and
       Minority Voting Rights.* Cambridge: Harvard University Press, 1987.
       316 pages.
       See entry 728.

1296   WATTERS, PAT. "The Negroes Enter Southern Politics." *Dissent* 13, no.
       4 (1966): 361–68.
       Watters reviews political developments in the South between the pas-
       sage of the Voting Rights Act in 1965 and the Democratic primaries in 1966.
       He examines SNCC's efforts to build an all-black political party in Lowndes
       County, Alabama, and its decision to exclude white workers on its staff.
       Although he doubts that black separatism will be a successful political strat-
       egy, he traces its origins to the disappointment felt by young activists follow-
       ing the 1964 Democratic convention.

1297   WILHOIT, FRANCIS M. *The Politics of Massive Resistance.* New York:
       George Braziller, 1973. 320 pages.
       See entry 1203.

1298   WIRT, FREDERICK M. *The Politics of Southern Equality: Law and
       Change in a Mississippi County.* Westport, CT: Greenwood Press,
       1970. 335 pages.
       See entry 425.

Voting

1299 ABNEY, GLENN F. "Factors Related to Negro Voter Turnout in Mississippi." *Journal of Politics* 36 (November 1974): 1057–63.
See entry 316.

1300 BROOKS, GARY H., and WILLIAM CLAGGETT. "Black Electoral Power, White Resistance, and Legislative Behavior." *Political Behavior* 3, no. 1 (1981): 49–68.
See entry 1218.

1301 BULLOCK, CHARLES S, III. "Congressional Voting and the Mobilization of a Black Electorate in the South." *Journal of Politics* 43 (August 1981): 662–82.
See entry 1219.

1302 COLBY, DAVID C. "The Voting Rights Act and Black Registration in Mississippi." *Publius* 16 (Fall 1986): 123–37.
See entry 331.

1303 EDDS, MARGARET. *Free at Last: What Really Happened When Civil Rights Came to Southern Politics.* Bethesda, MD: Adler & Adler, 1987. 277 pages.
See entry 1226.

1304 FOSTER, E. C. "A Time of Challenge: Afro-Mississippi Political Developments since 1965." *Journal of Negro History* 68 (Spring 1983): 185–200.
See entry 347.

1305 FOSTER, LORN S. "The Voting Rights Act: Black Voting and the New Southern Politics." *Western Journal of Black Studies* 7, no. 3 (1983): 120–29.
See entry 719.

1306 HAMILTON, CHARLES V. *The Bench and the Ballot: Southern Federal Judges and Black Voting Rights.* New York: Oxford University Press, 1973. 258 pages.
See entry 762.

1307 ———. "Southern Judges and Negro Voting: The Judicial Approach to the Solution of Controversial Social Problems." *Wisconsin Law Review* 65 (Winter 1965): 71–102.
See entry 764.

1308 HANKS, LAWRENCE J. *The Struggle for Black Political Empowerment in Three Georgia Counties.* Knoxville: University of Tennessee Press, 1987. 227 pages.
See entry 286.

1309 HOLLOWAY, HARRY. *The Politics of the Southern Negro: From Exclusion to Big City Organization.* New York: Random House, 1969. 374 pages.
See entry 1276.

1310 JOUBERT, PAUL E., and BEN M. CROUCH. "Mississippi Blacks and the Voting Rights Act of 1965." *Journal of Negro Education* 46 (Spring 1977): 157–67.
See entry 371.

1311 KEECH, WILLIAM R. *The Impact of Negro Voting: The Role of the Vote in the Quest for Equality.* Chicago: Rand McNally & Co., 1968. 113 pages.
See entry 211.

1312 _____. "Political Participation and Political Structures: The Voting Rights Act of 1965." *Phylon* 41, no. 1 (1980): 25–35.
Keech maintains that rapid gains in black voter registration occurred in southern counties regardless of their demographic characteristics, thus, the increase must be due to changes in the "opportunity structure" (i.e., passage and implementation of the Voting Rights Act).

1313 KERNELL, SAM. "Comment: A Re-Evaluation of Black Voting in Mississippi." *American Political Science Review* 67, no. 4 (1973): 1307–18.
See entry 373.

1314 KNICKREHM, KAY M., and DEVIN BENT. "Voting Rights, Voter Turnout and Realignment: The Impact of the 1965 Voting Rights Act." *Journal of Black Studies* 18 (March 1988): 283–96.
Knickrehm and Bent look at the impact of the Voting Rights Act on voter turnout and partisan alignment in Virginia between 1960 and 1981. Their data come from statewide elections, and cities and counties are their unit of analysis. They conclude "that in rural areas increased black voting. . . has been more than offset by increased white support of the Republican party."

1315 LAWSON, STEVEN F. *Black Ballots: Voting Rights in the South, 1944–1969.* New York: Columbia University Press, 1976. 474 pages.
See entry 722.

1316 _____. *In Pursuit of Power: Southern Blacks and Electoral Politics, 1965–1982.* New York: Columbia University Press, 1985. 391 pages.
See entry 1240.

1317 _____. "Preserving the Second Reconstruction: Enforcement of the Voting Rights Act, 1965–1975." *Southern Studies* 22, no. 1 (1983): 55–75.
See entry 681.

1318 _____. *Running for Freedom: Civil Rights and Black Politics since 1941.* New York: McGraw-Hill, 1991. 306 pages.
See entry 1284.

1319 LAWSON, STEVEN F., and MARK I. GELFAND. "Consensus and Civil Rights: Lyndon B. Johnson and the Black Franchise." *Prologue* 8 (Summer 1976): 65–76.
   See entry 682.

1320 LEVESQUE, RUSSELL J. "White Response to Nonwhite Voter Registration in the Southern States." *Pacific Sociological Review* 15 (April 1972): 245–55.
   See entry 1285.

1321 LEWIS, JOHN, and ARCHIE ALLEN. "Black Voter Registration in the South." *Notre Dame Lawyer* 48 (October 1972): 105–32.
   Lewis and Allen review the efforts of the civil rights movement to advance black political empowerment through voter registration, as well as some consequences of this activity. They emphasize the work of the Voter Education Project and point out remaining problem areas.

1322 LICHTMAN, ALLAN. "The Federal Assault against Voting Discrimination in the Deep South, 1957–1967." *Journal of Negro History* 54 (October 1969): 346–67.
   See entry 684.

1323 McMILLEN, NEIL R. "Black Enfranchisement in Mississippi: Federal Enforcement and Black Protest in the 1960s." *Journal of Southern History* 43, no. 3 (1977): 351–72. Reprinted in *We Shall Overcome*, edited by David J. Garrow, vol. 2, 679–700. Brooklyn, NY: Carlson Publishing, 1989.
   See entry 385.

1324 MARSHALL, BURKE. "Federal Protection of Negro Voting Rights." *Law and Contemporary Problems* 27 (Summer 1962): 455–67.
   See entry 689.

1325 MATTHEWS, DONALD R., and JAMES W. PROTHRO. *Negroes and the New Southern Politics.* New York: Harcourt, Brace and World, 1966. 551 pages.
   See entry 1288.

1326 _____. "Social and Economic Factors and Negro Voter Registration in the South." *American Political Science Review* 57 (March 1963): 24–22.
   Matthews and Prothro conducted a statistical analysis of the relationship between the rate of Negro voter registration in southern counties and the social and economic characteristics of those counties. They found that "personal attributes of Negroes . . . have relatively little to do with Negro registration rates." What does account for low black registration, they maintain, is discrimination by white officials. However, they caution that "reformers should not expect miracles in their efforts" to increase black registration through political and legal means.

1327   MAXWELL, GRACE R. "The Civil Rights Movement and Black Political
       Participation." In *The Civil Rights Movement in Florida and the
       United States*, edited by Charles U. Smith, 252–90. Tallahassee, FL:
       Father & Son Press, 1989.
       Maxwell documents the growth of black voter registration in the South
following the passage of the Voting Rights Act of 1965 and the resulting
increase in the number of black elected officials.

1328   MEIER, AUGUST. "The Dilemmas of Negro Protest Strategy." In *We
       Shall Overcome*, edited by David J. Garrow, vol. 2, 789–806. Brook-
       lyn, NY: Carlson Publishing, 1989. Orig. pub. in *New South* 21 (Spring
       1966): 1–18.
       Meier comments on the strategies of civil rights organizations following
the passage of the 1965 Voting Rights Act. He compares the political strategies of blacks in Alabama and Mississippi, especially the issue of whether to
form independent political organizations or to work within the Democratic
party. He does not consider direct action to be an outmoded strategy, but
sees a combination of direct action and political threats emerging as a common strategy. He also discusses the "political dimension of various programs
for improving the lot of the poor."

1329   MURRAY, PAUL T. "The Struggle for Political Power in a Black Belt
       County." *Humanity and Society* 12 (August 1988): 239–53.
       See entry 219.

1330   SALAMON, LESTER, and STEPHEN VAN EVERA. "Fear, Apathy, and Dis-
       crimination: A Test of Three Explanations of Political Participa-
       tion." *American Political Science Review* 67, no. 4 (1973): 1288–
       1306.
       See entry 405.

1331   SITTON, CLAUDE. "Bullets and Ballots in Greenwood, Mississippi." In
       Freedom Now! The Struggle for Civil Rights in America, edited by
       Alan F. Westin, 87–94. New York: Basic Books, 1964. Orig. pub. in
       the *New York Times*, 6 April 1963, 20.
       See entry 412.

1332   STRONG, DONALD S. *Negroes, Ballots, and Judges*. Tuscaloosa: Univer-
       sity of Alabama Press, 1968. 100 pages.
       See entry 796.

1333   THERNSTROM, ABIGAIL. "The Odd Evolution of the Voting Rights Act."
       Public Interest 55 (Spring 1979): 49–76.
       See entry 727.

1334   _____. *Whose Votes Count? Affirmative Action and Minority Voting
       Rights*. Cambridge: Harvard University Press, 1987. 316 pages.
       See entry 728.

1335   THOMPSON, KENNETH H. *The Voting Rights Act and Black Electoral Participation.* Washington, DC: Joint Center for Political Studies, 1982. 45 pages.
  See entry 729.

1336   WATTERS, PAT, and REECE CLEGHORN. *Climbing Jacob's Ladder: The Arrival of Negroes in Southern Politics.* New York: Harcourt, Brace and World, 1967. 389 pages.
  An excellent account of the struggle for the vote in the Deep South during the early 1960s. The authors describe the obstacles faced by civil rights workers while organizing voter registration campaigns in the Deep South. Included in an appendix is an interview with Annelle Ponder and Fannie Lou Hamer, in which they describe the beating they endured following their arrest in Winona, Mississippi, in June 1963.

1337   WIRT, FREDERICK M. *The Politics of Southern Equality: Law and Change in a Mississippi County.* Westport, CT: Greenwood Press, 1970. 335 pages.
  See entry 425.

Schools

1338   ANDERSON, MARGARET. *The Children of the South.* New York: Farrar, Straus & Giroux, 1966. 208 pages.
  See entry 440.

1339   BLAUSTEIN, ALBERT P., and CLARENCE CLYDE FERGUSON, JR. *Desegregation and the Law: The Meaning and Effect of the School Segregation Cases.* 2d ed. New York: Vintage Books, 1962. 359 pages.
  See entry 746.

1340   BLOSSOM, VIRGIL T. *It Has Happened Here.* New York: Harper & Row, 1959. 209 pages.
  See entry 245.

1341   CRAIN, ROBERT L. *The Politics of School Desegregation: Comparative Case Studies of Community Structure and Policy-Making.* National Opinion Research Center Monographs in Social Research. Chicago: Aldine Publishing Co., 1968. 390 pages.
  See entry 1266.

1342   DURAM, JAMES C. *A Moderate Among Extremists: Dwight D. Eisenhower and the School Desegregation Crisis.* Chicago: Nelson-Hall Publishers, 1981. 306 pages.
  See entry 665.

1343   DYKEMAN, WILMA, and JAMES STOKELY. "Courage in Action in Clinton, Tennessee." *The Nation*, 22 December 1956, 531–33.
       See entry 443.

1344   FREYER, TONY. *The Little Rock Crisis: A Constitutional Interpretation.* Westport, CT: Greenwood Press, 1984. 186 pages.
       See entry 250.

1345   GRAGLIA, LINO S. *Disaster by Decree: The Supreme Court Decisions on Race and the Schools.* Ithaca, NY: Cornell University Press, 1976. 351 pages.
       See entry 760.

1346   HUCKABY, ELIZABETH. *Crisis at Central High: Little Rock, 1957–58.* Baton Rouge: Louisiana State University Press, 1980. 222 pages.
       See entry 252.

1347   INGER, MORTON. *Politics and Reality in an American City: The New Orleans School Crisis of 1960.* New York: Center for Urban Education, 1969. 114 pages.
       See entry 310.

1348   JONES, LEON. *From Brown to Boston: Desegregation in Education, 1954–1974.* 2 vols. Metuchen, NJ: Scarecrow Press, 1979. 2175 pages.
       This two-volume annotated bibliography on school desegregation contains references to 2,839 articles, 441 books, and 1,766 legal decisions.

1349   KILPATRICK, JAMES J. *The Southern Case for School Segregation.* New York: Crowell-Collier Press, 1962. 220 pages.
       See entry 1181.

1350   KLUGER, RICHARD. *Simple Justice: The History of Brown v. Board of Education and Black America's Struggle for Equality.* New York: Alfred A. Knopf, 1976. 823 pages.
       See entry 614.

1351   MORRIS, WILLIE. *Yazoo: Integration in a Deep Southern Town.* New York: Harper's Magazine Press, 1971. 192 pages.
       See entry 391.

1352   ORFIELD, GARY. *The Reconstruction of Southern Education: The Schools and the 1964 Civil Rights Act.* New York: John Wiley & Sons, 1969. 376 pages.
       See entry 698.

1353   PANETTA, LEON. *Bring Us Together: The Nixon Team and the Civil Rights Retreat.* Philadelphia: Lippincott, 1971. 380 pages.
       See entry 699.

1354 PELTASON, JACK W. *Fifty-Eight Lonely Men: Southern Federal Judges and School Desegregation.* New York: Harcourt, Brace and World, 1961. 270 pages.
   See entry 788.

1355 QUAY, RICHARD H. *In Pursuit of Equality of Educational Opportunity: A Selective Bibliography and Guide to the Research Literature.* New York: Garland Publishing, 1977. 173 pages.
   This bibliography of works on school desegregation contains references to 1,435 books and articles and 254 bibliographies. None are annotated.

1356 SMITH, BOB. *They Closed Their Schools: Prince Edward County, Virginia, 1951–1964.* Chapel Hill: University of North Carolina Press, 1965. 281 pages.
   See entry 460.

1357 STUDENT NONVIOLENT COORDINATING COMMITTEE. "Enforcement of the Educational Provisions of the Civil Rights Act of 1964." In *The Great Society Reader*, edited by Marvin E. Gettleman and David Mermelstein, 294–305. New York: Random House, 1967.
   See entry 726.

1358 VANDER ZANDEN, JAMES W. "Accommodation to Undesired Change: The Case of the South." *Journal of Negro Education* 31 (1962): 30–35.
   Vander Zanden traces three stages in the implementation of school desegregation in the South: (1) from 17 May 1954 to 31 May 1955, which was characterized by disbelief and attempts to "buy time," (2) 31 May 1955 to late 1957, during which "die-hard, adamant resistance became the order of the day," and (3) following the Little Rock crisis when "the full resources of the federal government" were committed to enforcing desegregation decisions.

1359 ——. "Turmoil in the South." *Journal of Negro Education* 29 (Fall 1960): 445–52.
   Vander Zanden presents a list of thirty propositions that relate to public disorders and violence accompanying school desegregation. The main thrust of his propositions is that change happens most smoothly when public officials have a firm and clear policy in support of desegregation.

Theory

1360 CHONG, DENNIS. *Collective Action and the Civil Rights Movement.* Chicago: University of Chicago Press, 1990. 261 pages.
   Chong applies rational choice theory to the civil rights movement. He addresses two major questions: (1) how do individuals decide whether or

not to participate in social movements and (2) how do these individual decisions translate into collective outcomes?

1361   DAVIES, JAMES C. "The J-Curve of Rising and Declining Satisfactions as a Cause of Some Great Revolutions and a Contained Rebellion." In *The History of Violence in America: Historical and Comparative Perspectives*, edited by Hugh Davis Graham and Ted Robert Gurr, 690–730. New York: Praeger Publishers, 1969. Reprinted in *Violence in America*, edited by Hugh Davis Graham and Ted Robert Gurr, 415–36. Beverly Hills, CA: Sage Publications, 1979.
       See entry 1003.

1362   GESCHWENDER, JAMES A. "Social Structure and the Negro Revolt: An Examination of Some Hypotheses." *Social Forces* 43, no. 2 (1964): 248–56.
       See entry 1004.

1363   HIMES, JOSEPH S. *Racial Conflict in American Society*. Columbus, OH: Merrill Publishing Co., 1973. 205 pages.
       See entry 46.

1364   MCADAM, DOUG. "The Decline of the Civil Rights Movement." In *Social Movements of the Sixties and Seventies*, edited by Jo Freeman, 279–329. New York: Longman, 1983.
       See entry 1105.

1365   _____. *Political Process and the Development of Black Insurgency, 1930–1970*. Chicago: University of Chicago Press, 1982. 304 pages.
       See entry 1009.

1366   MCADAM, DOUG, and KELLY MOORE. "The Politics of Black Insurgency, 1930–1975." In *Violence in America: Protest, Rebellion, Reform*, 3rd ed., edited by Ted Robert Gurr, vol. 2., 255–85. Newbury Park, CA: Sage Publications, 1989.
       See entry 1010.

1367   MORRIS, ALDON D. *The Origins of the Civil Rights Movement: Black Communities Organizing for Change*. New York: Free Press, 1984. 354 pages.
       See entry 1016.

1368   OBERSCHALL, ANTHONY. "Mobilization, Leaders, and Followers in the Civil Rights Movement in the United States, 1950 to 1970." In *Social Conflict and Social Movements*, 204–41. Englewood Cliffs, NJ: Prentice Hall Press, 1973.
       Oberschall presents his analysis of the civil rights movement using the resource mobilization perspective. He stresses the importance of outside support and the impact of outside societal events in "bringing about a loosening of social control which permits mobilization of the collectivity's resources." These include "the federal government, Northern liberals, college

students, churches, and . . . the effects of national news media coverage."
He also emphasizes that successful social movements require "a prior base
grounded either in associations or in communal groups." This theme has
been further developed by Aldon Morris in *The Origins of the Civil Rights
Movement* (1984, see entry 1016).

1369   PIVEN, FRANCES F., and RICHARD CLOWARD. *Poor People's Movements:
       Why They Succeed, How They Fail.* 1977. Reprint. New York: Vintage
       Books, 1979. 381 pages.
       See entry 80.

1370   VON ESCHEN, DONALD, JEROME KIRK, and MAURICE PINARD. "The Or-
       ganizational Substructure of Disorderly Politics." *Social Forces* 49
       (1971): 529–43.
       See entry 1049.

1371   WEST, CORNEL. "The Paradox of the Afro-American Rebellion." In *The
       Sixties without Apology,* edited by Stanley Aronowitz, 44–58. Minne-
       apolis: University of Minnesota Press, 1984.
       See entry 104.

1372   YANCEY, WILLIAM L. "Organizational Structures and Environments: A
       Second Look at the NAACP and CORE." *Social Science Quarterly* 51
       (June 1970): 25–30.
       See entry 607.

Historiography

1373   BURSON, GEORGE S., JR. "The Second Reconstruction: A Historiograph-
       ical Essay on Recent Works." *Journal of Negro History* 59, no. 4
       (1974): 322–36.
       Burson reviews a large number of studies of the civil rights movement
published between 1960 and 1973. He also points out several important
sources of primary information on the movement. He concludes that "thus
far the historian's contribution (to the understanding of the Civil Rights
Movement) has been modest."

1374   CARSON, CLAYBORNE. "Civil Rights Reform and the Black Freedom
       Struggle." In *The Civil Rights Movement in America,* edited by
       Charles W. Eagles, 19–38. Jackson: University Press of Mississippi,
       1986.
       Carson's essay is primarily a review and critique of past scholarship on
the civil rights movement. He stresses the need to see the movement as a
series of local struggles, each with its own distinctive goals, tactics, and
leadership. It is a serious mistake, he argues, to view the civil rights movement as an effort by national leaders and organizations to secure passage of
federal legislation.

1375 FISCHER, ROGER A. "Capstone for a Generation: Martin Luther King, Jr., and the Civil Rights Movement in Civil Rights Historiography." *Choice* 27, no. 6 (1990): 911–15.

Fischer reviews the eighteen-volume series *Martin Luther King, Jr., and the Civil Rights Movement* (1989, see entry 135), edited by David J. Garrow. He outlines three directions for future research on the civil rights movement: (1) to redirect the focus from King to the movement as a whole, (2) to fill obvious voids in the study of key individuals and critical communities, and (3) to interpret the meaning of the movement for the broader society.

1376 GARROW, DAVID J. "The Age of the Unheralded." *Progressive* (April 1990): 38–43.

Garrow reviews several key works on the history of the civil rights movement that reinforce his contention that "the transformation of the American South stemmed far more from direct involvement by thousands of relative unknowns than from the efforts of a few established organizations and prominent individuals."

1377 LAWSON, STEPHEN F. "Civil Rights." In *Exploring the Johnson Years*, edited by Robert A. Divine, 93–125. Austin: University of Texas Press, 1981.
See entry 679.

1378 ———. "Freedom Then, Freedom Now: The Historiography of the Civil Rights Movement." *American Historical Review* 96, no. 2 (1991): 456–71.

Lawson undertakes a comprehensive review of recent scholarship on the civil rights movement. He distinguishes three general types of studies of the movement: (1) works that focus on leaders and events of national significance and see the struggle as "primarily a political movement that secured legislative and judicial triumphs," (2) research in which the focal point was local communities and grass-roots organizations and their efforts to create new social identities for African Americans, and (3) studies that use an interactive model that "connect[s] the local with the national," and examine external influences on the movement, internal dynamics of local organizations, and the ideological roots of the freedom struggle. His essay includes references to most major studies of the movement published between 1970 and 1990.

1379 MACK, THURA, and JANETTE PRESCOD. "The Struggle for Civil Rights: A Selected, Annotated Bibliography of Research Collections and U.S. Government Documents, 1963–1985." *Choice* 28, no. 6 (1991): 887–92.

Mack and Prescod list fifty-two government publications and eighteen research and microform collections dealing with various aspects of civil rights. Included are reports of government agencies such as the Civil Rights Commission and collections from civil rights organizations such as CORE and the NAACP, as well as FBI files on Martin Luther King, Jr., Malcolm X, and the Black Panther party.

1380   ROGERS, KIM LACY. "Decoding a City of Words: Fantasy Theme Analysis and the Interpretation of Oral Interviews." *International Journal of Oral History* 7, no. 1 (1986): 43–56.
See entry 313.

1381   ———. "Oral History and the History of the Civil Rights Movement." *Journal of American History* 75, no. 2 (1988): 567–76.
Rogers argues that oral history is a "critical source for scholars seeking to understand the civil rights movement and social movements in general." She points out that it can provide evidence of the local genesis of the movement, the radicalism of its grass-roots base, and changes in individual and collective consciousness. Rogers also reviews the holdings of major oral history collections dealing with the civil rights movement.

1382   ZANGRANDO, ROBERT L. "Manuscript Sources for Twentieth Century Civil Rights Research." *Journal of American History* 74 (June 1987): 243–51.
Zangrando reviews manuscript sources in five categories: files of civil rights organizations, personal and public papers of individuals involved in civil rights, files of liberal advocacy groups, records of government agencies, and papers of major political leaders. Not included, however, are oral histories of movement participants, which are generally considered a major resource for researchers.

Bibliographies

1383   CARSON, CLAYBORNE, dir. *A Guide to Research on Martin Luther King, Jr., and the Modern Black Freedom Struggle.* Stanford, CA: Stanford University Libraries, 1989. 185 pages.
This bibliography was produced by the staff of the Martin Luther King, Jr. Papers Project. It is divided into seven sections: manuscripts and microform collections, reference works, works by King, works and articles on King and the black freedom struggle, dissertations and theses, government documents, and audio/visual materials. Many, but not all, entries are annotated.

1384   FISHER, WILLIAM H. *Free At Last: A Bibliography of Martin Luther King, Jr.* Metuchen, NJ: Scarecrow Press, 1976. 169 pages.
This extensive bibliography of works by and about King is divided into four sections: works by King, works specifically on King, works that include King, and reviews of books by King. A one-sentence annotation is included for each entry. Periodical literature is heavily represented.

1385   JONES, LEON. *From Brown to Boston: Desegregation in Education, 1954–1974.* 2 vols. Metuchen, NJ: Scarecrow Press, 1979. 2175 pages.
See entry 1348.

1386 MACK, THURA, and JANETTE PRESCOD. "The Struggle for Civil Rights: A Selected, Annotated Bibliography of Research Collections and U.S. Government Documents, 1963–1985." *Choice* 28, no. 6 (1991): 887–92.
See entry 1379.

1387 PYATT, SHERMAN E. *Martin Luther King, Jr.: An Annotated Bibliography.* Westport, CT: Greenwood Press, 1986. 154 pages.
This comprehensive bibliography contains 1,277 entries (including cross-references) dealing with the life and work of Martin Luther King, Jr. The work is organized into ten sections: works by King, biographical studies, SCLC, marches and demonstrations, major awards, FBI and government operations, philosophy, King's assassination, and commemorations and eulogies. Each entry has a one-sentence annotation. In addition to articles and books, the bibliography includes dissertations, government documents, and FBI files.

1388 QUAY, RICHARD H. *In Pursuit of Equality of Educational Opportunity: A Selective Bibliography and Guide to the Research Literature.* New York: Garland Publishing, 1977. 173 pages.
See entry 1355.

1389 WEATHERSPOON, FLOYD D. *Equal Employment Opportunity and Affirmative Action: A Sourcebook.* New York: Garland Publishing, 1985. 437 pages.
This book includes a comprehensive annotated bibliography of 1,133 books and articles dealing with various aspects of equal employment opportunity, affirmative action, and major legal cases in these fields. Also included are copies of laws and administrative guidelines dealing with equal employment opportunities.

Author Index

251

Subject Index

ABOUT THE AUTHOR

Paul T. Murray is associate professor of sociology at Siena College. A student civil rights volunteer, his articles on American race relations and civil rights have been published in such journals as *Social Problems*, *Journal of Black Studies, Humanity and Society*, and *Virginia Magazine of History and Biography*. He has also served as a consultant and expert witness to the U.S. Department of Justice, Civil Rights Division, and the Lawyers' Committee for Civil Rights Under Law.